"This is a very important, courageous and origi Israeli government leaders succumbed to Tur close down the 1982 conference that was a milestone event in the struggle against denials of historically known genocides. With intellectual integrity, Charny criticizes the disrespect of the State of Israel to other genocides. When you deny another's genocide, you betray your own genocide; when you deny genocide of the present or of the past, you prepare the ground for a new one. It also presents a particularly fascinating in-depth picture of Elie Wiesel's complicated role in the process. Charny is a brave scholar—one of the rare academics who risks speaking about Israeli crimes such as the State of Israel selling weapons to other governments that commit genocide or about crimes toward the Palestinian people during the War of Independence—the Nakba. This is a significant text that will probably be of wide interest in the world, and at the same time it will probably be an unexpected read for many people in Israeli society."

—From the Foreword by Yair Auron, Prof. Emeritus, Open University of Israel, author of *The Banality of Denial: Israel and the Armenian Genocide*

"I applaud Prof. Charny's relentless yet respectful crusade and especially this seminal book that sheds disturbing light on our country's deplorable mishandling of the issue, yet upholds a hope for its positive transformation. Like many others I am unable to comprehend official Israel turning a blind eye to the Armenian Genocide by Turkey. No *realpolitik* can justify such immoral conduct, nor the false claim that it may cost Jewish or Israeli lives. As a scholar of Medicine's role in the Holocaust, my colleagues and I summon health professionals to become Genocide Watchers and do their utmost to identify and prevent such calamities. We also call on all health professionals to incorporate in their professional identity the dangers of the inherent potential for abuse of power in healthcare. These obligate a full and transparent acknowledgement of the Armenian Holocaust (in which unfortunately once again physicians played a decisive role)."

—Shmuel Reis, MD, MHPE, Family Physician; Academic Director, Center for Medical Education, and Professor, Faculty of Medicine, Hebrew University Jerusalem; Conference Coordinator, International Workshop on Study of Medicine in and after the Holocaust

"Charny dissects the Israeli government's unscrupulous and shameful non-recognition of the Armenian Genocide with the precision of an academic scalpel. He uses the Israeli Freedom of Information Act to reveal the ugly political untruths from never-before-seen archival documents of Israel's Foreign Ministry about the Israeli government's [...] failed attempt to block an academic conference held in 1982 in Israel on the Jewish Holocaust, the Armenian Genocide, and other genocides. Even though he is a patriotic Israeli citizen,

Charny places his humanitarianism ahead of his nationalistic feelings. This book vindicates him as an honest scholar and a good human being who exposes the lies of his own government, insisting that Israel should have been the first country to recognize the Armenian Genocide, not the last."

—Harut Sassounian, Publisher, *California Courier*, outstanding Armenian-American newspaper; former President, United Armenian Fund; President, Armenia Artsakh Fund for the development of Armenia

"[This book] is bound to be a classic in the literature of genocide studies. It is a fascinating, disturbing and revelatory work. The book addresses the planning and implementation of the first international conference ever held on the subject of genocide (other than the Holocaust), and Turkey's allout efforts to pressure the State of Israel [to persuade] Charny to disinvite all Armenians [...] from the conference. To assert that Charny's stance was courageous does not even begin to speak to the courage he displayed. A must-read for anyone interested in what it means to take a moral stand and not bend, and for anyone interested in the history of the founding of the field of genocide studies."

—Samuel Totten, Prof. Emeritus, University Arkansas; author of *Genocide Pioneers*

"The book you are holding is a must-read. Here are a Turk, Armenian, and Jew coming together to deliver an intensely poignant and meaningful message to us all: those who deny the reality of a genocide perpetrated upon others largely lose their credibility when speaking of genocides perpetrated against themselves. These documents show us how those who deny the Armenian genocide on the pretext of national security are indirectly admitting their own capability to carry out precisely such a crime themselves."

—Taner Akçam, Professor, Genocide Studies, Clark University, author of *Killing Orders: Talat Pasha's Telegram's and the Armenian Genocide*

"Israel Charny's book revisits one of the turning points in the study of human barbarity: the First International Conference on the Holocaust and Genocide held in Tel Aviv in 1982. In what amounts to a historical whodunit, he shows how systematic attempts to isolate the Holocaust experience of World War II from the Armenian genocide that preceded it at the height of World War I were deflected, and a new norm of comparative genocide studies was established. Since then, the specificities of each attempt at eradicating a group because of its beliefs, ethnic background or geographic origin—be they Jews, Armenians, Yazidis, Bosnians, Tutsis, Rohingyas or any other people—are studied within the context of features common to a long list of efforts to eliminate marginalized and discredited communities. This change—which now has been picked up by Black Lives Matters and similar movements—owes a great deal to the courage of Professor Charny and his colleagues, who stood up to immense political and psychological pressures to insist on the unwavering equality of all human beings—not only in life and sickness, but also in death and remembrance."

—Naomi Chazan, Prof. Emerita, Political Science, Hebrew University Jerusalem; former Deputy Speaker, Israeli Knesset, and Former Director, Truman Peace Institute, Hebrew University Jerusalem

"Israel Charny is one of those indefatigable scholars—Jonathan Swift is another—whose fierce indignation is necessary to our age and who fight the most necessary battles at the right moment. Charny's latest work proclaims that every genocide is unique but that none has the right to claim unique suffering, and that denial is the final stage of genocide. He thus speaks to the future as well as the past. He holds his own Israeli government to account for its failure to acknowledge the 1915 Armenian mass murders as genocide. He even proves that the Israeli authorities invented threats to the Jewish community in Turkey in 1982 in a vain attempt to curtail a Jerusalem Holocaust and genocide conference he helped to arrange—and thus curtail all discussion on the Armenian genocide. At the same time, he makes no cheap shots—he admires Israel even when he undermines its outrageous denial."

—Robert William Fisk, Middle East correspondent, *The Independent*

"This book tells an important and fascinating story. Drawing on revealing, newly declassified Israeli documents, it deals with a major moment not only in the formation of the field of genocide studies, but in global intellectual history, not to mention behind-the-scenes diplomatic skullduggery. This was a key point at which states, scholars, and public figures were challenged to come to terms over the past and future of genocide, its meaning for surviving victims, and its continuing threat to humankind. The book movingly illuminates these challenges, interactions, successes and failures, personal and political. The author deserves congratulations on his pioneering role in the unfolding events, and for assembling this conclusive, multifaceted account. The Foreword and the various contributed chapters are written by a stellar team of highly qualified, respected scholars and authors. I very strongly recommend this book."

—Ben Kiernan, Whitney Griswold Professor of History, Yale University; Founding Director of the Genocide Studies Program, 1994–2015

ISRAEL'S FAILED RESPONSE TO THE ARMENIAN GENOCIDE

DENIAL, STATE DECEPTION, TRUTH VERSUS POLITICIZATION OF HISTORY

The Holocaust: History and Literature, Ethics and Philosophy

Series Editor

Michael Berenbaum (American Jewish University)

ISRAEL'S FAILED RESPONSE TO THE ARMENIAN GENOCIDE

DENIAL, STATE DECEPTION, TRUTH VERSUS POLITICIZATION OF HISTORY

ISRAEL W. CHARNY

WITH THREE CONTEMPORARY UPDATES BY A TURK, AN ARMENIAN, AND A JEW:

RAGIP ZARAKOLU
Intrepid publisher in exile in Sweden after multiple Turkish jails (also his wife died in prison, and his son has been jailed), who stands up heroically to fascism

RICHARD HOVANNISIAN
A profoundly creative doyen of Armenian scholarship, who was one of the leaders of the Armenian scholars at the conference in Tel Aviv in 1982

MICHAEL BERENBAUM
Former Research Director of US Holocaust Memorial Museum in Washington, DC, who was responsible for the museum's brilliantly successful contents

BOSTON
2021

Library of Congress Cataloging-in-Publication Data

Names: Charny, Israel W., author. | Zarakolu, Ragıp, 1948- author.
| Hovannisian, Richard G., author. | Berenbaum, Michael, 1945- author.
Title: Israel's failed response to the Armenian genocide : denial, state
deception, truth versus politicization of history / Israel W. Charny;
with three contemporary updates by a Turk, an Armenian, and a Jew:
Ragip Zarakolu, Richard Hovannisian, MIchael Berenbaum.
Other titles: Holocaust (Boston, Mass.)
Description: Brookline, MA : Academic Studies Press, 2021. | Series: The
holocaust: History and literature, ethics and philosophy | Includes
bibliographical references and index.
Identifiers: LCCN 2021006227 (print) | LCCN 2021006228 (ebook)
| ISBN 9781644695234 (hardback) | ISBN 9781644696026 (paperback)
| ISBN 9781644695241 (adobe pdf) | ISBN 9781644695258 (epub)
Subjects: LCSH: Wiesel, Elie, 1928-2016. | Peres, Shimon, 1923-2016.
| International Conference on the Holocaust and Genocide (1st : 1982 :
Tel Aviv, Israel) | Armenian Genocide, 1915-1923--Congresses. |
Armenia--History--1901---Congresses. | Israel--Foreign
relations--Armenia. | Armenia--Foreign relations--Israel.
Classification: LCC DS195.5.C4675 2021 (print) | LCC DS195.5 (ebook) |
DDC 956.6/20154--dc23
LC record available at https://lccn.loc.gov/2021006227
LC ebook record available at https://lccn.loc.gov/2021006228

ISBN 9781644695234 (hardback)
ISBN 9781644696026 (paperback)
ISBN 9781644695241 (adobe pdf)
ISBN 9781644695258 (epub)

Book design by PHi Business Solutions
Cover design by Ivan Grave

Published by Academic Studies Press.
1577 Beacon Street
Brookline, MA 02446, USA
press@academicstudiespress.com
www.academicstudiespress.com

DEDICATION

It's a longstanding habit of mine, but each time it feels affirmative and renewing, and gives heartfelt pleasure.
I DEDICATE THIS BOOK,
as so many others I wrote, first and foremost to
MY DEAR WIFE AND BEST FRIEND THESE forty-plus YEARS
JUDY SCHOTT-KATZ CHARNY

I also add a dedication to each of my six dear children and their spouses and beloved children—our thirteen grandchildren.
Our children: ADAM, RENA, ANNA, MICHELE, DAVID, AVIV
Our grandchildren: ZACHARY, MATAN, HALLEL, YUVAL, TAL, MAAYAN, ORI, RONI, TAMAR, SHIRA, NATHAN, LIA, ANNA
And always a dedication to **LIFE!** *for all human beings everywhere. There is nothing more precious.*

Contents

Preface

This preface was published in a book, edited by Richard Hovannisian, of selected papers on the Armenian Genocide that were presented at the First International Conference on the Holocaust and Genocide in Tel Aviv in 1982. Regrettably, it is as appropriate as ever for a mankind that still "doesn't get it."

ONE IS EITHER FOR HUMAN LIFE OR NOT

Israel W. Charny[1]

I am honored and pleased to have been invited to write the preface to this important volume, and gratified that much of the work it contains was first developed for and presented at the International Conference on the Holocaust and Genocide, held in Tel Aviv in 1982. Although in a basic philosophical sense the task is endless, I am sure that the excellent papers presented here constitute a major contribution to our knowledge of the Armenian Genocide. The Armenian Genocide was a cataclysmic event to the Armenian people—indeed, to all people—and to the very process we call civilization. To study the Armenian Genocide is to do honor to the Armenian people and their history, and it is also to affirm a commitment to protect and fight for the rights of all peoples.

I write this piece shortly after returning to Jerusalem from Boston, where I participated in a noteworthy conference on the theme, "Seventy Years after the Genocide: Lessons from the Armenian Experience." I am impressed by the increasing range and depth of scholarship on the Armenian Genocide. I also sense an upsurge of pride in one's Armenian heritage, a greater resoluteness in articulating the story of the injustice done to the Armenians. In

---

1   This preface is reproduced, with permission, from Richard G. Hovannisian, ed., *The Armenian Genocide in Perspective* (New Brunswick, NJ: Transaction Publishers, 1986), 5–7.

addition, it is very heartening that an increasing number of Armenian scholars and leaders are ready to join scholars and leaders of other ethnic, national
and religious communities in studying the history of different genocides in a
broad human rights perspective, and out of a shared concern for the future
fate of all peoples.

I would like to think that the milestone conference in 1982 and the continuing work of our Institute of the International Conference on the Holocaust and
Genocide have something to do with these developments. If I have understood
my Armenian colleagues correctly, the conference was the first time that the
Armenian case was presented in an international forum of scholars. I remember vividly the deep concern and sometimes outright anxiety of Armenian
participants when the conference organizers took a stand against the Turkish
government's heavy pressures to have the Armenian topic removed from the
conference and against the Israeli government, which, to the unending shame
of many of us, succumbed to Turkish demands and attempted to close down
the conference. It was a powerful lesson that Armenians and Jews and all other
peoples- must stand together in a common battle against those responsible for
past events of genocide, and against all those who seek to deny the truth of such
past events.

I often wonder what it meant to Armenians to see some of us Jews, and
our beloved Jewish state, bow to *realpolitik* and agree to suppress Armenian
history. Even in 1985, upon returning to Israel from Boston, I found that the
government had attempted to pressure the mayor of Jerusalem, Teddy Kollek,
not to participate in a meeting at the Hebrew University on Mt. Scopus in
commemoration of the Armenian Genocide. Happily, I have also been
encouraged by a strong editorial in the *Jerusalem Post* (April 25, 1985) insisting that "no political considerations can supersede the imperative against
joining the forgetters and distorters of the genocide of another people." This
is the Israel I believe in, and the voice of human integrity that I am always
thrilled to hear.

Nonetheless, it is a fact that among the people who experienced the
Holocaust there are individuals who are willing to collaborate with the killer-
apologists of another people because it serves their immediate sense of self-
interest. This sobering restatement of truth about human nature and the
potential evil that exists in people is not unrelated to the very dynamics from
which sprang both the Armenian Genocide and the Holocaust.

Sadly, a readiness to court violence and to revel in power is present in all
peoples. Thus, in the burst of a new Armenian pride these last years, there has

also emerged a terrorist movement that has claimed the lives of Turkish diplomats, their families, and other innocent people. Although many of us can readily understand the deep rage felt by the Armenians against the Turkish government, which is currently engaged in massive campaigns to obliterate the history of the Armenian Genocide, the killing of innocent people cannot be the way for those of us who believe that the essential evil in all genocide is the preempting of another human being's inherent right to life.

Similarly, the Jewish national experience in its reconstituted homeland instructs us again in the truth about human nature. Even a victimized people, with their deep sensitivity to suffering, must guard against the hubris of power, the corruption of pragmatism, and the lure of militarism.

One can but hope that the ethical traditions of Judaism and the basic democratic structure of the State of Israel, along with the never-to-be-forgotten legacy of the Holocaust, will prevail in reestablishing the Israeli commitment to "purity of arms," that is, a commitment to power only for self-defense, and never for inflicting or cooperating in a reckless destruction of another people. We who have been victims have a profound responsibility to guard against wanton violence even in our struggles against our oppressors. Each and every human being, at any given time in human history, has a connection with all the genocides that have taken place in the past, and with the potential for genocide against any people whatsoever in the future. One is either for human life or not. There is no such thing as indifference on this issue.

The new forms of mass murder available today on our planet threaten the continuation of human existence. It is the responsibility of us all to be aware of the dangers of nuclear holocausts, multiple genocides, or omnicide that can obliterate millions of human beings belonging to many different groups.

We should not forget Pastor Niemoeller's brilliant epigraph to the Holocaust:

> *First they came for the Jews*
> *And I did not speak out—*
> *Because I was not a Jew.*
> *Then they came for the communists*
> *And I did not speak out—*
> *Because I was not a communist.*
> *Then they came for the trade*

Unionists and I did not speak out—
Because I was not a trade unionist.
Then they came for me—
And there was no one left
To speak out for me.

Foreword. Who Really Lied? The Turks, Armenians, and Jews Revisited

Yair Auron, Professor Emeritus, Open University of Israel

"We Zionists look upon the fate of the Armenian people with a deep and sincere sympathy; we do so as men, as Jews, and as Zionists."
—Shmuel Tolkowsky, 1918 (Tolkowsky was secretary to Chaim Weizmann, who later became the first president of Israel—Ed.)[1]

This book is a major contribution to the study of the Armenian Genocide and the process of denial of known genocides altogether. Three major scholars of genocide also contributed to the writing of the book: Ragip Zarakolou (a Turk); Richard Hovannisian (an Armenian); and Michael Berenbaum (a Jew). Bringing in these three leaders in their various ethnic groups is a very symbolic, meaningful and wise decision, each of them being a distinguished representative both of their identity groups and of the quest for human decency.

A big part of the book deals with issues concerning the 1982 conference in Tel Aviv. Charny was probably the first one to use the concepts of "Holocaust" and "genocide" together, instead of the concepts of "Holocaust" and "genocide" separately. This new notion is meaningful in the study of the Holocaust and in the study of genocide, as well as in the interrelations between them. By using comprehensive new sources and newly declassified government documents, Charny gives new perspectives on the hostile attitude of Turkey and Israel towards the conference. He analyzes the development of the pioneering international conference on genocide that was a milestone event in the struggle against denials of historically known genocides. Charny has been dealing with the domain of individual denial and collective denial for many years.

---

1   Cited in Yair Auron, *The Banality of Denial: Israel and the Armenian Genocide* (New Brunswick, NJ: Transaction Publishers, 2003, reprinted, Routledge, 2004).

Charny originated the idea of the conference and also played an important role in its organization as well. He took a stand, successfully, against the Turkish and the Israeli governments. When he encountered heavy pressures to have Armenian topics excluded from the conference, and even demands to exclude the participation of Armenian scholars, he stood firm and his efforts were outstandingly successful. The book also describes and provides new sources of information about the hostility of various Israeli government leaders who succumbed to the Turkish demands and attempted to close down the conference, and it presents a particularly fascinating in-depth picture of Elie Wiesel's complicated role in the process.

Over the years, the Turkish government has attempted to disrupt academic conferences and public discussions of genocide many times and has even intruded in some Holocaust conferences in response to spontaneous audience comments about the Armenian Genocide. Charny once told me about a Holocaust conference in London organized by the late publisher Robert Maxwell, where, after a denier had finished his shpiel, Charny proposed that the chair, who had allowed the denier's comments entirely civilly, censure the denier, and what then happened is that the audience spontaneously rose and left the session. As we know, the Turkish government has devoted itself to bizarre denial for decades and is currently still engaged in a massive campaign to obliterate the Armenian Genocide.

The 1982 conference took place even though some of the speakers canceled their participation due to Israeli and Turkish pressures. The conference was an important "target" for the Turks. This was due to the papers presented at the conference. This was many years ago when there was much less recognition of the Armenian Genocide. These papers constituted a major contribution to the knowledge of humanity about the genocide. They described the injustice that had been done to the Armenians. The significance of that knowledge was not just to Turkey, Armenia, and Israel, but also for all humanity in a world where a significant portion of the population did not recognize the Armenian Genocide and tried to avoid the injustice that had been done to the Armenians.

Where there is denial the Armenians are victims twice. Their first victimization is the genocide itself. The genocide had a beginning and an end, whereas their second victimization is the process of denial. This process has continued for many years, its damages can last for generations.

The genocide of the Circassian people is another good example. The Circassians suffered from a long genocide for 101 years. That genocide was committed by the Russians (1763–1864). It ended 156 years ago. Actually, today's generations are the seventh and eighth generations after the genocide. Nevertheless, the young generations of today continue the struggle for the recognition of the

Circassians' genocide. We have to admit that it does not have any real chance to be recognized. It is a forgotten and denied genocide. Nevertheless, it is a very significant element in the identity of their younger generations today. These young people struggle for genocide recognition. Even more, they struggle for their survival. The same is true for the third and fourth generation of Armenians. They struggle for genocide recognition. It is a significant element in their identity.

Let us quote some sentences from the remarkable and landmark book of Judith Lewis Herman, *Trauma and Recovery*, published in 1982. Herman is a professor of clinical psychiatry at Harvard Medical School and a scholar of trauma, dealing with the aftermath of violence. She points out the difference between a natural disaster, an "Act of God," and "Human Disaster, committed by human beings." This analysis has great relevance to our discussion here. This is what Herman wrote: "When the traumatic events are of human design, those who bear witness are caught in the conflict between victim and perpetrator. It is morally impossible to remain neutral in this conflict. *The bystander is forced to take sides* (my emphasis)."[2]

The main part of the book deals with the political and moral behavior of the State of Israel. With intellectual integrity, Charny criticizes the disrespect of the State of Israel to other genocides. When you deny another's genocide, you betray your own genocide; when you deny genocide of the present or of the past, you prepare the ground for a new one. Therefore, the significance of recognition or non-recognition of the genocide of the past or the present is not only related to the past, but also to the present and the future. Those who would be future perpetrators understand that genocide can be committed, in most cases, without any real punishment.

The State of Israel is selling weapons to other governments that commit genocide while these governments are still committing genocide. This is a huge moral failure that also betrays the legacy of the Jewish Holocaust.

Charny also shows the closeness or similarities between the Jewish Holocaust and the Armenian Genocide. He does this by showing the difference between the two events. The attitude of the book towards the Armenian Genocide and the Jewish Holocaust is the closeness between the two, forming a paradigm of genocide and evil in our world in the twentieth century and in the present century.

In this regard we have to mention the role of the "third party," for example, those people and states that remained indifferent while facing the genocide.

2   Judith Herman, *Trauma and Recovery* (New York: Basic Books, 1982), 1.

In many cases, Israel is one of the countries with an attitude of indifference. This is another serious moral issue. Charny quotes Pastor Niemoller's brilliant epigraph to the Holocaust to show the similarity between the situations of the two peoples, the Armenian and the Jews:

> *Then they came to me*
> *And there was no one left*
> *To speak out for me* [Armenian or Jew—Y.A.]

This book is truly a significant text. Moreover, it is quite probably an unexpected one for many people in Israeli society, especially due to its dealing with unrevealed events that took place during the war of 1948. Charny is one of the rare academics who risks speaking about Israeli crimes toward the Palestinian people during the War of Independence—the Nakba, the catastrophe of the Palestinians. This complex and painful issue has not been sufficiently studied and discussed. Its influence is perhaps more subconscious than conscious and affects Israeli attitudes toward other genocides, including the Armenian Genocide. Charny is a brave scholar to use the terms "genocidal killing" and "genocidal expulsion" of the Palestinians that only a few Israeli academies would use. In my opinion, Charny can be proud of it. One of his claims is that Israel denies its own actions—this is another moral failure. For him, it is one aspect of the road that had led Israel from being the "good guys" to become the "bigger liars."

The essential evil in all genocide, writes Charny, is preempting other human beings' inherent right for life. For Charny, the most basic choices in life are: for human life or against life. This is a decisive example of the "human attitude" in the author's writing about genocide. He cares about human life more than about the politics of it all even as he sheds a great deal of light on the political maneuvering, strategies, and lies.

To sum up: **this is a very important, courageous, and original book.** This important work is based on Charny's humanistic approach. He proposes new perspectives while analyzing people and states that commit crimes that they deny. It is a significant text that will probably be of wide interest in the world, and at the same time it will probably be an unexpected text for many people in Israeli society.

In 2003, I wrote in *The Banality of Denial: Israel and the Armenian Genocide*:

> Over the years I have been troubled by a sense of oppressive discomfort and criticism of the evasive behavior, verging on denial of the various

governments of Israel regarding the memory of Armenian Genocide. I decided to examine both the overt factors and deeper and more complex factors leading to such behaviour, which to me seems morally unacceptable, particularly since we Jews were victims of the Holocaust. As an Israeli Jew, I aspire in my academic work to describe, analyze, and comment on the attitude of my state and society as honestly as I can, and in so doing, to change this attitude. My goal in writing this book, as in the first one, is to uncover the truth—with as much precision as possible.[3]

---

3   Yair Auron, *The Banality of Denial.*

Introduction

SUMMARY: THE "GOOD GUYS" (ISRAEL) TURN OUT TO BE THE BIGGER LIARS

Previously classified and secret documents have now revealed clearly how extensive Israel's role was in the Turkish and Israeli governments' ruthless efforts to suppress historical truth and academic freedom in the famed First International Conference on the Holocaust and Genocide in Tel Aviv in June 1982.

The newly available documents from the Israeli Ministry of Foreign Affairs (henceforth IMFA) reveal that Turkey indeed pressured Israel to remove the subject of the Armenian Genocide from the conference. However, the startling fact that has now been exposed is that repeated statements by Israel's Foreign Ministry that Turkey was actually threatening to harm Jewish lives were made up by Israel itself. It was Israel that set out on the cruel juggernaut effort to cancel the conference based on entirely fabricated stories of Turkish threats to Jewish lives. At first the threats were defined as aimed at Jews in Turkey and this is what appeared in early *New York Times* stories, but then the Ministry clarified—though at first as top secret until this too became international news—that the most serious threat was that Turkey might stop giving safe passage to Jewish refugees escaping from Iran and Syria through Turkey and therefore their lives were at risk.

This conference was the first known international academic conference on genocide ever; it introduced the first known linkage of "Holocaust and genocide" ever; and it was the first ever to host Armenian scholars—including famed Profs Richard Hovannisian and Vahakn Dadrian—speaking of the forgotten and denied Armenian Genocide.

The IMFA indeed may have been seeking to protect the Jewish refugees and Israel's relationship to Turkey in general, but Israel went ruthlessly far in its efforts to suppress any mention of the Armenian Genocide and even to demand cancelling the participation of Armenian scholars, and if not then to close the conference down entirely.

In a later chapter we will also describe and analyze the complex and surprising history of Elie Wiesel's responses to the pressures to remove the topic of the Armenian Genocide and/or close the conference down in entirety. Beginning with his role as official president of the conference and continuing with his initial adamant refusal to remove the Armenian Genocide from the program, Wiesel proceeded to waffle his positions. He resigned his role as president and then, more than disappointingly, proved to be an aggressive opponent of the conference who influenced many people not to attend and not to provide financial support they had promised. He himself "did us dirty" quite directly when he cancelled the financial grant he had promised from his foundation—and he knew all too well how hard we were working and the range of expenses we had undertaken.

Without taking away from Wiesel being a hugely heroic symbol of Holocaust agony and survival, as well as his going on to be a courageous promoter of the meaning of the Holocaust as calling for the life safety of *all* peoples everywhere, we report here the extensive damages Wiesel's actions did to the conference, and our own hurt, frustration and anger, but we still offer a thoughtful and not entirely unsympathetic analysis of his motivations in doing so and of his basic greatness.

Four Israeli leaders (in the middle right to left: Prof. Israel Charny, Prof. Yehuda Buer, MK Yossi Sarid, and Prof. Yair Auron) paying homage at the Eternal Flame at the Armenian Genocide Museum in Yerevan.

Figure 1. View of a conference session at the Tel Aviv Hilton. The microphone is in the hands of conference chair, Israel W. Charny.

CHAPTER 1

The First International Conference on the Holocaust and Genocide in June 1982 in Tel Aviv Was a Milestone Event on Many Levels

In 1982—soon to be forty years ago—a most original conference took place in Tel Aviv, the First International Conference on the Holocaust and Genocide.

1. This was the first known international conference ever on the subject of genocide.
2. To the best of our knowledge, this was the first known use of a linkage between the concepts "Holocaust" and "genocide."
3. This conference was the first known international forum ever in which the subject of the Armenian Genocide was to be discussed.
4. As the events unfolded, the conference became one of the most notorious and widely known instances of Turkish government efforts to censor any identification or mention of the Armenian Genocide.
5. The relentless efforts of the Israeli government over several months, utilizing a variety of severe pressures to close the conference down, were a startling exposé of the extent to which Israel (a democratic government) would go to suppress historical truth and academic freedom.
6. The above also demonstrated the extent to which Israel—for all its history of having suffered a terrible Holocaust—was prepared to deny and censor the genocide of another people—the Armenian people.

7. The organizers' steadfastness, and one dare say about ourselves also our courage in standing up to both university (job) pressures and the powerful attacks by the Israeli government, became a celebrated event in the history of battles for academic freedom.

As the originator and director of the conference, at its conclusion I wrote an article entitled, "The Conference Crisis: The Turks, Armenians and the Jews," in a book edited by me with Shamai Davidson, the co-director of the conference, *The Book of the International Conference on the Holocaust and Genocide. Book 1. The Conference Program and Crisis.*[1]

The Turks had set off an intense political process after learning of the impending conference from a *Jerusalem Post* article on March 29, 1982[2] and/or a second article in the *Jerusalem Post* on April 20, 1982[3] by demanding the Israeli government cancel any and all lectures on the Armenian Genocide. The conference—which was originally scheduled to open at Yad Vashem in Jerusalem and continue in Tel Aviv for several days—included six papers on the Armenian Genocide out of 150 scheduled papers overall.

At the outset Turkish threats were reported "against Jewish lives." These threats were at first interpreted as being threats against the Jewish population of Turkey itself, but then slowly but surely it was revealed to me and others by the IMFA that, without exactly retracting the idea that there were threats against Turkish Jews, the most serious threat that alarmed Israel was that the Turks would prevent the ongoing safe passages of Jews escaping from Iran and Syria through Turkey, which was giving them safe passage. I was told this explicitly by the IMFA, and then also by Jak Veissid, the self-identified head of the Turkish Jewish community who had one day turned up unannounced on my clinic doorstep in Tel Aviv. Progressively more and more remarks about this threat were then made publicly. The bubble of secrecy finally burst in entirety

---

1 Israel W. Charny, "The Turks, Armenians and Jews," in *The Book of the International Conference on the Holocaust and Genocide*, ed. Israel W. Charny with Shamai Davidson (Tel Aviv: Institute of the International Conference on the Holocaust and Genocide, 1983), 269–315. This was followed by another book: Israel W. Charny, ed., *Toward the Understanding and Prevention of Genocide* (*Selected Presentations at the International Conference of the Holocaust and Genocide*) (Boulder, CO: Westview Press, and London: Bowker Publishing, 1984). See also Richard G. Hovannisian, ed., *The Armenian Genocide in Perspective*, which grew largely out of the conference.

2 Michal Yudelman, "World Conference on Genocide for June," *Jerusalem Post*, March 29, 1982.

3 Judy Siegel, "Learning from the Holocaust," *Jerusalem Post*, April 20, 1982.

when Elie Wiesel, who was the identified president of the conference, called the *New York Times* in Paris on June 3, 1982 and referred to their being actual threats to Jewish lives, following which, slowly but surely, the ominous threat to Jewish refugees, added to the threat against Jews in Turkey, became more and more known.

Under these frightening circumstances, the position that I and my colleagues took was that if actual lives were in danger, we would indeed consider taking measures to postpone or close the conference. However, we insisted that under no circumstances would we agree to the initial demand of the IMFA that we remove the six papers on the Armenian Genocide (as noted, out of the 150 scheduled papers overall) nor would we agree to the emerging insulting and unforgivable demand that Armenian scholars not be permitted to participate. The government said that if we acceded to these demands we could proceed freely with the rest of the conference. I was more than angry at the government intrusion, its demands to censor the epochal Armenian Genocide, and at the blatant discrimination of Armenian scholars—though I was not sure if the latter further offensive demand had been initiated by Turks or by Israelis.

Headlines of Five Stories in *New York Times* Tracking the Drama of Threats to the Conference by Turkey and Israel, but the Conference Does Take Place Successfully

1. Special to the *New York Times*, June 2, 1982
   "Parley on Genocide in Doubt, Pressure by Turkey Reported"

2. Special to the *New York Times*, June 3, 1982
   "Israel Set to Oppose Parley After Threat to Turkish Jews"

3. *Associated Press*, June 4, 1982
   "Genocide Seminar with Armenians to Go Forward"

4. Special to the *New York Times*, June 5, 1982, by Marvine Howe
   "Turkey Denies It Threatened Jews on Tel Aviv Parley on Genocide"

5. Special to the *New York Times*, June 22, 1982
   "Genocide Seminar, Opposed by Israel, Opens"

Three Stories in *Jerusalem Post* at the Outset Announce Expectations for the Conference and a Decision to Open Despite Pressures from Turkey and Israel

---

Jerusalem Post, March 29, 1982, by Michal Yudelman
"World Conference on Genocide Set for June"

Jerusalem Post, April 30, 1982, by Judy Siegel
"Learning from the Holocaust"

Jerusalem Post, June 4, 1982
"Genocide Meeting to Go Ahead Despite Threats from Turkey"

We appreciate the permission of the *Jerusalem Post* to reprint the three stories which now follow:

Just imagine our Jewish-Israeli response to a non-totalitarian government that would promote Holocaust denial and exclude Jewish speakers from a bona fide academic conference!

Nonetheless, given the profound seriousness of the threats to actual lives, at no time was I or were my colleagues dismissive or disrespectful. I promised sincerely that we would give deeply serious consideration to the developing information, and that our decisions would always give the highest consideration, first and foremost, to protecting lives.

This may be the reason that there are times in the IMFA documents where there are surprising notes that they believe that I might be yielding to their demands—the sincerity of my concern for Jewish lives apparently mixed with the wish fulfillment of the Ministry representatives to give them a hope that I would cave in and accept the instructions of the government as well as my university and several other prominent institutions and leaders like Elie Wiesel, all of whom were requesting, cajoling, and insisting that I follow the government's demands.

As noted, the great Elie Wiesel was the president of the conference. The subject of his role developed as a sub-drama in its own right. I had invited

World conference on genocide set for June

By MICHAL YUDELMAN
Jerusalem Post Reporter

TEL AVIV. — Some 400 representatives from all over the world will attend a conference on the Holocaust and genocide to be held in June, conference executive director Prof. Israel Charny told the press yesterday.

The conference, which will open in Jerusalem's Yad Vashem and continue in Tel Aviv, will concentrate on the relevance of genocide to our present and future.

The conference will deal with the Holocaust and genocide in an interdisciplinary manner, with attorneys, sociologists, philosophers, clergymen, journalists, political scientists, researchers, psychologists, anthropologists, writers, artists and others taking part.

"Even today, genocide occurs but does not becomes public knowledge due to a conspiracy of silence," Charny said. He noted that the conference will deal with genocide such as occurred in Biafra, Uganda, Afghanistan and the Armenian massacre.

The role of mass media in the dissemination of information and the increasing number of "historical revisionists" denying that the Holocaust ever took place will as also be discussed.

Los Angeles businessman Mel Mermelstein, a Holocaust survivor who successfully sued one such group of revisionists will be among the participants.

Also participating will be Armenian churchmen and scientists, who will conduct a special session on the Turkish genocide against the Armenian people.

Conference president Elie Weisel, professor of Holocaust studies at Boston University, will address the opening ceremony at Yad Vashem and lecture several times at the conference.

The conference is co-sponsored by Hunter College of the City University of New York and the Henrietta Szold National Institute for Research in the Behavioural Sciences of Jerusalem, and in conjunction with the Holocaust Survivors Memorial Foundation of New York.

Figure 2. *Jerusalem Post*, March 29, 1982.

Wiesel to be president of the conference some years earlier and he had agreed graciously (he wrote me that he was in need of *mitzvot* [good deeds] and so he agreed also to speak to the conference without his usual financial remuneration), and he took an active role along with us in developing the plans for the

Learning from the Holocaust

By JUDY SIEGEL/Jerusalem Post Reporter

AN INTERNATIONAL conference aimed at trying to prevent genocide or to intervene when it occurs, and at learning from the Holocaust, will be held in Jerusalem and Tel Aviv in June with delegates from about 20 countries.

Planned over the past three years by Prof. Yisrael Charny of Tel Aviv University and a few of his colleagues, the International Conference on the Holocaust and Genocide will bring to Israel experts in the fields of political science, international law, communications, atomic energy and human rights. "This is the first major interdisciplinary conference on this subject," says Prof. Charny, who has paid for expenses so far out of his own pocket. "We expect to act as a professional pressure group and call attention to cases of potential or actual genocide," he told The Jerusalem Post, adding that the history of the Nazi period might have been very different if Kristallnacht had been covered on TV in the way that the Vietnam War was brought to every living room."

Over 200 delegates are expected from around Israel, with an equal number arriving from places like Sri Lanka, Norway, Brazil, the U.S., Japan and the Philippines. (Israelis may register by writing to

Eli Wiesel

POB 29784, Tel Aviv, or by calling 03-654571.)

Holocaust writer Eli Wiesel, who is chairman of the U.S. Holocaust Council, will be president of the conference. At the opening on June 20 at Yad Vashem, he will speak about remembering the Holocaust, and later, at the Tel Aviv Hilton, he will read a paper on warning against genocide.

Frank Reynolds, the well-known ABC TV journalist, will speak on the role of communications in preventing genocide. "I look forward to the conference as an opportunity to learn and as a responsibility to share views on a subject so important as to numb the senses. It seems to me that is precisely what must never again be allowed to happen — the numbing of the senses," Reynolds told Charny.

CHARNY, THE author of the soon-to-be-published book How Can We Commit the Unthinkable: Genocide, the Human Cancer, expects the conference delegates to maintain regular contact and act as a lobby, using a "genocide early warning system" that is being developed to pinpoint potential murderers of whole peoples. "We don't dare say that we will eliminate genocide," he explains. "But we want to try to reduce it — not to cure the disease-but to fight against it."

Fumikasu Inoue, a Japanese architect who is developing a model for a Holocaust study centre and memorial in Israel, is leaving for Japan to promote participation in the genocide conference. He told The Post that there is great interest in the Holocaust in his native country, and that residents of Krose, a town near Hiroshima, are trying to raise $1 million to build a memorial to the victims of Auschwitz, to tell the world "not only no more Hiroshima, but never again Auschwitz." He hopes to bring some Hiroshima survivors who speak English to attend the conference and talk about what happened to them.

Figure 3. *Jerusalem Post*, Tuesday, April 20, 1982.

conference. When the time came that the Israeli government first demanded that we withdraw the subject of the Armenian Genocide from the conference, Wiesel joined us, meaning specifically myself and Shamai Davidson, MD, a wonderful psychiatrist-psychoanalyst who was the director of Shalvata Hospital, a major psychiatric center in Israel, who himself specialized devotedly in treating Holocaust survivors, and who as noted had the role of co-director of the conference. The three of us adamantly refused to follow the dictates of the IMFA to remove the subject of the Armenian Genocide and/or the Armenian scholars from the conference.

Further, even during the unfolding hectic politics of threats, sanctions and retaliations by Israel against the conference and against me that followed during

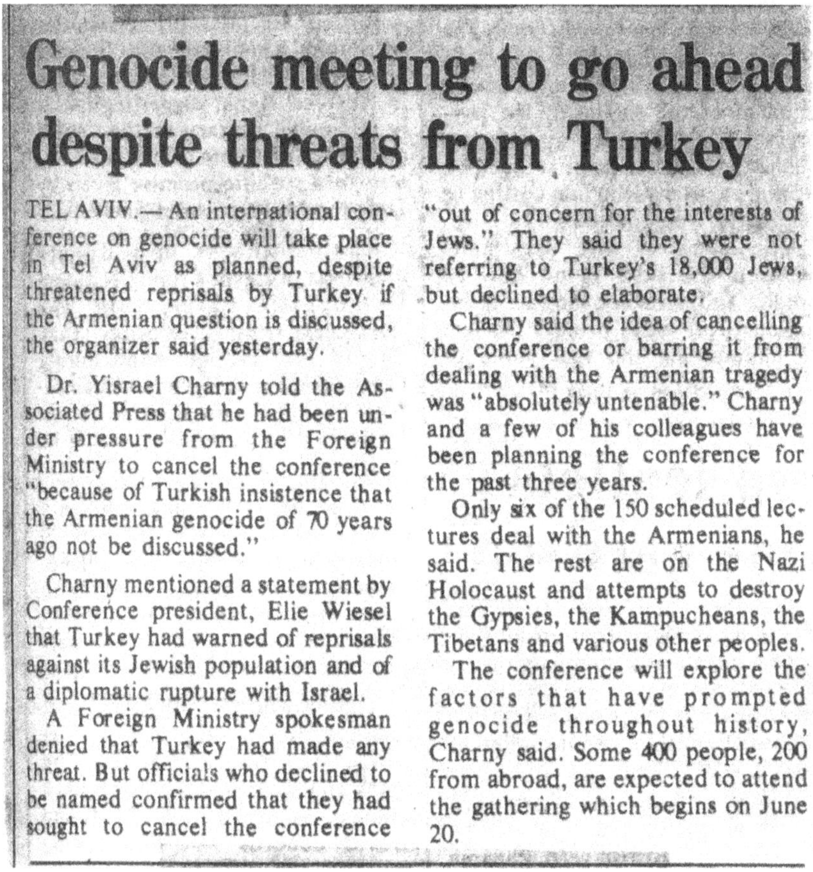

Genocide meeting to go ahead despite threats from Turkey

TEL AVIV.— An international conference on genocide will take place in Tel Aviv as planned, despite threatened reprisals by Turkey if the Armenian question is discussed, the organizer said yesterday.

Dr. Yisrael Charny told the Associated Press that he had been under pressure from the Foreign Ministry to cancel the conference "because of Turkish insistence that the Armenian genocide of 70 years ago not be discussed."

Charny mentioned a statement by Conference president, Elie Wiesel that Turkey had warned of reprisals against its Jewish population and of a diplomatic rupture with Israel.

A Foreign Ministry spokesman denied that Turkey had made any threat. But officials who declined to be named confirmed that they had sought to cancel the conference "out of concern for the interests of Jews." They said they were not referring to Turkey's 18,000 Jews, but declined to elaborate.

Charny said the idea of cancelling the conference or barring it from dealing with the Armenian tragedy was "absolutely untenable." Charny and a few of his colleagues have been planning the conference for the past three years.

Only six of the 150 scheduled lectures deal with the Armenians, he said. The rest are on the Nazi Holocaust and attempts to destroy the Gypsies, the Kampucheans, the Tibetans and various other peoples.

The conference will explore the factors that have prompted genocide throughout history, Charny said. Some 400 people, 200 from abroad, are expected to attend the gathering which begins on June 20.

Figure 4. *Jerusalem Post*, Friday, June 4, 1982.

the ensuing months, to the best of my knowledge at the time Wiesel remained firm on the subject, though at the same time he was to go on to resign as president of the conference after I had refused to accept the dictates of the IMFA to cancel the conference in entirety.

NEWLY ACCESSED DOCUMENTS OF ISRAEL'S MINISTRY OF FOREIGN AFFAIRS TELL ANOTHER STORY[4]

SECRET

Date: April 20, 1982

To: Ankara and Istanbul

From: Director, Diaspora Desk, Israel Ministry Foreign Affairs Jerusalem

Document No. 6663   [our page no. 34]

... We are continuing to act to minimize and shrink the Armenian subject to every extent possible through all possible means ...[5]

However, now newly released documents from the secret and classified records of the IMFA reveal that, at least according to the Foreign Ministry, there were indeed moments when Wiesel tilted towards some measure of censorship of the Armenian Genocide, and certainly that after he resigned as president he played an immensely active role in personally contacting, one after the other, various leader-participants in the conference such as intended keynote speakers and workshop chairs, distinguished public figures who were to attend, and one source of financial support after another, to urge them to cancel their participation and/or support of the conference. The following are some further illustrative documents of Wiesel's aggressive collaboration with the IMFA to limit and/or close down the conference:

---

4   The excerpts given from Israel government files are from the Israel Ministry of Foreign Affairs files on the International Conference on the Holocaust and Genocide. Note that these files contain some other documents that are still classified, but all the documents that are cited in this article have been released by the Israeli Records Archive under the law that requires public access to records after a given number of years.

　　Note that we are refraining from reproducing names of Ministry officials who are signed on to the various documents since there is no intention here of shaming or criticizing individual government officials as such. We do, of course, very much intend to criticize and indeed shame our otherwise so dear State of Israel for a bevy of violations of basic integrity beginning with the time-honored scandal of the failure to recognize the Armenian Genocide—and it turns out other genocides as well, and continuing with playing *realpolitik* "dirty ball" of out-and-out lying, manipulating, and implicating others. This is not the Israel many of us dreamt of having in fulfillment of a new dignity of the Jewish people.

5   Israel Ministry of Foreign Affairs, April 20, 1984, ISA-mfa-mfa-000368i, 143.

SECRET/IMMEDIATE
Date: June 6, 1982
To: Stockholm
From: Israel Ministry Foreign Affairs Jerusalem
Document No. 4061   [our page number 130]

In a conversation with Elie Wiesel this morning, he requested that you convey to Per Ahlmark [*Per Ahlmark was leader of the Swedish liberal party, 1975–1978, and Deputy Prime Minister, 1976–1978—Ed.*] that he will appreciate very much if Per Ahlmark will not participate in the conference.[6]

CLASSIFIED/IMMEDIATE
Date: June 7, 1982
To: Israel Ministry Foreign Affairs Jerusalem
From: Stockholm
Document No. 7132   [our page number 132]

Please convey to Elie Wiesel from Per Ahlmark.
Dear Elie,
I'm sorry to hear about the conference. I'll go to Israel as a journalist for my paper, *Expressen*. I will not be Repeat not be a participant of the conference. If we do not meet in Israel this time—let's meet soon some other time some other place. Yours—Per Ahlmark[7]

CLASSIFIED/URGENT
Date: Date not clear but apparently June 9, 1982
To: Middle East Desk, Israel Ministry Foreign Affairs Jerusalem
From: Israel General Consul New York
Document No. 287   [our page number 137]

I spoke now with Jack Eisner [*Jack Eisner headed the Holocaust Survivors' Memorial Foundation based in New York. On May 13, 1982, he issued a check for $10,000 to the conference but before it was deposited into the conference account payment was stopped—Ed.*] and he advised me he won't participate in conference and that he supports the position of the government and Elie

6   Israel Ministry of Foreign Affairs, June 6, 1982, ISA-mfa-mfa-000368i, 147.
7   Israel Ministry of Foreign Affairs, June 7, 1982, ISA-mfa-mfa-000368i, 38.

> Wiesel. He also told me he has stopped funding the conference and that he has issued a Stop Payment to check he gave Charny for the conference. He repeated his position and repeated his request we advise Wiesel of his [Eisner's] action.
>
> P.S. I sent telegrams of Wiesel to several people.[8]

In Chapter 3, I will discuss the Elie Wiesel story in further depth. In brief, it is my belief that Wiesel was guided by a mixture of motives beginning with his profound loyalty and caring for the State of Israel, his genuine alarm at the reports by Israel that Jewish lives were at risk, continuing with his lifelong ambivalence about recognizing too strongly the genocides of other peoples as if in competitive comparison to the Holocaust, as well as by personal motives for remaining popular and accepted by the highest authorities of Israel.

We learned from many people who had registered for the conference as active presenters, and whose identities appeared in a full preliminary program that we distributed in April, that they were literally called personally by the Israeli Embassy in their country and asked not to attend!

Moreover, in June many people who checked into hotels in Tel Aviv reported that they were called in their hotel rooms and were actually told the conference was cancelled!

Throughout this drama there were no doubts whatsoever that Turkey was exerting pressures to drop the Armenian subject and/or stop the entire conference, but when push came to shove the Turkish government violently denied that they had or were making any threats against Jewish lives. In fact, there is documentation that shows the Turks even proposed to Israel that it was the Armenians who were setting them up with the false charges that the Turks were making threats against Jewish lives—and in general pictured the Armenians as using the conference "as an instrument to attack Turkey."

> CLASSIFIED
> Date: June 10, 1982
> To: Middle East Desk, Israel Ministry Foreign Affairs Jerusalem
> From: Israel General Consul in Istanbul
> Document No. 390 [our page number 139]

---

8   Israel Ministry of Foreign Affairs, [June 9, 1982], ISA-mfa-mfa-000368i, 37.

[*The consul is reporting on a conversation with a Turkish diplomat—henceforth D—about the response of the Chief of Staff of the Turkish Foreign Ministry— henceforth G*].

D said that Turkey is very appreciative of the efforts that are being made by the Israel Foreign Ministry on the conference on the Holocaust. G reported that he said to Vassid [*the head of the Turkish Jewish community— Ed.*]: Don't get overly upset by the reports of threats as it were against the Jewish community in Turkey. It is possible that these vicious rumors are coming from Armenian sources.[9]

Slowly but surely, Turkish officials issued denials that they were threatening Jewish lives. *But who was to believe the Turks?* After all their record as absolute liars about history and then grotesque manipulators of *realpolitik* power was totally clear, so how in the world was one going to accept the denials of threats of violence from such nefarious dirty players?

From April to June 1982 the Israeli government succeeded in bringing about Elie Wiesel's resignation as president of the conference and, as noted, embarked on an active campaign to damage and even force the closing down of the conference, including bringing about a withdrawal of Yad Vashem from being the official hosts of the official and value-defining conference opening, withdrawal of Tel Aviv University from being a co-sponsor and withdrawal of its Rector, Prof. Yoram Dinstein, from chairing the closing Summation Session of the conference, cancellation of a good number of distinguished speakers and lecturers such as Prof. Yehuda Bauer and attorney Alan Dershowitz (in those days known as a powerful human rights advocate), cancellation of several hundred registrants, and censorship of any news of the conference in the Israeli press. The ministry was ostensibly riding high and yet they still were failing in their basic goal because the Armenian speakers were arriving after all, the Armenian Genocide was on the program, and over 300 registrants still were on their way—a number that is not insignificant for any academic conference.

IMMEDIATE
Date: June 6, 1982
To: Ankara and Istanbul
From: Israel Ministry of Foreign Affairs Jerusalem
Document No. 3964   [our page number 127]

---

9   Israel Ministry of Foreign Affairs, June 10, 1982, ISA-mfa-mfa-0003677, 279.

A *Haaretz* story of this date stated that "Turkey firmly denied all reports that Turkey had threatened to harm Jews in Turkey in response to the participation of Armenia in a conference on genocide that was scheduled to take place in Tel Aviv." The *Haaretz* article continued that the *New York Times* of the previous day had published a statement that the Israeli representative in Ankara had informed the Turkish Foreign Ministry that "all official Israeli institutions have cancelled their participation in the conference, and that many of the registered participants had been asked not to participate in the conference. He expressed the hope that the organizers would decide to cancel the conference if it shrunk into a small private seminar. He also said that to the best of his knowledge Turkey had not threatened to harm Jews."[10]

THE STORY OF YAD VASHEM'S WITHDRAWAL FROM THE CONFERENCE

For all practical purposes we also lost the support of other institutions that were our sponsors, Hunter College of the City University of New York, and in Israel, the Szold National Institute for Research in the Behavioral Sciences in Jerusalem. Hunter College, where I had been teaching psychology some summers, never withdrew formally. They simply stopped participating. The Szold Institute, to which I was intimately connected as a Senior Fellow, had to drop out because it was a government institution. It was there that, over an eight-year period, I had collaborated intensely, week after week, with Dr. Chanan Rapaport, the Institute's director, on the historic development of a Genocide Early Warning System (GEWS).[11] Chanan Rapaport and I remain appreciative friends to this day, but his hands were tied.

---

10 Israel Ministry of Foreign Affairs, June 6, 1982, ISA-mfa-mfa-000368i, 45.
11 Genocide Early Warning System (GEWS) by Israel W. Charny and Chanan Rapaport. Original presentation 1977 in a pamphlet by the Szold National Institute for Research in the Behavioral Sciences, Jerusalem, Israel. This was the earliest known development of an early warning system for genocide.

   Subsequent major publication as "Toward a Genocide Early Warning System," chapter 13 in Israel W. Charny and Chanan Rapaport, *How Can We Commit the Unthinkable? Genocide: The Human Cancer* (Boulder, CO: Westview Press, 1982), 283–331; and "Appendix: The Flow of Normal Life Processes in Individuals, Families, Groups and the Societal System that Can Culminate in Genocidal Destructiveness," ibid., 344–347. The chapter has since been republished in a variety of publications.

   The book was republished as a paperback: Israel W. Charny and Chanan Rapaport, *Genocide: The Human Cancer* (New York: Hearst Books, 1983). In 1998 there appeared a Portuguese translation with a new Introduction and updated bibliography. In 2019 the original English edition was republished by Routledge with a Kindle edition.

The story of Yad Vashem's withdrawal is a dramatic one. Notwithstanding the fact that they too as a government institution were ordered to cancel their relationship with us, there seemed to remain somehow a welcome tension in the two main leaders with whom we had agreed on the Opening Ceremony and Program of the conference, Dr. Yitzchak Arad, who was the director, and Gideon Hausner, chair of the international board, who had been the famous prosecutor in the history-making trial of Adolph Eichmann. The two seemed concerned about the lack of integrity of cancelling an agreement and a program that we all had negotiated so thoughtfully. Given that they really had no explanation or excuse, they then retreated to a core disagreement they had with us but which they had managed to "swallow" and bypass in our original agreement: Yad Vashem believed that the Holocaust was in a uniquely unique category of its own, therefore was not really comparable with other genocides. Our conference obviously addressed genocide as a universal human problem, and even the special meanings of the Holocaust in our history as humans did not remove it from the collective subject matter of genocides or remove it from comparative study with other genocides.

But why did this trouble them now when it had not stopped them from negotiating the original agreement? The simplest guess is that, although they didn't say so, their boss—the government—told them to cut us off. Nonetheless, at the same time there developed evidence that they had gotten in trouble with their own community, and that they were being attacked by close colleagues for doing business with us heretics.

The letter announcing the cancellation of the opening of the conference at Yad Vashem in Jerusalem was written on April 29, 1982 by Arad, with a further notation by his signature that the letter was written with the agreement of Hausner. They were clearly uncomfortable, but they were also adamant and put their finger directly on the key issue for them. It was not Turkey's demands to get rid of the Armenian Genocide subject. It was the uniqueness of the Holocaust, and the fact that some of their own staff gave them hell for ever agreeing to host

---

Studies validating the GEWS, including the finding that demonization or attribution of severe danger to the other **together with** dehumanization of the same people target is a frequent and especially virulent early-warning indicator, were completed on the Armenian Genocide by Astourian; DeChamps and DeChamps on the Rawandan Genocide; and Paulino on a threatened genocide in the Dominican Republic. See Stephan Astourian, "The Armenian Genocide: An Interpretation," *The History Teacher* 23, no. 2 (1990): 111–160; Elisabeth and Phillipe DeChamps, "Le Gènocide Rwandais: Deux Ans Après: Le Modelle d'Israel W. Charny," *Dialogue* 190 (April/May 1996): 10–32; and Edward Paulino, "Anti-Haitianism, Historical Memory, and the Potential for Genocidal Violence in the Dominican Republic," *Genocide Studies and Prevention* 1, no. 3 (2006): 265–288.

our Opening, for we were, after all, quite *unkosher*, notwithstanding their "respect for the conference." Arad wrote as follows (translated from the Hebrew):

> Following the public announcement of the program of the First Interna-
> tional Conference on the Holocaust and Genocide, a number of members
> of the directorate of Yad Vashem expressed their opposition to opening
> the conference in Yad Vashem. In their judgment, the conference program
> is likely to erase the unique nature of the Shoah and move it into a general
> framework of horrific acts and mass murders in our century.[12]

Notwithstanding the above, Dr. Arad went on to convey the previously quoted respect for the conference and also made a point of inviting us *yes* to open the conference with a visit to the basic Yad Vashem Memorial of the Eternal Flame before then returning by buses to Tel Aviv for the actual deliberations of the conference. In other words, the presentations by anyone associated with Yad Vashem, most specifically by Elie Wiesel and Gideon Hausner who had been scheduled to speak to us within the reverent setting of the Yad Vashem memorial, were out.

Yea, Arad also acknowledged that they had originally confirmed the program for the full Opening at Yad Vashem, and *yes*, he wrote in a gentleman-like way apologizing for the logistical mayhem they were causing us. Together with the fact that they had strained to convey their respect for the conference and to invite us not-quite fully-Untouchables to a memorial session, there was some consolation to us when never before had the Holocaust and the universal problem of genocide met. But clearly it was a big loss for the very major purpose we had set ourselves to bring the study of Holocaust and all genocides together into a shared and unified study of this most terrible of repeated human behaviors— over and over again killing masses of "others."

THE SMOKING GUN REVEALED: A SENIOR ISRAELI DIPLOMAT IN TURKEY KNEW NOTHING AT ALL ABOUT THREATS TO JEWS!

The government continued to hope that its relentless attacks would bring more cuts in the conference program and resources and kept up its relentless campaign which by now had moved from its big gun of claims of Turkish threats

---

12 Yitzchak Arad, with the explicit agreement of Gideon Hausner, Letter to Prof. Israel Charny, April 29, 1982. Personal communication.

against Jews in Turkey to its big gun of threats that Turkey would cut off life-saving escape routes of Jews fleeing Iran and Syria through Turkey.

What is now being revealed for the first time is that previously classified documents of the IMFA make it entirely clear that **the alleged threats to detain or to possibly return the escaping Jews from Iran and Syria to their countries of origin were fabricated—made up—no less than by the Israeli government and attributed to the Turks.** *See the full English text of the Israeli Consul's letter below. The original text in Hebrew is available upon request.*[13]

The classified letter that follows, translated from the Hebrew, from Israel's General Consul in Istanbul to Jerusalem is dated June 17, 1982. This was the first day that two-day pre-conference workshops were already taking place in Tel Aviv in preparation for the full conference a few days later, but the Consul is full of praise for his colleagues for succeeding in achieving "the progressive reduction of the conference" and still even predicts "its virtual expected cancellation." At the same time he goes on, somewhat incredulously, to question the "one point which it seems to me has been the driving central concept in our overwhelmingly intense efforts to cancel the conference ... the hints that were made about the subject of the safe passage of Jews from Iran and Syria through Turkey."[14] Amazingly, the Consul goes on to say definitively that "**The subject was unknown to me**" [*bold mine –Ed.*]."

The statement just quoted was permitted for dissemination by the Israeli government censor, so I see no reason not to note also the existence of still another statement that strengthens our report even as I avoid giving identifying information of the number of the document because this one is still marked as requiring permission of the censor even though it adds absolutely no additional knowledge. Of course, the whole arrangement is a joke—the law requires release of old records after so many years, and the Records Authority complies but then continues to insist on clearance of no few documents with the censor. The additional statement we have found in another IMFA record also concludes adamantly that there were no threats made.

So that now we were trapped by Israeli lies about threats that didn't exist but were attributed to a government that is a known liar about the basic truth of their previous Ottoman government committing a major genocide, that their

13 A translation of the full text into English of the Consul letter appears shortly in the article. The Hebrew original of the letter of the Israeli Consul is available upon request to en-cygeno@gmail.com.
14 Israel Ministry of Foreign Affairs, June 17, 1982, ISA-mfa-mfa-000300tj, document no. 404, 80, 82 [our page numbers 151–152].

new Atatürk government continued, in which 1.5 million Armenians—as well as millions more of Assyrians, Yezidis, Greeks and smaller numbers of other "non-Turks" as well were murdered.[15]

In addition, throw in for good measure the pressures of Tel Aviv University against this writer, who was then an untenured associate professor of psychology in the School of Social Work, and throw in the very powerful and successful efforts to cancel the funds that had been committed to support the conference so that we faced very serious financial deficits (some of which led me personally to be unable to meet my own basic financial obligations at the time such as payments for health insurance). Ironically, the demonstrably real threats—though granted of financial and professional annihilation and not our physical lives—now were against me and Kenes, the company that was organizing the conference.[16]

Figure 5. General Consul of Israel.

---

15 See the Special Issue of the web magazine, *Genocide Prevention Now* (*GPN*), which was published for several years by the Institute on the Holocaust and Genocide in Jerusalem with the support of the Carnegie Corporation: *Genocide Prevention Now* 5 (2011): *Special Issue on Co-Victims of the Armenian Genocide: Assyrians, Yezidis, Greeks*, http://www.ihgjlm.com/genocide-prevention-now-special-issue-5/.

16 This is an opportunity to express the greatest appreciation to Mr. Gideon Rivlin, the owner and manager of Kenes Tours, who were our excellent congress organizers, for his unqualified as well as financially generous support of the conference as he saw it being subjected to enormous political and economic pressures. For Mr. Rivlin too it was a matter of principle.

In one letter from Rivlin to the IMFA he notes resolutely that the company organizing the conference could withdraw from the entire conflict because they were simply "contractors"

CLASSIFIED
Date: June 17, 1982 | 404 | file ISA-mfa-mfa-00030tj
To: Head, Middle East Desk Jerusalem
From: Israel General Consul Istanbul
Document No.: 404   [our page numbers 151–152]
Copies to: Associate Director (name), Assistant Director; Director of Dias-
pora; Representative of Israel in Ankara
Subject: Holocaust Conference—Interim Summary

It is hard to predict if the conference were to take place at its scheduled time
[*the Consul is already under the belief that the conference has been postponed
or cancelled—all italic comments in brackets are by the author-editor, Israel W.
Charny*] despite the recent events in the wake of IDF's activity in Lebanon
[*Israel invaded Lebanon on June 6, 1982*], but the stage to which we have
arrived as described by you in your letter constitutes a "good derived from
bad" situation [*translation from the Hebrew*, meaz yatza matok].

In my opinion despite the strong criticism [*articles had begun to appear
in the Israeli press criticizing the government's efforts to censor the conference*],
the progressive reduction of the scope of the conference heading towards its
expected virtual cancellation was an outcome that one is to celebrate from
the point of view of the relationships between Turkey and Israel. I believe
that the positive influence of this development is already showing in the
behaviors and statements being made by the Turks with regard to "Operation Peace for Galilee." It is hard to believe the statements would have been so
restrained had the conference actually taken place, they are now restrained,
certainly in comparison to the reactions coming from Europe on the matter
[*meaning Operation Galilee*]. Additional signs in this direction include the
pleasant atmosphere in recent deliberations between Middle East officials in
Ankara with our diplomatic representative, who has been summoned twice
by them. It is my opinion that not only the postponement or cancellation of
the conference have brought about a reduction of tension in the attitude of

---

who were engaged to execute the conference, and that the responsibility for the cancellation
of the conference—and all the legal suits that could develop—could be laid on me as the
originator and leader of the conference. A bit of terror struck me as I read this and I realized
that I could well have been in very deep waters of many legal and financial complications. But
it is almost as if Gideon Rivlin is writing with tongue in cheek, because he goes on to open
the next paragraph saying deliciously, "But I will not do that."

the Turks to us, but also all the press reports, including the article of Elon in *Haaretz* [*well known columnist Amos Elon, who was the author of the best-selling "The Israelis: Founders and Sons," published a major article in Haaretz on June 11, 1982 entitled, "Their Holocaust: As a Result of Turkish Pressures the Foreign Ministry Demands Cancellation of an International Conference in which One of the Subjects was Scheduled to be the Holocaust of the Armenian People."*] that conveyed clearly to the Turks our good intentions to them and the difficulties encountered in a democratic society [*referring to limits on government overriding academic freedom*], and the efforts we invested in order to bring to a maximum reduction of the influence of this conference even if it were to take place and Armenians would participate in it. These press reports also had the potential of clarifying to the military regime in Turkey what limitations there are on a democratic government when it seeks to limit academic freedom.

[*Bold is by me—Ed.*] **I want to take this opportunity to comment on one point which it seems to me has been the driving central concept in our overwhelmingly intense efforts to cancel the conference. I am referring to the hints that were made about the subject of the safe passage of Jews from Iran and Syria through Turkey. The subject was unknown to me until Mr. Veissid** [*head of Turkish Jewish community who had appeared at my Tel Aviv clinic to convey to me the grave dangers to the lives of Jews if the conference were to take place*] **returned from Israel and informed me that to his great astonishment he found that "all the arguments he had prepared against the conference were now trivialized in the face of the decisive argument that was now conveyed to him that Turkey had threatened that if the conference would take place as planned, they would detain the Syrian and Iranian Jews who were escaping across the border to Turkey" but then Veissid himself adopted this argument out of "a feeling of terrible responsibility to my Jewish brothers" and on this basis he made the effort to convince Dr. Charny and others to cancel the conference.**

By the way, here in Turkey there were no signs whatsoever of a relationship between this subject [*escaping Jews*] **and the conference. Further, I would like to comment that whoever knows the fierce commitment of the Turks in their traditions and principles not to detain refugees, would not entertain any thought whatsoever that Turkey was capable of endangering the lives of the Jews by returning them to the Syrians and Iranians. Moreover, this is a period in which Turkey is**

> making every effort to improve her image in the world, and to me it is inconceivable that she would have done something so evil as the above and thus would have invited severe criticism against her from the free world.
>
> To conclude, "good derived from bad" [*see first paragraph*] and our efforts that were publicized had an impressive effect on the Turks that is likely to serve us further in later events ...
>
>
> Yours truly,
> (Israel General Consul Istanbul)[17]

The further price I paid was that I was never to be granted tenure by Tel Aviv University. In fact, all the committees involved in the Via Dolorosa ("Way of Suffering") tenure process did vote for my tenure, only for the Rector, the same Professor Yoram Dinstein (who later became president of the university) to refuse to sign the final authorization. Dinstein had been approached by me much earlier to be a member of the Organizing Committee, and even more than that to be the chair of the closing Summation Session of the conference, and had agreed to do so. Once the pressures of the Israeli government began, he pulled out. In the classified documents of the Israel Foreign Ministry there is a letter in which he conveys that Tel Aviv University would not be supporting the conference, and in which he also lies that he had met with me several times to discuss my failure to invite actual meetings of the Organizing Committee, but given my failure to answer his critique properly he had decided to withdraw even before the diplomatic crisis. The real truth is that Dinstein never met with me and I was to learn of the university pulling out and was told that I was in "big trouble" with the university by the chairman of my department when we were both in the bathroom urinating next to one another. This was shortly after I had returned from a conference of Amnesty International in Amsterdam to which I had been invited with Professors Leo Kuper (UCLA) and Irving Louis Horowitz (Rutgers) to present our newly emerging academic works on genocide which were then signaling the possible emergence of a new full-fledged discipline of genocide studies.[18]

---

17 Israel Ministry of Foreign Affairs, June 7, 1982, ISA-mfa-mfa-00030tj, 80, 82.

18 Following Raphael Lemkin's 1944 trailblazing work (Raphael Lemkin, *Access Rule in Occupied Europe* [Washington, DC: Carnegie Endowment for International Peace, 1944]) and creation of the concept of "genocide" towards the end of World War II, there was one

When all is said and done, now many years later, and for me in my truly old age, I can say that I am genuinely proud of my conduct, and paradoxically grateful to the government and to my university for setting before me a fundamental challenge to choose between personal, professional and financial security and basic ethical values. Regarding Tel Aviv University, of course it hurt deeply, and in my own way of thinking may have contributed psychosomatically to my development of cancer a few years later. But I still feel I was privileged to live out such a basic challenge between self-interest and critical ethical values. I'm also happy to add that I sued Tel Aviv University and won a substantial out of court settlement, let alone that there soon came five years when I was simultaneously drawing my Tel Aviv pension while serving as a professor and head of an innovative department that I had been invited to establish at the Hebrew University of Jerusalem. It was a "Turkish delight."

Two Collections of Papers Presented at the Conference:
Two volumes of papers that were presented at the conference were published at the time:

Israel W. Charny, ed., *Toward the Understanding and Prevention of Genocide: Proceedings of the International Conference on the Holocaust and Genocide* (Boulder, CO: Westview Press, 1984). Republished by Routledge Publishers, 2019.

Richard G. Hovannisian, ed., *The Armenian Genocide in Perspective* (New Brunswick, NJ: Transaction Publishers, 1986).

English-language book on genocide published in Holland: Pieter Drost, *The Crime of State*, 2 vols. (Leyden: A. W. Sythoff, 1959). There then followed many years in which we know of no publications on genocide as a process until three books published respectively by Horowitz in 1976 (Irving Louis Horowitz, *Taking Lives: Genocide and State Power*, 3rd ed. [New Brunswick, NJ: Transaction Books, 1982, 1st ed., 1976]), Kuper in 1981 (Leo Kuper, *Genocide: Its Political Use in the Twentieth Century* [London: Penguin, 1981, republished, New Haven, CT: Yale University Press, 1982]), and Charny in 1982 (Israel W. Charny and Chanan Rapaport, *How Can We Commit the Unthinkable?*). A partial exception is Richard Arens, ed., *Genocide in Paraguay* (Philadelphia, PA: Temple University Press, 1976). However, this noteworthy and valuable book is about the specific case of the genocide of the *Aché* Indians and not about genocide overall as a process.

With Lemkin's book and his creation of the word-concept "genocide," the three books by Kuper, Horowitz, and Charny became the intellectual foundation for a new academic discipline of genocide studies.

להלך התיכת ומרייסדיים:

חתימה	תפקיד בעמותה	משלח יד	מען	ת. זהות	ת. לידה . ח	משפחה . ח	שם פרטי

(in Hebrew) Signatures of Profs. Israel W. Charny, Shamai Davidson, and Elie Wiesel (in that order from the top) on document submitted to the Non-Profit Authority of the Israel Ministry of Justice to establish the Insitute on the Holocaust and Genocide

Figure 6. Signatures (in Hebrew) of Profs. Israel W. Charny, Shamai Davidson, and Elie Wiesel (in that order from the top) on document submitted to the Non-Profit Authority of the Israel Ministry of Justice to establish the Institute on the Holocaust and Genocide.

The clear-cut success of the First International Conference on the Holocaust and Genocide in 1982 enabled Israel Charny, Shamai Davidson, and Elie Wiesel to submit a request to the Non-Profit Authority of the Ministry of Interior of the State of Israel to establish a long-term institute. In fact, the three had joined together in an institute beginning in 1979, but now they proceeded to register the institute legally. The institute was legally confirmed on July 23, 1983, at this point with the name, "The Permanent Conference for Research on the Holocaust and Genocide," and was situated legally at the Shalvata Mental Health Center located in Hod Hasharon. Israel. A few years later, on November 5, 1988, the government approved changing to its long-term name, Institute on the Holocaust and Genocide with its location in Jerusalem.

The above reproduction carries the signatures of the three founders of the Institute on the original application to the Ministry to establish it as a non-profit organization responsible for annual financial reporting and subject to the auditing and supervision of the government of Israel. The work of the Institute through all the years has been voluntary with no income to senior staff with the exception of the office/publications coordinator.

See further history in Israel W. Charny, ed., *Encyclopedia of Genocide*, 2 vols. (Santa Barbara, CA: ABC-Clio, 1999) (see below for information on the contents of this book and its other editions).

international Council of the Institute on the Holocaust and Genocide in Jerusalem

SUPPLEMENT 1: PROGRAM OF CONFERENCE

How does One Summarize the Learning that Took Place at the First International Conference on the Holocaust and Genocide?

Obviously, the very impressive richness of the program, the wide scope and variety of ethnicities of presenters, and the wide range of their scholarly disciplines suggests that a rich intellectual process took place.

As to how to summarize the content, I think the summaries will be happily different for a good many. A good number of Holocaust survivors, for example, found themselves comforted and confirmed by the genuine depth of interest in the Holocaust and in the basic causes of genocide. People working with survivors, on the other hand, were very aware of how their subject was treated by different practitioners and different cultures. Those conceived with the proliferation of mega weapons of mass destruction and the emerging danger of what Prof. John Somerville (USA) and Shingo Shibata (Japan) characterize as "omnicide" have their perspective on the conference's genuine awareness of the new risks to humankind. **And so on—including the contributions of the first generation of scholars of what is yet to become the field and academic discipline of Holocaust and genocide studies,** such as myself, Leo Kuper, and Helen Fein. Obviously, our summaries of the coverage of the conference would emphasize the very focus on genocide, a concept that was never at the center of any international professional meeting, as far as we know. Finally, there are some scholars who are talking about how human beings kill each other off terribly cruelly and frequently, how they organize such campaigns, and what is driving them. We ourselves were so grateful for the conference we had initiated and organized.

The Armenian Genocide was, both very legitimately and inadvertently, a major form of the conference; and certainly for Armenians it was a new level of recognition and invitation and by the international intellectual community in general, and by Jews/Israelis, or from another angle by Holocaust scholars and leaders of Holocaust memorials. *Asbarez,* a major Armenian-American newspaper, drew a very meaningful perspective of the broad meaning of the conference for genocide scholarship.

> The presence of the Armenians was an issue that often erupted into debate. Yet as the conference proceeded and papers by Jewish and Armenian specialists on various aspects of genocide and its effects on survivors and their descendants were read, the value of comparative study became

increasingly apparent. Historians, journalists, sociologists, professors of literature, psychiatrists and psychologists all contributed the insight of their disciplines to the common knowledge, creating a dialogue that could only serve to deepen understanding of one of the most perplexing forms of human behavior: the organized attempt to exterminate a race or ethnic group. The conference also helped to give scholars, accustomed by the nature of research to study in isolation, and by their chosen area of concentration to probe the depths of human behavior, to benefit from that sense of release derived from shared experience.[19]

An even broader effort to summarize some of the many intriguing lectures appeared in another leading Armenian-American newspaper, the *Armenian Mirror Spectator*. Understandably, we see here a particular emphasis of the meaning for the Armenian community, but it is in the context of participation and interest in a variety of other subjects that were presented.

The Conference, which was designed to lead "towards understanding, intervention and prevention of Genocide," failed to come up with any concrete formulas to deal with the problem of Genocide.

But most of the participants came away from the conference with a strong sense of accomplishment, as if they had, perhaps, embarked on a process that would, by the momentum begun at the conference, go ahead to make a real contribution to the problems it considered.

As Prof. Charny put it [*quoting a famous Talmudic dictum—Ed.*], "It's not for us to finish the job, but very much our task to begin it."

The four-day conference included moments of bitterness, antagonism, and disagreement, but also many instances of mutual understanding, enlightenment and hope.

Rev. Franklin Littell, of Temple University, led a fascinating session on the problem of teachers who deny the Holocaust. "How can we maintain standards worthy of a republic of learning," was a focus of this session, with many wondering why universities cannot enforce higher standards of scholarship in their faculties.

The participants included Mel Mermelstein, a survivor of the Auschwitz concentration camp in Germany, who described the legal action taken by him against the "Institute of Historical Review," an organization which publishes material casting doubt on the facts of the Jewish Holocaust and

19 "Conference on Genocide Held with Armenian Scholars," *Asbarez*, July 10, 1982.

which challenged him to prove that Jews were gassed at Auschwitz. Mr. Mermelstein took the Institute to court, suing for libel, injurious denial of an established fact, and defamation of his family. One year after first filing the suit, a judge ruled that the Holocaust is "not reasonably open to dispute." Mr. Mermelstein stressed the importance of challenging the statements of those who distort history. And while his search for legal remedy has been a long and expensive one, he believes that it is extremely important.

Marjorie Housepian Dobkin spoke on "The Price of Collaboration: News from Turkey 1915–1923," in which she traced the extensive reporting of Armenian massacres that appeared in the press in the United States at that time.

In his interesting presentation, Israel Charny discussed "The Missing Principle in Psychopathology: Disorders of Pseudocompetence and Evil." Dr. Charny explored the problem of defining normality and abnormality following the Holocaust. He pointed out that ... the Holocaust could not have been carried out without the support of "normal" and "rational" community leaders. But how can people who commit such murders be considered "normal," Prof. Charny wondered? Such a phenomenon requires a new definition of dysfunction to include the person who surrenders his independence and can no longer think for himself or make rational judgments.

Archbishop Shahé Ajamian who represented the Armenian community on the organization committee for the Symposium and who delivered the opening address, commented at the end that the conference represented "a huge step forward in bringing the Armenians to the attention of the international community."

This was achieved first because the high quality of the Armenian papers attracted a great deal of attention, the Archbishop said. Second, he pointed out, all other speakers were placed in a position of being either for or against the Armenian participation. Finally, because there was Turkish pressure and because the conference suffered as a result, the Armenian issue became the central issue of the conference.

The Armenian community must now follow up the conference by keeping in touch with the organizers so that future events, inside or outside Israel, will include Armenians. It is now up to the Armenians to take advantage of the situation and to be certain that "the Armenian Genocide is included in an adequate way in all future publications and activities," Abp. Ajamian said.[20]

---

20 "A New Conspiracy of Silence is Intolerable," *The Armenian Mirror Spectator*, July 3, 1982.

THE CONFERENCE PROGRAM

Following the above, we present the key information about the topics of session and names of chairs and speakers. This information was taken from the original two printed pamphlets (approximately eighty pages) that were distributed to conference participants, but everything was in an intense dynamic flux. Presenters were busy deciding whether they would come to Israel, and even if they did or if they themselves lived in Israel, whether they would participate in the conference or not. An endless parade of dramatic scenes ensues where seminars or speakers are cancelled, and in many cases such as in respect of plenaries, speakers were replaced.

The following program should be regarded first of all as the basic structure risks that had been prepared for the groundbreaking event. We organizers were too busy to maintain formal records of who came and/or didn't, and maybe that's just as well although the reader will see that some instances become clear in various chapters of the book.

Finally, for those who want to see what the State of Israel, from Prime Minister to Foreign Minister, to a long line of foreign ministry officials, and what the great academic authorities of Tel Aviv University in particular—especially its Rector Prof. Yoram Dinstein—absolutely needed to censor, shut down, and discredit: here is the *Terrible Program* of the First International Conference on the Holocaust and Genocide. How could Israel/Tel Aviv University tolerate such material and such speakers?!

Program of the First International Conference on the Holocaust and Genocide, Tel Aviv, 1982

Pre-Conference Intensive Dialogue Workshops
Tel Aviv, 2 days, June 17–18, 1982, preceding the Conference, June 20–24

First International Conference on the Holocaust and Genocide,
Tel Aviv, June 20–24, 1982

Pre-Conference Intensive Dialogue Workshops:

Twelve workshops were planned following an opening plenary session with **Elie Wiesel**. *The Israeli government had a fully detailed preliminary program which we* *had distributed internationally in April and thus succeeded in contacting a large number of the scheduled workshop leaders and requested-advised them to cancel. The five starred workshops did take place, and a group discussion format was arranged for registrants whose workshop leader had not arrived.*

1. **Yehuda Bauer**: Jewish-Gentile Relationships in Nazi-Occupied Europe
2. **Ben Whittaker**: Genocide, Real and Potential: Minority Group Rights
3. **Alan Dershowitz**: The Role of Law in Combatting Genocide
4. **Frank Reynolds** (ABC Network): The Performance of the Media during the Holocaust: Lessons for Contemporary and Future Situations
5. **Saul Mendlovitz**: A World Perspective of Genocide
6. **Laurie Wiseberg**: The Response of Governments, Inter-Governmental Organizations and Non-Governmental Organizations to Genocide
7. ***Rev. Franklin H. Littell**: Teaching the Holocaust and Genocide
8. ***Shamai Davidson, MD**: Coming to Terms with the Past and Living with Memories of the Unlivable in the Lives of Survivors and their Families
9. ***Robert J. Lifton, MD:** Psycho-historical Aspects of the Holocaust and Genocide
10. ***John Somerville and Shingo Shibata**: Nuclear Weaponry and Ecocidal Technology: The Extension of the Threat of the Holocaust and Genocide to All Mankind
11. **Rabbi Marc Tanenbaum**: Dehumanization as a Prelude to Genocide: Developing an Early Warning System
12. **Sidra Ezrachi and John Felstiner**: Creation in the Shadow of Catastrophe: The Artistic Response to the Holocaust

International Conference on the Holocaust and Genocide
June 20–24, 1982, Tel Aviv

Selected Program Sessions

Sunday, June 20, 1982: Opening of the Conference

The conference was originally scheduled to open at Yad Vashem in Jerusalem where it was to be addressed by **Elie Wiesel, Yitzhak Arad,** Director of Yad Vashem, and **Gideon Hausner,** who had been the prosecutor at the Eichmann trial. However, the Israeli government prevailed on Yad Vashem to cancel its participation.

An intense process followed of securing a hall at the Tel Aviv Hilton, where the conference already was scheduled to continue from the following day on and to securing a new plenary speaker for the opening. At least two distinguished Jewish leaders personally agreed to take the role but then cancelled in the hours approaching the opening with tales of the pressures that had been thrust upon them. The day was then saved when a wonderful acceptance was received from beloved Member of Knesset, **Ora Namir,** who in later years served first as Israel's Minister of Welfare and later as Ambassador to China. Ora absolutely opposed the government censorship and gave an inspiring send-off to the conference.

The second half of the evening of the opening session was devoted to a full briefing of the audience by the director of the conference, Israel W. Charny, as to all the political dynamics and attacks on the conference that had taken place, and then followed a fully open dialogue with the audience and their questions and comments. As is noted elsewhere in this book, at least two of the comments from the audience became fuller statements by two of the scheduled major participants in the conference, who had indeed arrived in Israel but then decided not to participate. One was Rabbi Marc H. Tanenbaum, director, National Inter-Religious Affairs, American Jewish Committee, who received a telephone order from his office in New York to withdraw his participation and was obviously upset, but complied with his orders and sought to rationalize them. The other person was Jack Eisner, president of the Holocaust Survivor's Memorial Foundation, who had contributed $10,000 to the conference but then instructed the bank to stop payment. Eisner made a point of saying that as a survivor and a person loyal to the State of Israel, he was pleased with what he had done, but that as a human being he was not really happy with himself.

Note (repeating the earlier clarification): The following are from the published program that was distributed at the conference and did reflect advice of cancellations up to the time we went to press. However, it should be understood that some of the lecturers scheduled below also chose not to attend the conference.

Monday, June 21, 1982

Opening Plenary: Chairs, **Israel W. Charny and Shamai Davidson, MD**
Opening of Proceedings: Why Remember? Suffering as a Link between Two
Peoples: **Archbishop Shahé Ajamian, Armenian Patriarchate, Jerusalem**

Between Holocaust and Genocide, an Attempt at a Definition: **Yehuda Bauer**
Deadly Endings: Models of Genocide Past and to Come: **Helen Fein**
The Role of Law in the Prevention of Genocide: **Alan Dershowitz**

> **Workshop 1**: Psycho-Historical Aspects of the Holocaust and Genocide,
> **Robert J. Lifton, Md.**

The Cognitive Approach and Preventing Genocide: Chair, **Louis René Beres;**
    Dan Bar-On, Richard Flantz, Richard Laurence, Barbara Harff
Balancing the Individual and Broad Psychosocial Factors: Chair, **Eva Fogelman;**
    Dieter D. Hartmann, Alan S. Zuckerman, John K. Roth
Teaching through Experience—Explanation and Discussion: Chair, **Nira Kfir;**
    Helen H. Waterford, Rina Neher-Bernheim, Harrison M. Davis
Long-Term Effects of Survival: Chair, **Shamai Davidson, MD; Netta Kohn**
    Dor-Shav, Judith Hemmendinger, Stephen Karr, Harvey Peskin, Alen
    J. Salarian
Confronting Destruction and Genocide: Chair, **Rabbi Emanuel Rackman;**
    Rudolf G. Roden, Rabbi Robert Reeve Brenner, Yaffa Eliach
Special Session on Southeast Asia: **Marc H. Tanenbaum, david hawk**

> **Workshop 2:** Teaching the Holocaust—Experiences, Priorities, and Reac-
> tions: **Neil H. Katz, Alan L. Berger**

The Price of Indifference: Chair, **Rev. Franklin H. Littell; Vahakn N. Dadrian,**
    Chester L. Hunt, Arlene Rossen Cardozo, Yosef Nedava
The What and When of Rescue and Rehabilitation: Chair, **Monty N. Pen-**
    kower; Haim Genizi, Robert W. Ross, Romani Rose, Andre Krump-
    erman, MD
The Artistic Response: Chair, **John Felstiner; Ruth Schenfeld, Leo Hamalian,**
    Frieda W. Aaron, Hana Yaoz-Kest
Educating the Professional and the Professional Educating the Adolescent:
    Chair, **Chaim Schatzker; Richard Libowitz, Margaret Sternstrom,**
    Father Robert Bullock, Marilyn B. Feingold, Henry Hausdorff, Isaiah
    Kuperstein
Long-Term Effects of Survival II: Chair, **Harvey Peskin; Hillel Klein, Sarah**
    Moscovitz, Yael Danieli, Abraham J. Peck
Children in a War of Terror—Northern Ireland, Southern Lebanon, and Israel:
    Chair, **Judith Issroff, MD; Ofra Ayalon, Judith Issroff, MD, Rona Fields**

Track Sessions under the Direction of **Rev. Franklin H. Littell, Yehuda Bauer, Alan Dershowitz, Robert J. Lifton, MD, Shamai Davidson, MD, John Sommerville and Shingo Shabata, Rabbi Marc Tanenbaum, Sidra Ezrachi and John Felstiner, Leo Kuper**

Evening Event: Holocaust through the Eyes of a Survivor, **Jack P. Eisner**, play excerpt, "Adam's Purim Party," based on **Yoram Kanuk**'s novel, acted by **Neve Tzedek Theatre Group**, director **Nora Chilton**, with **Oded Kotler, Edna Fliedel** and others

Tuesday, June 22, 1982

Plenary 2: Chairs, **Alan Dershowitz, Avadis Sanjian**
Forms of Consecration of Power and Myth—Prior to Genocide: **Uriel Tal**

After Auschwitz: Repression or Lining Out the Lessons: **Rev. Franklin H. Littell**
"Domestic" Genocide: An Enquiry into Preliminary Warning Signals: **Leo Kuper**

Workshop 3: Psycho-Historical Aspects of the Holocaust and Genocide II: **Robert J. Lifton, Md**

Can Religion Meet the Challenge of Tomorrow?: Chair, **Rabbi Marc Tanenbaum; Julius Moravcsik, Abraham J. Peck, Rev. Monsignor Vincent A. Yzermans**
Social and Political History: Chair, **Yehuda Bauer; Zvi Bacharach, Robert G. L. Waite, George M. Kren, Edy Kaufman, Daan Bronkhorst**
The Holocaust—Was It Predictable?: Chair, **Werner Bratz; Dov Segal, Luba K. Gurdus, Rev. Charles Carrol**
Transmission of Effects of Survival: Chair, **Maria Rosenbloom; Axel Russell, Sophie Kav-Venaki, Ari Nadler, Leora Goder, Sarah Shiryon, Herman Musaph**

Special Session on Law and Prevention: Chair, **Alan Dershowitz; Mario J. Bendersky, Allan Gerson**
Designing The Monument—The Architect's Response to the Holocaust: **Fumikatsu Inoue**

Workshop 4: United Nations. A Comparative Approach to Genocide and a Program of Action: **Leo Kuper**

Reevaluating Values and Ethics: Chair, **John K. Roth; Eva Fogelman, Gustav Dreifuss, B. Lange, Edna R. Johnson**

Preventing Another "Eichmann": Chair, **Ronald Aronson; Aryeh Barnea, Miriam Rieck, William Richards and Luis Kutner**

Paths to Genocide: Chairs, **Edy Kaufman and Daan Bronkhorst; Phuntsog Wangyal, Lyman H. Legters, Fritz Greussing, Shlomo Aronson**

Transmission of Effects of Survival II: Chair, **Axel Russell, MD; Helene Frankle, Chaim Deutsch, Stanley Schneider, Zoli Zlotogorski, Dina Wardi-Schwarz**

Using the Past to Educate for the Future: Chair, **Robert W. Ross; Maurice Goldstein, Julius Lieblein, Dorothy Kobak**

The Holocaust and God: Chair, **Rev. Franklin H. Littell, MD; A. Roy Eckardt, Andre Neher, Rabbi Reeve R. Brenner**

Track Sessions—continued from Monday

Evening Event:

The Paradoxes of Genocide: **John R. Silber**

Warning against Genocide: **Elie Wiesel**

Wednesday, June 23, 1982

Plenary 3: Chairs, **John Somerville, Leo Kuper; Robert Jay Lifton, MD, Emil L. Fackenheim, Israel W. Charny, Shamai Davidson, MD**

The Threat of Genocide and Its Relationship to Survival—Refugee Experience: **Ron Baker, Simon Phillips, Rachel Pearson**

Denial—Before, During, and After: Chair, **Helen Fein; Richard G. Hovannisian, Melvin Mermelstein, Shlomo Bresnitz, Avedis K. Sanjian**

The Artistic Message: Chair, **Sidra Ezrachi; Luba K. Gurdus, Andre L. Stein, Yishai Tobin**

Societal Madness: Chair, **John K. Roth; Ronald Aronson, Arnold Krammer, Tilman Zulch, Upendra Nath Mishra**

Powerlessness—a Factor in Genocide: Chair, **Rabbi Marc H. Tanenbaum; Monty N. Penkower, Alice L. Eckardt, Judith Issrof**

Oral History: Chair, **Shamai Davidson, MD; Shohig Sherry Terzian, Lilli Kopecky, Helen H. Waterford**

Therapeutic Considerations with Survivors and Their Children: Chair, **Sophie Kav-Venaki; H. Z. Winnik, Yael Danieli, Nira Kfir, Florabel Kinsler**

The Power of Politics and Commerce: Chair, **Vahakn N. Dadrian; Arlene Rossen Cardozo, Marjorie Housepian Dobkin, Robert W. Ross**

Prevention and Responsibility: Chair, **Marcia Sachs Littell; Louis Rene Beres, David Kader, Frances Gaezer Grossman, Vigen Guroian**

Evaluations of Different Concepts regarding the Ideology of Genocide: Chair, **Leo Kuper; Ted R. Gurr, Richard H. Dekmejian, Gerard A. Vanderhaar, Kurt Jonassohn**

Replication of Psychosocial Studies: Chair, **Hillel Klein, MD; Maria Rosenbloom, Jerry V. Differ, Norman Solkoff**

Various Group and Community Modalities for Holocaust Survivors and Their Offspring: Implications for Other Traumatized Populations: Chair, **Bella Savran; Helene Frankle, Yael Danielli, Eva Fogelman, Florabel Kinsler, Bella Savran**

The Endless History of Genocide: Chair, **Yehuda Bauer; William Richards, Melvin Mermelstein, Leita Kaldi**

Exchange Sessions: Chairs: **Yocheved Howard and Ephraim Howard; Mikhail Agursky, Morris C. Beckwitt, MD, Mordechai Benyakar, S. Mibashan, J. Friedmann, J. Agmon, Robert J. Daly, MD, Arthur M. Green and Regina M. Green, Judith Issroff, MD, Dina Wardi-Schwarz, Shalom Litman, MD, Ephraim M. Howard, Yocheved Howard**

Track Sessions— continued from Tuesday

Evening Session: Special Conference Forum with Active Audience Participation: The Denial of Genocide and the Rewriting of History

Thursday, June 24, 1982

Chairs, **Vahakn n. Dadrian and Robert Seltzer; John Somerville, Shingo Shibata, Rabbi Marc H. Tanenbaum, Sidra Ezrachi, John Felstiner**

Track Sessions—continued from Wednesday

Conference Summation Panel and Discussion

Chair, **Israel W. Charny**; Participants—Chairpersons of all the Track Groups: **rev. Franklin H. Littell, Yehuda Bauer, Alan Dershowitz, Robert J. Lifton, Shamai Davidson, MD, John Somerville, Shingo Shibata, Rabbi Marc H. Tanenbaum, Sidra Ezrachi, John Felstiner, Leo Kuper**

Figure 7. Professors Shamai Davidson and Israel Charny standing in front of the Wailing Wall in Jerusalem following the end of conference celebration at the Armenian Patriarchate.

CELEBRATION OF THE CONFERENCE AT THE ARMENIAN PATRIARCHATE IN THE OLD CITY OF JERUSALEM

The Armenian Patriarch of Jerusalem, His Beatitude Yeghishe Derderian, invited the conferees on a tour of the Armenian Patriarchate and the city of Jerusalem. More than one hundred participants in the conference made the trip, beginning their visit to the Old City of Jerusalem with a tour of the Cathedral of St. James, built in the twelfth century. Several gifts brought to Jerusalem by Armenian pilgrims over the century, now guarded in the St. James Treasury, had been assembled in the sanctuary for the scholars to see. Archbishop Karekin Kazanjian, Dean of the Theological Seminary of the Brotherhood of St. James, explained the richly embroidered vestments, chalices and other items created and given as an expression of piety.

The scholars were then guided through the monastery complex. During a brief stop at the Patriarchate library, where they were greeted by Librarian Sahag Kalaijian, the scholars heard a concise summary of Armenian History by Prof. Richard Hovannisian.

Mr. Momjian thanked Drs. Israel Charny and Shamai Davidson for their unwavering support for the inclusion of the Armenian scholars and their papers in the conference program.

The Patriarch, in turn, honored Charny and Davidson, presenting them with copies of the art book, *Armenian Art Treasures of Jerusalem*, whose introduction is written by Prof. Avedis Sanjian of UCLA. He likewise presented copies of this exquisite volume to Helen Fein, Franklin Littell, and John Somerville in gratitude for their transcendent sense of justice which could not be altered by political pressures, and for their sympathy towards the American experience.

Conferees stated afterwards that the visit to the patriarchate was a moving experience.[21]

---

21 "International Conference on Holocaust and Genocide Held with Armenian Experience," *Armenian Observer*, July 14, 1982.

SUPPLEMENT 2: RESPONSES OF PARTICIPANTS IN THE FIRST INTERNATIONAL CONFERENCE ON THE HOLOCAUST AND GENOCIDE

The conference as a whole was as splendid an achievement on the intellectual plane as it was a triumph on the moral plane. It was a significant and unforgettable experience for all of us. **John Somerville, professor emeritus of Philosophy, City University of New York, president, Union of American and Japanese Professionals against Nuclear Omnicide**

It was a pleasure to be part of the Holocaust conference. The conference was well organized, efficiently run and conducted in excellent taste under very trying circumstances. **Aba Beer, national chairman, National Holocaust Remembrance Committee, Canadian Jewish Congress**

I would like to express my profound appreciation for the experience in Tel Aviv of both the pre-conference workshops and international conference. That so much could be accomplished in spite of the turmoil created by the people who objected to the conference was most remarkable. **F. Burton Nelson, professor of Theology and Ethics, North Park Theological Seminary, Chicago**

I recognize the risk, ambiguity, and moral complexity related to any threat on human lives. With that assumed and said, I want to praise the leadership of the conference for their disciplined refusal to "knuckle under." The conference on the whole was without doubt one of the finest I have ever attended. **Ronald E. Santoni, professor of Philosophy and Chair, Denison University**

The organizers are to be congratulated for their intense and astute efforts at making the conference a truly meaningful event. It was an extremely powerful experience. I appreciate more than I can express your interest in the Gypsy situation. The concern of the conference will be communicated to all my Gypsy friends in the United States as well as internationally. **Leita Kaldi, Gypsies United, USA**

The conference gave me very much indeed, I returned home with moving experiences. And no more will the Armenian Genocide be just a remote issue. **Dieter Hartmann, Dr. rer. soc., West Germany**

The conference was a learning and stirring event/experience for me. I'm grateful that it occurred, and that I could participate. **John Felstiner, Department of English, Stanford University**

Who would oppose a program which would combine reverence for the Jewish victims of Nazi Germany with a determination that nothing like the holocaust should ever again happen to any people? With the wisdom of hindsight, however, it becomes clear that it was impossible for such an important event to avoid causing controversy. The conference was an achievement that it was held and that it did achieve so many of its aims. **Ronald Aronson, Wayne State University**

I congratulate you on the success of the conference. As events unfolded, the conference was held during a time of great stress in the Middle East which also provided a clear demonstration of the need for the conference and the issues which it explored. I am very pleased that I was able to attend. **Sidney Altman, MD, president, Amhai—Association for Mental Health Affiliation with Israel**

I want to congratulate you for the courage with which you stuck to your guns. **Martin Wangh, MD, Harry S. Truman Research Institute for the Advancement of Peace, Hebrew University, Jerusalem**

The conference was stimulating and provided much helpful material. I hope you will hold additional international gatherings. **Alan L. Berger, Chairman, Jewish Studies, Syracuse University**

I compliment and congratulate you. The International Conference on the Holocaust and Genocide will stand out as an extraordinary effort at investigating atrocities from varying perspectives. All the attendees shared my enthusiasm. **Esther K. Ansfield, Department of Comparative Literature, University of Wisconsin**

The International Conference on the Holocaust and Genocide will pass into the annals of history with a meaningful distinction. The conference emphasized the need to monitor the potential for new acts of genocide around the globe, particularly in relation to nuclear proliferation and ecocidal technology, extending the threat of Holocaust to humankind as a whole. We hope this worthwhile conference will be remembered as the first in a chain which will evolve into a permanent commission for the prevention of genocide in the world. **Luba K. Gurdus,** *Martyrdom and Resistance*

Thanks for the great experience of the conference. I learned a great deal—re. Armenians, Tibetans, Cambodians, Iranians, etc., and above all the pain of the HOLOCAUST! **Dorothy Kobak, Temple University**

The conference gave me very much indeed, I returned home with moving experiences and no more will the Armenian Genocide be just remote issue. **Dieter Hartmann, Dr. iur., Dr. rer. soc., West Germany**

Some prominent Jews and Israelis are supporting Turkish propaganda to downplay and even deny the Armenian experience. The presentations at the conference are the best hope of integrity and scholarship in the study of genocide. **Vahakn N. Dadrian, professor of Sociology, State University of New York**

Thank you for your labor in making the conference happen despite the many obstacles and frustrations. I know most in attendance found it to be an important and stimulating meeting. **David Kader, professor of Law and associate dean, Arizona State University, College of Law**

I am glad to learn that your initiative-which has already granted us the important conference-is going on. So does the brave and just attitude you have taken in the Armenian matter. **Aryeh Barnea**, Hebrew University

The Armenian Assembly is deeply grateful to you for your courageous demonstration of commitment and tenacity. Were it not for your conduct, the Republic of Turkey would have once again succeeded in its international campaign of intimidations. I thank you for your steadfast defense of academic freedom in the face of monumental pressure. Our organization looks forward to additional occasions for cooperative activity. **Ross Vartian, executive director, Armenian Assembly of America**

Officials of the Republic of Turkey once again attempted to silence any commentary about the Armenian Genocide of 1915–23. If Turkish demands had been met, I would not be here today addressing this conference. If Turkish demands had been met, Professors Dekmejian, Dobkin, Grigorian, Guroian, Hamalian, Hovannisian, Nedava, Oshagan, Solarian, Sanjian, and Terzian would have been excluded from this unique and vitally important gathering. If Turkish demands had been met, Executive Director Charny and Organizing Committee member, Archbishop Ajamian, could not have honored the stated purpose of this enclave—to memorialize and study the Holocaust as well as all past and present acts of genocide.

In the United States, the Turkish government is making a continuous effort at excluding the experience and lessons of the Armenian Genocide from the US Holocaust Museum and Educational Projects. Turkish officials will once again attempt to force decision-makers to choose between Turks and Armenians yet we expect that the United States will also reject the Republic of Turkey.

Remembrance and vigilance, at whatever cost, are the only courses of action available to people and nations of goodwill who seek to prevent future crimes against humanity. It is in this spirit that I extend the profound gratitude of all Armenians, those who stood for these principles on this occasion. **Set Momjian, former US representative to the United Nations; member, US Holocaust Memorial Council; chairman, Armenian Assembly of America Committee on the Armenian Genocide**

Exceptionally touching remarks came from the secretary-general of the Public Committee of Auschwitz and Other Extermination Camps who herself had been a *sonderkommando*:

The organizers did a fantastic job in making the conference a success despite all the hardships. The pre-conference workshops accomplished their purpose well. The conference itself tried to move towards universal Judaism, and the linkage to other genocides did not prevent the participants from stressing the uniqueness of the Holocaust. **Lilli Kopecky, secretary general, Public Committee of Auschwitz and Other Extermination Camp Survivors in Israel; adjunct professor, Emory University**

SUPPLEMENT 3: PRESS AND OTHER PUBLIC RESPONSES TO THE FIRST INTERNATIONAL CONFERENCE ON THE HOLOCAUST AND GENOCIDE, JUNE 1982

Nuclear Threat and the Holocaust

One of the first conferences to take the bold step of linking nuclear holocaust with the Holocaust suffered by the Jews. **International Fellowship of Reconciliation**

Despite the Demand of the Foreign Ministry (under Pressure from Turkey) the Conference on Genocide will Take Place

For years we spoke of the conspiracy of silence that the nations of the world maintained about the Holocaust for reasons of expediency or political exploitation, and now we know that this can also happen to us. **Nachum Barnea**, *Davar* [daily newspaper, Tel Aviv], June 4, 1982

Genocide Seminar with Armenians to Go Forward in Tel Aviv

June 3 (AP)—A conference on genocide will convene as planned despite reported Turkish threats of reprisal and pressure from Israeli authorities to cancel it. The organizer, Israel Charny said the idea of cancelling the conference or avoiding the Armenian issue was "absolutely untenable." *New York Times*, Friday, June 4, 1982

The Turkish Demand of Israel: Don't Speak about the Armenians

The government of Turkey threatens worsening relations with Israel if an International Conference on Genocide takes place this month in Tel Aviv. The Conference organizers reply: The Jews, who were the victim of a world conspiracy of silence, won't agree to a new conspiracy of silence. **Yoav Karni**, *Yediot Achronot* [daily newspaper, Tel Aviv], June 6, 1982

Their Holocaust

The Conference organizers were willing to avoid publicizing of the Armenian contribution in the deliberations, but not to cancel it. Impossible, they held, that Jews should comply with the Turks in denying the Armenian Genocide—at a time when the world is trying to deny the Holocaust of the Jewish people to the point of denying the existence of the gas chambers in Auschwitz. **Amos Elon**, *Haaretz*, June 11, 1982

Genocide Parley Opens despite Turks

Despite persistent and comprehensive efforts by the Foreign Ministry to prevent the convocation, the International Conference on the Holocaust and Genocide began yesterday in Tel Aviv's Hilton Hotel. "We cannot exclude the Armenian subject from the conference. They too suffered genocide and our conference is devoted to the whole phenomenon, not just what happened to the Jews at the hands of the Nazi," said Prof. **Shamai Davidson**, Co-Director of the Conference. "When it comes to genocide there is always someone who wants to keep something quiet," he said. *Jerusalem Post*, June 21, 1982

Turkish Threat to US Reported

The counsel for the United States Holocaust Memorial Council said yesterday that a Turkish diplomat had threatened retaliation if the fate of Turkish Armenians was included in a proposed Washington museum on the German death camps of World War II. The American official, Monroe H. Freedman, said he had been warned that, if the Armenian issue was to be part of the museum, "The physical safety of Jews in Turkey would be threatened and Turkey might pull out of NATO." Mr. Freeman said that the Turkish diplomat, Mithat Balkan, who is an embassy counselor in Washington, had made the threats during luncheon meetings in 1981. Mr. Balkan denied having said that the physical safety of Jews in Turkey would be endangered. "I never said such a thing," he said. "No man in his right mind would even think of such a thing." *New York Times*, June 22, 1982

Genocide Seminar, Opposed by Israel, Opens

An international academic conference on Nazi death camps and other genocidal horrors opened today despite efforts by the Israeli Government to have it called off. Dr. Frances Gaezer Grossman of Scarsdale, N.Y. who is with the Post-Graduate Center for Mental Health in New York City said here that she returned a call from the Israeli Consulate in New York on Tuesday a few hours before flying to Israel. "It was an affront to my dignity as a human being and as a Jew, [that] a Jew should be told he cannot go to an academic conference or there will be a pogrom." *New York Times*, June 22, 1982

Memories of Armenians

There is considerable irony in the fact that Israeli official bodies should be so hesitant about recalling the Turkish atrocities, which, as Hitler himself made clear, served as a model for the Nazi "Final Solution." Moreover, the book in which Franz Werfel immortalized Armenian suffering, *The Forty Days of Musa Dagh*, was required reading for Zionist youth in the days before Auschwitz and even afterwards. **Nechemia Meyers, *Los Angeles Jewish Opinion*,** June 1982

Israeli Government against Holocaust Congress

Experts from twenty countries discussed this week the historical, medical and psychological aspects of genocide. The theme was not only the Holocaust during the Nazi period but other genocides. Until the last minute, the Israel government had tried to cancel the congress. Participants from all over the world were informed by phone or writing not to attend the conference. It was suggested to move the congress to another country. The organizers refused—in my opinion rightly so. Israel sees itself as a shelter for all Jews. Therefore, it particularly should not allow other countries, where human rights are of no value, to apply pressure. **Heiner Lichtenstein, Broadcast Report on WDR/IDR T**, West Germany, June 26, 1982

The Armenian Genocide—"Yok"

Behind the scenes they said to it that the conference had almost no media coverage. How shall we protest the indifference of the world toward our people if we ourselves silence the memory of another people's holocaust? **Gabriel Stern, *Al Hamishmar*** [daily newspaper, Tel Aviv], August 13, 1982

Turkey Denies It Threatened Jews over Tel Aviv Parley on Genocide

Ankara, Turkey. The Turkish Government categorically denied today that any threat had been made to Jews here in retaliation for Armenian participation in a scheduled international conference in Tel Aviv on genocide. **Marvin Howe, *New York Times*,** June 5, 1982

TURKISH ENVOY DENIES REPORT THAT JEWS IN TURKEY WOULD BE HARMED IF HOLOCAUST MEMORIAL INCLUDES MASSACRE OF ARMENIANS

[*As the time for the conference approached, the* New York Times *reported the Counsel for the United States Holocaust Memorial Council said that a Turkish diplomat had threatened retaliation against "the physical safety of*

Jews in Turkey" if the proposed museum included the Armenian Genocide. The following is a continuation of the story a year later and now at the level of the Turkish Ambassador to the United States—Ed.]

The Turkish Ambassador to Washington has denied that he has ever implied that Jews in Turkey would be threatened if the 1914–1915 massacre of Armenians in Turkey is included in the Holocaust Memorial Museum being planned for Washington. Ambassador Şükrü Elekdağ said he was issuing a statement denying a report in a *Washington Post* article on the museum April 13, in which a "White House source" implied that the inclusion of the massacre in the museum "might have an impact on Jews in Turkey. The proposition that Turkish citizens of the Jewish faith are, in any sense, potentially threatened by the Turkish government or the non-Jewish majority of the Turkish population is utterly groundless. **Şükrü Elekdağ**. *Jewish Telegraphic Agency (JTA)*, April 26, 1983

Provides Understanding of Many Events of Genocide

The Conference succeeded in expanding its central focus on the Holocaust into a larger perspective that provides understanding of many events of mass murder and genocide. **Daan Bronkhorst**, *Amsterdam Volskrant*, June 25, 1982

Conspiracy of Silence

It was with a shock of disbelief and incredulity that we were informed that the Israeli Government had succumbed to Turkish pressures not to support nor officially recognize this conference. It reminds us of the conspiracy of silence which helped bring about the Holocaust in the first place. **L. Fortus** and twenty-five other signatories from Israel, the United States, Holland and Canada. Letter to editor, *Jerusalem Post*, June 28, 1982

Turkish Threats Fail to Halt Holocaust Parley

The Israeli government publicly admitted it had attempted to force cancellation of the conference. Set Momjian, a member of the US Holocaust Memorial Council and former US Representative to the United Nations and the UN Commission on Human Rights thanked Dr. Israel Charny and Dr. Shamai Davidson for their courage in standing behind the Armenians and refusing to bow to Turkish threats and pressures from the Israel government. *California Courier*, July 8, 1982

SUPPLEMENT 4: "THEIR HOLOCAUST," AMOS ELON, HAARETZ, JUNE 11, 1982[22]

Translated from the Hebrew

As a result of pressure from Turkey, the Foreign Office demands that the International Conference, in which one of the subjects was to have been on the genocide of the Armenian nation, be cancelled.

Two psychologists of note, Professors Israel Charny and Shamai Davidson (Universities of Tel Aviv and Bar Ilan), decided two years ago to initiate an International Scientific Conference in Tel Aviv on the Holocaust and Genocide. These men are perplexed by the question of the destructive drive in man and invited many people from all sphere of the Behavioral Sciences as well as theologians and legal experts—Jews and non-Jews—survivors of the Holocaust, and historians of the genocide of other peoples: in the USSR, Hiroshima, South-East Asia, and of the Armenians in Turkey, to present papers at the Conference.

There was positive affirmation for this initiative. The author, Elie Wiesel, accepted the Presidency of the Conference and was to address the opening plenary session. Distinguished persons from across the globe joined the Organizing Committee, among them the Presidents of Boston and Notre Dame Universities (USA) and from Israel, Professor Yoram Dinstein, Rector of Tel Aviv University; Yitzhak Arad, Director of Yad Vashem, and Professors Yehuda Bauer, Uriel Tal, Shmaryahu Talman, and others. June 20, 1982 was set as the ceremonial opening at Yad Vashem in Jerusalem. Mr. Gideon Hausner was to give a presentation on "Future Holocaust." The closing ceremony was to have taken place under the chairmanship of the Rector of Tel Aviv University.

Everything was set: about 200 noted scientists across the world, and almost 100 Israelis assured their active participation when suddenly a serious crisis erupted.

Mr. Moshe Gilboa of the Overseas Publications Department of the Foreign Office confronted the Conference Organizers with the firm request that the Committee cancel the Conference—or change the program.

What had happened? Apparently, among the 130 programmed lectures and discussion panels, about half a dozen focused on the Armenian Genocide of 1915 when the Turkish regime massacred between 1,000,000 to 1,500,000

---

22 Amos Elon was an Israeli journalist and writer. He was the author of the bestseller, *The Israelis: Founders and Sons* (Harmondsworth: Penguin, 1983).

Armenians (*plus, as we shall later note, a similar number of victims of still other peoples-Ed.*), Panels had also been prepared on the Soviet Gulag, Hiroshima, and the destruction of the tribes in Australia. But these issues did not worry Mr. Gilboa of the Foreign Office—only the sessions on the Armenians disturbed him.

Why? It would appear that we are so isolated in the world today that any lowly extortionist—and this time it is the Turkish government—can, or tries, to force our hand.

The Foreign Office pressed on determinedly for cancellation of all proceedings related to the Armenian Genocide. According to them, if this was not done, serious international interests, and perhaps Jewish communities abroad, would be harmed.

The Conference organizers doubted the moral implications of this claim and refused to accept the demands of the Foreign Office quite so easily. They were willing to avoid publicizing of the Armenian contribution in the deliberations, but not to cancel it. It is not possible, they claimed, for a government that opposes surrender to terrorists and hijackers, to submit to the Turkish demands and thereby suppress the spirit of liberty and academic discussion in the State of Israel.

Impossible also, they held, that Jews should comply with the Turks in denying the Armenian Genocide—and this at a time when the world is trying to deny the Holocaust of the Jewish people to the point of denying the existence of the gas chambers in Auschwitz.

The Foreign Office is not persuaded by this claim. It is not the first time they have tried to silence the voice of criticism concerning Turkey, or the expression of public opinion on the extermination of the Armenians. In 1978, following an official Turkish protest, they got Israel TV to shelve a documentary film on the Armenian Quarter in Jerusalem, in which the massacre of the Armenians in Turkey (1915) was treated as a side issue only. In 1978 an attempt to prevent the screening of the anti-Turkish film, *Midnight Express*, failed.

On the present occasion, when they realized that Professor Israel Charny was not willing to change or to cancel the proceedings or the Conference, they used other means. The heaviest guns were fired from New York, where senior Israeli diplomats hurried to the home of Elie Wiesel and demanded from him that he rescind his agreement to act as President of the Conference. At first this was refused them. He had been an active participant in the work of the Preparatory Committee, and Professor Charny is his friend. Wiesel also feels close to his ideology and wrote the preface to Charny's new book, *Genocide: The Human Cancer*. The Foreign Office were not put off by his refusal. They continued to put pressure on him. "The Turks are threatening us," they told Wiesel. Wiesel answered, "Stand up to the pressure of the Turks." But when they told him that a delegation of Jews from Turkey appeared in Israel and warned that there would be "reprisals" if the Conference took place in its original design, Wiesel yielded. He could not stand up to this emotional pressure. He sent a telegram to Professor Charny in which he demanded:

> In the name of conscience, postpone our important Conference or relocate it in another country in accordance with the request of the very highest officials of the Israel Government who fear Conference at this moment could jeopardize vital interests of the Jewish people.

When Charny refused, Wiesel resigned.

The steamroller pressed down on one after another: on Tel Aviv University, on Vad VaShem. Professor Dinstein, rector of the University, first suggested that a lecturer be invited from Turkey to balance the Armenian claims. Afterwards he, too, resigned from the Committee.

The Director of Yad Vashem, Yitzhak Arad, informed the Conference organizers that the opening ceremonial session "cannot take place at the Auditorium of Yad Vashem as was promised"; Mr. Arad said this week in reply to the question that Yad Vashem had left the Committee because of "the opposition of the Foreign Office, which was brought to our knowledge in no uncertain way."

Was that enough? Mr. Arad admitted that there was another reason. After he examined the Conference program, it appeared that the Organizers had made a "too widespread use of" and, in his opinion, abused the term "Holocaust."

How? "For years we have been struggling to convey that the term Holocaust belongs only to us," explained Mr. Arad. "One should not include the catastrophes of others. But this is what the Conference organizers are doing."

Is this so? Do they not differentiate between the meaning of the Holocaust and that of Genocide, even in the official name of the Conference? "Definitely not," said Mr. Arad. He does not understand what all these Armenian lecturers are doing in this Conference.

Mr. Gideon Hausner, who expressed the view that the Armenian Holocaust forecast the Holocaust of the Jewish people, also resigned from the Committee "because of the convincing intervention of the Foreign Office" and because, in his opinion, "the Conference can reduce and blur the Holocaust in comparison with other great catastrophes."

Also, the Holocaust Memorial Foundation associated with the American Memorial Council for the Holocaust, under the chairmanship of Elie Wiesel, which promised financial assistance to the Conference organizers this week stated that they will not participate in the Conference and they will not finance it "because the Turkish Government threatens reprisals."

With this kind of logic prevailing among the heads of the Foundation which was established to encourage remembrance and not denial, there were those this week who remembered Hitler's statement in 1939, on the eve of the Holocaust: "Who speaks today of the annihilation of the Armenians? The world believes in success alone."

The Foreign Office spokesman continues to state that there is no Turkish pressure on Israel. Nevertheless, they demand that the Conference be cancelled "because of the concern for injury to humanitarian Jewish interests." He is not ready to define or to describe these interests.

We are dealing with—and this is not the first time—an official bureaucracy which reminds the world whether they like it or not of our Holocaust, but for which the Holocaust of others is only a subject for political exploitation, like the annihilation of the Christians in Lebanon.

The victim is always egocentric. This is a manifestation of his system of defense and surviving, but the rigid egocentricity of Yad Vashem people arouses the embarrassing question in regard to the boundary between the natural chauvinism—the survivor and the cheap opportunism practised by types who think it worth the exercise.

Is not self-censorship frequently worse than external censorship? And what would Messrs. Hausner and Arad say if the Italian Government should prevent the Holocaust of the Jewish people in 1940 to 1945 from being mentioned at an International Scientific Conference on Holocaust and Genocide in Rome?

The authorities hoped that as a result of the resignation of Prof. Dinstein, of Mr. Hausner, of Mr. Arad, and of Elie Wiesel, that the number of participants at the Conference would be drastically reduced, and perhaps it would not take place at all. One who did announce that he would participate in all circumstances was the Armenian Archbishop in Jerusalem, Shahé Ajamian, who complained: "The Government is tending once again to surrender to pressure by the Turks. Thank God that there are people like Charny and Davidson who are faithful to their principles."

Professor Charny telegraphed Elie Wiesel, as follows: "The Conference will take place even if only the traditional ten participate. The price of denying history of the murder of truth always expresses itself in human life."

CHAPTER 2

The Conference Really Did Take Place and Very Meaningfully

Recently I was speaking to a very esteemed colleague in genocide studies in Israel and he referred to the "famous Holocaust and Genocide Conference" in 1982 having been cancelled because of the severe Turkish/Israeli pressures.

Over the years I hear a good number of people making this error, and this mistaken conclusion that the conference was cancelled also has made its way into professional publications, for example, a very detailed analysis of "A Unique Denial: Israel's Foreign Policy and the Armenian Genocide," by Eldad ben Aharon in the *British Journal of Middle Eastern Studies*.[1] The author describes Israel's opposition to the conference at length, but never a single word that it did take place. At one point he is involved in reporting a conversation that the Israeli Consul in Turkey had with Turkey's Secretary of State, and he refers to the latter saying, "If Armenian participants had attended the conference …" thus implying they never were there.[2]

I have corresponded with Ben Aharon and he has conveyed in return his regrets about the lack of clarity that the conference indeed took place. In a more recent article, Ben Aharon states clearly, "Eventually it took place in Tel Aviv with the participation of 300 people."[3]

---

1   Eldad Ben Aharon, "A Unique Denial: Israel's Foreign Policy and the Armenian Genocide," *British Journal of Middle Eastern Studies* 42, no. 4 (2015): 638–654.
2   Ibid., 11.
3   Eldad Ben Aharon, "Between Ankara and Jerusalem: The Armenian Genocide as a Zero-Sum Game in Israel's Foreign Policy (1980s–2010s)," *Journal of Balkan and Near Eastern Studies* 20, no. 5 (2018): 459–476.

OTHER EXAMPLES OF REPORTING THAT THE FIRST INTERNATIONAL CONFERENCE ON THE HOLOCAUST AND GENOCIDE IN 1982 WAS CANCELLED

Robert Fisk, "US Academics Join Rush to Deny Turkish Massacre of Armenians: Slaughter Viewed as Accident of First World War," **London Independent**, July 2, 1997.

Yet despite the support of Jewish academics for acknowledgment of the earlier Holocaust, Israel failed the Armenians in 1982 when it gave way to pressure from Turkey and forced the cancellation of a conference on the Jewish Holocaust and its 6 million victims in which Armenians would have described their own genocide. Elie Wiesel, the Jewish Holocaust survivor, pulled out of the conference after pressure from the Israeli Foreign Ministry. Turkey is today Israel's most powerful Muslim ally.

California Courier, June 14, 2018, republishing an editorial by the New York-based **Jewish Week Media Group**, June 6, 2018. The *California Courier* is a very prominent Armenian-American newspaper which in turn is the source for many other Armenian publications especially but not only in the United States. The Jewish Week Media Group serves a range of Jewish-American publications in New York and nationally and is also distributed internationally to other Jewish publications.

Both the *Courier* and the *Jewish Media* publications reported that "in 1982, Israel, under pressure from Turkey cancelled the Holocaust conference in which Armenians would have described their people's genocide. Nobel Peace Laureate Elie Wiesel pulled out of the gathering, reportedly after Turkey threatened reprisals against Turkish Jews."

Haaretz, April 19, 2019. In a review of the book *The Impossible People in a Global Perspective*, by eminent Holocaust historian, Yehuda Bauer, veteran reporter Hanoch Marmari wrote correctly that the opening of the conference had been planned to take place at Yad Vashem but was cancelled in response to the demand of Israel's Foreign Ministry in response to pressures by Turkey to prevent the participation of Armenian scholars and to remove any deliberations about the Armenian Genocide. However,

Marmari then continued, "In the wake of the cancellation of the program at Yad Vashem, the majority of scheduled participants in the conference cancelled, among them a Holocaust historian who was already well know at the time, Yehuda Bauer. Even if several spontaneous sessions did take place, the conference as a whole evaporated."

The Israeli government also resorted to its prerogatives for censoring news that ostensibly could endanger Israeli security—which normally apply to information of potential military significance – by censoring from the Israeli press any mention of the conference's forthcoming workshops on June 17–18, 1982 and news of the convening of the larger conference on June 24–27. (This also caused some serious discomfort to some participants who travelled to Jerusalem on the June 24 for the planned opening session at Yad Vashem, which had been cancelled due to government pressures). Nonetheless, there were some writers such as Nachum Barnea, a leading reporter in Israel to this day, who braved the censor's ruling. On June 4, 1982, Barnea wrote in the leading newspaper of the Labour movement, *Davar*:

Despite the Demand of the Foreign Ministry (under Pressure from Turkey) the Conference on Genocide will Take Place

For years we spoke of the conspiracy of silence that the nations of the world maintained about the Holocaust for reasons of expediency or political exploitation, and now we know that this can also happen to us.[4]

At the same time, a wide range of reporters around the world began to pick up the trail of the unfolding drama. The *New York Times* in particular reported in a sequence of no less than five articles over several days what was happening. On the same June 4, 1982, the *Times* reported decisively an Associated Press story:

Genocide Seminar with Armenians to Go Forward in Tel Aviv

A conference on genocide will convene as planned despite reported Turkish threats of reprisal and pressure from Israeli authorities to cancel it. The organizer, Israel Charny said the idea of cancelling the conference or avoiding the Armenian issue was "absolutely untenable."[5]

---

4   Nachum Barnea, "Despite the Demand of the Foreign Ministry (under Pressure from Turkey) the Conference on Genocide Will Take Place," *Davar*, June 4, 1982.
5   "Genocide Seminar with Armenians to Go Forward Tel Aviv," *New York Times* (AP), June 4, 1982.

Already on June 1, the Associated Press was reporting—see, for example, the *Philadelphia Inquirer*—that "a world conference will convene here as planned despite Turkish threats of reprisal and pressure from Israeli authorities to cancel it."[6]

The *Jerusalem Post* also reported, "Genocide Meeting to Go Ahead despite Threats from Turkey"—little did they know that the headline should have read "Pressures and Threats from Turkey and Israel"—and referred to worldwide coverage of the story by the Associated Press.[7]

Once the conference opened news coverage continued and accelerated; thus on June 22, the *New York Times* reported:

Genocide Seminar, Opposed by Israel, Opens

An international academic conference on Nazi death camps and other genocidal horrors opened today despite efforts by the Israeli Government to have it called off. Dr. Frances Gaezer Grossman of Scarsdale, N.Y. who is with the Post-Graduate Center for Mental Health in New York City said here that she returned a call from the Israeli Consulate in New York on Tuesday a few hours before flying to Israel. "It was an affront to my dignity as a human being and as a Jew," she said in the meeting hall of the Hilton Hotel here, "that, after the Holocaust and the establishment of Israel, a Jew should be told he cannot do to an academic conference or there will be a pogrom."[8]

Because of the pressures, the conference opening which was to have taken place at Yad Vashem in Jerusalem was moved to Tel Aviv, and as noted out of the originally scheduled 600 registrants some 300 participants turned up which in itself is a meaningful number for a professional event. The conference is clearly recognized and is honored to this day as a milestone event. To all accounts the conference that did take place was deeply moving and soon earned recognition as a defining event in the development of a new discipline of genocide studies (see, for example, Terrence Des Pres, in the *Yale Review*).[9] For the Armenians specifically,—led by Hovannisian and Dadrian—the conference was noted

---

6   Marcus Eliason, "Genocide Conference Rejects Threats," *Philadelphia Inquirer* (AP), June 1, 1982.

7   "Genocide Meeting to Go Ahead despite Threats from Turkey," *Jerusalem Post*, June 4, 1982.

8   "Genocide Seminar, Opposed by Israel, Opens." *New York Times*, June 22, 1982.

9   Terrence Des Pres, "On Governing Narratives: The Turkish-Armenian Case." *Yale Review* 75, no. 4 (1986): 517–521.

deeply and appreciatively as a first-time ever recognition in an international setting of their disastrous tragic genocide.

The responses to the conference from participants were also virtually unanimous in their respect and in their applause for our standing up to the intense government efforts to remove the subject of the Armenian Genocide and if not to cancel the conference in its entirety (see following the previous chapter, "Responses of Participants").

The Israeli press too, after recovering from the government's manipulative censorship of information about the conference before it convened, was generous in its praise both of our topical focus and of our standing up for our academic and intellectual freedom. Yoram Kaniuk, famed Israeli writer, himself a Holocaust survivor, wrote in the *Maariv* newspaper, after he had phoned Elie Wiesel to ask why he had withdrawn from the conference, "I thought that if it's impossible to study genocide in Israel because of threats to Jews, what is the justification for Israel's existence?"[10]

In the newspaper of the Labour movement, *Al Hamishmar*, there was the observation that behind the scenes the government saw to it that the conference had almost no media coverage. "How shall we protest the indifference of the world towards our people if we ourselves silence the memory of another people's holocaust?"[11]

As one can see, there was a great deal of intense emotional response from many people to the drama, and intriguingly much of such emotion continues to be expressed to this day. News of the forthcoming publication of this book, for example, evoked a wave of unsolicited greetings and congratulations from both Jewish and Armenian leaders in particular. At the time of the conference, a good number of articles in the Israeli press also named names and criticized a number of those who had dropped out of the conference after first agreeing to be among the featured lecturers and leaders, including, of course, Elie Wiesel, Professor Yehuda Bauer, and also Professor Yoram Dinstein and Tel Aviv University—the remarks about the latter in particular obviously did wonders for my career at the university.

In sum, the definitive and decisively correct statement of the facts is that the First International Conference on the Holocaust and Genocide did take place quite fully even in the face of the quite extreme pressures of the government

---

10 Yoram Kaniuk, "One Day in the Life of a Human Being" [Hebrew], *Maariv*, July 2, 1982.
11 Gabriel Stern, "The Armenian Genocide—'Yok!'" [Hebrew], *Al Hamishmar*, August 13, 1982.

of Israel which was complying with the demands of the Turkish government to cancel any reference to the Armenian Genocide. The conference took place with an attendance of 300 people—after an earlier expectation of an attendance of 600—before the Israeli government literally called people listed in the preliminary program to cancel. The conference included the screening of films on the Armenian Genocide by Dr. Michael Hagopian and six papers by Armenian scholars including Richard Hovannisian, Vahakn Dadrian, and Ronald Suny. We were honored by considerable reporting in the world press including the *New York Times* and *Jerusalem Post*, in addition to praiseworthy editorials and columns in newspapers, as well as professional articles in books and magazines, for our sterling victory for academic freedom. Additionally, the conference was especially celebrated by the world Armenian community as the first academic conference in the world up until that time that gave recognition to the Armenian Genocide.

As Mark Twain might have said, the many references that nonetheless appeared and continue to pop up in the press and scholarly articles that declare that the conference died were grossly exaggerated. It is a little like the obscenities of never-ending denials of the actual Armenian Genocide or the Holocaust—or the genocides of many other peoples which become subject to denial. The escapists and whitewashers of the realities of human life, liars, and bigots never stop.

A PAUSE TO THANK TWO KEY PARTICIPANTS FOR THEIR LEADERSHIP IN THE CONFERENCE

This seems an appropriate place to express respect and appreciation to two outstanding people who, in the heights of confusion and tensions that reigned as messages of cancellation of participation in the conference poured in from so many sources, truly rose to the occasion as principled and brave leaders.

The first is the late MK (Member of Knesset) Ora Namir, of the Labor Party, who in later years became Minister of Welfare and then moved on to be Israel's ambassador to China. At the last minute of our opening day of the conference, Ora Namir agreed to become the critical Plenary Speaker in our Opening Evening Session which had been moved from Yad Vashem to the Hilton Hotel in Tel Aviv. Namir was forthright and charming. No genocide is to be denied or not recognized. No democratic government has the right to censor and control an academic conference. With the legitimation she, a distinguished member of the Knesset, gave to our conference, she removed decisively a possible negative aura in which we could have been defined in the public view as disloyal Israelis. It was following her talk that I conducted the open dialogue with the audience and the consensual feeling that emerged from the evening was an enthusiastic respect for what we were doing. We were the dedicated tellers of truth about genocides—our own Holocaust, the Armenian Genocide, and the genocides of all peoples. We were decent human beings and good Jews and Israelis who fought off governmental corruption. We ended the day with a good feeling that our audience (and as we have seen later, the press) were rallying warmly behind us.

A second special person is the late Rev. Prof. Franklin Littell, an American Methodist minister who for many years had identified the meanings of the Holocaust as crucial for the development of genuine Christian thinking and experience, and the basis for a crucially wholesome evolution of our Homo sapiens species.

A frequent visitor to the Hebrew University of Jerusalem (which Franklin jokingly referred to as "the finest German university outside of Germany"), I had periodic opportunities for very welcome conversations with him over the years including one memorable discussion in an isolated hallway on the Mount Scopus campus of the university where he introduced me to his work on identifying emergent fascist-Nazi type governments. Clearly this was an important contribution in its own right, and for me it also sparked my thinking on identifying a wider range of what I came to call Genocide Early Warnings.

Unlike a number of his close colleagues at Yad Vashem and Hebrew University, Franklin was far too principled to agree either to censorship of the topic of genocide studies—in this case, the Armenian Genocide, or to submit to government or other institutional demands to deny basic free speech. He hated fascism. So in addition to the several roles Franklin had accepted originally for the conference both as a pre-conference workshop leader and as a subsequent lecturer, he now stepped into a number of positions in the conference that had been abandoned by the original invitees. Throughout the week of the workshops and conference, Franklin was a steadily meaningful source of encouragement and dignity who helped us all to stand up firmly in response to the blows that rained down on us.

SO WHO LIED TO WHOM AND WHO THREATENED WHOM?

For sure it was not the Armenians who lied. They are, to begin with, to this day, more than 100 years later, the undisputed victims of the big Turkish lie that there never was an Armenian Genocide. And they are the unintended victims of a tragically myopic and unethical *realpolitik* political orientation by Israel to take care of its own self-interests. I have real doubts if Israel actually gains anything from this policy, which is also seen in response to genocidal attacks against other peoples, at the expense of forthright policies of respect, memorial, caring, empathy, and powerful protests of the travails of other peoples including outright crimes against humanity and genocide.

In the scenario that we were playing out, it was obvious that the major villains were as usual the Turks, with their clear-cut bizarre history of pressures on lectures and talks, monuments, magazine articles, books, movies, and whatever, who were pressing the Israeli government not to allow a conference that would bring up the Armenian Genocide. And then, even more ominously, it was the Turkish officials who were reported threatening actual Jewish lives—which we understood at first to refer to Jews in Turkey and were later elaborated further into threats against Jews escaping from Iran and Syria.

One would never conceive that Israel, the home of the Jewish people and, notably, a democracy, would be the one to make up a huge lie that the Turks had threatened actual Jewish lives. *Boker tov*—meaning "Good morning" in Hebrew. **The Jews made up the threats and then put their governmental might into a relentless campaign to cancel an academic conference on Holocaust and genocide.**

Along the way, a variety of otherwise dear people, such as Elie Wiesel, Professor Yehuda Bauer, and institutions (such as the American Jewish Committee, whose Rabbi Marc Tanenbaum was to address the conference), the American Jewish Congress (whose Rabbi Arthur Herzberg agreed up to the last minute to be the Opening Session speaker and then withdrew under great pressure), Yad Vashem (which had agreed to be the venue for our opening session), and Tel Aviv University (which had agreed to be a co-sponsor of the conference, with its rector playing a major role as chair of the closing session) were all sucked into being collaborators to the malicious manipulations of governments and thereby in effect collaborators to denial.

A WORD OF SOME DEFENSE

Now I will offer a possible word of some defense of the actions of the State of Israel, but at the same time will not at all relent from an explicit moral analysis and a blistering critique of the government's policies.

The defense is that the Israeli government may have genuinely feared that the Turkish retaliation to the conference, which the Turks clearly wanted censored or cancelled, would turn into Turkey ending the safe passage they were giving to Jewish refugees, and given the gravity of the issue one can respect the Ministry's genuine concern and intention. Real human lives would be the issue, and academic matters and the integrity of the historical record pale before such a consideration. One can even understand possible attributions to us as irresponsible non-conformists and uncooperative citizens for failing to heed legitimate government instructions about our responsibilities to our beloved State of Israel.

However, the story of Israel's failures to recognize the Armenian Genocide, which in plain English constitute denials of the authenticity of the genocide, go back a long way before this specific conference, to many instances when there were no concerns about Jewish lives being lost that were invoked to justify the denials. Israel's informal policy of non-recognition of the Armenian Genocide through all the years continues to this day, though most Israeli people and the culture as a whole very much recognize and honor the Armenian Genocide). Israel's denials are a profound moral failure that has no justification whatsoever.

The accepted argument against my last statement is, of course, the basic conception of *realpolitik* which says that a nation conducts its relationships on a purely pragmatic basis without reference to truth, integrity, or decency, and with a disregard of the facts of history whenever fake news serves one's purposes better. I reject this conception vigorously, and also add from what I shall call a *realsurvival* point of view (as contrasted with *realpolitik*) that such a policy will erode the basic spirit of a people and consequently will render them far less capable of defending their own real security.

Moreover, the maneuvers and policies that Israel exercised were in their own right so dastardly and injurious to a great many people in Israel and around the world, and to so many institutions and to the basic values of academic freedom, that they convey a disturbing ugliness of excessive use of government power.

There is also no doubt that an underlying commitment was in play of a long-time almost official Israeli ideology—certainly of Yad Vashem and also many others—that there can be no comparisons of other genocides to the uniqueness of the Holocaust.[12] The implication is that it is best not to get too

---

12 In contrast, Vahakn Dadrian, a brilliant scholar of the Armenian Genocide, has described "the convergent aspects" of the Armenian Genocide and the Holocaust. There are also many other scholars—Armenian and Jewish—who have seen the Armenian Genocide as a template or "dress rehearsal" for the Holocaust and have cited Hitler's famous remark, "Who remembers the Armenians?," as he dispatched his troops to kill Jews. See Vahakn N. Dadrian,

involved or to pay too much attention to other genocides. I have literally wit-nessed scenes in ostensibly scholarly and professional contexts where refer-ence to a genocide other than the Holocaust has been treated as a serious and immoral violation of academic and public correctness.

From their side, the Turks got into the same act of refusing to relate what happened to the Armenians in any way to the history of the Holocaust. The *New York Times* reported that a Turkish Foreign Ministry spokesman, Nazmi Akiman, said, "We are not against the conference in Tel Aviv but oppose any linkage of the Holocaust to the Armenian allegations of genocide." The *Times* continued: "He said the Armenians had first tried to identify their case with the killing of millions of Jews in Germany during World War II when they tried to establish a presence in the Holocaust Museum in Washington last year. Turkey protested the attempt then, and the Armenians were kept out."[13]

The regrettably mistaken point of view of the incomparability of the Hol-ocaust was quite prevalent and strong for many years in many circles especially of Jewish scholars. Hopefully this point of view has lessened in recent years, but it can still be found as the prevailing policy or at least politically correct narrative in a variety of Jewish-Israeli institutions, for example, at Yad Vashem. This exclusivity expresses and engenders a kind of superiority and devaluation of other genocides and the peoples who were their victims, which I believe one should also note is characteristic of the very perpetrators of genocides who dehumanize the victim people and establish their own people or race or reli-gion or ideology as superior to all others.[14]

"The Convergent Aspects of the Armenian and Jewish Cases of Genocide: A Reinterpreta-tion of the Concept of Holocaust," *Holocaust and Genocide Studies* 3, no. 2 (1988): 26–70.

13   Marvin Howe and Special to the *New York Times*, "Turkey Denies It Threatened Jews and Tel Aviv Parley on Genocide," *New York Times*, June 5, 1982, https://www.nytimes.com/1982/06/05/world/turkey-denies-it-threatened-jewes-over-tel-aviv-parley-on-genocide.html.

14   Israel W. Charny, "The Psychology of Denying Other Victims of a Genocide—A Quest for Ex-clusivity and Superiority—Disturbingly, Not Unlike Similar Motives in Those who Commit Genocide," *Genocide Prevention Now* 5 (2011). GPN is no longer accessible on the internet, but many of its articles are posted on the website of the Institute on the Holocaust and Genocide. The above article can be found at http://www.ihgjlm.com/the-psychology-of-denying-other-victims-of-a-genocide-a-quest-for-exclusivity-and-superiority-disturbingly-not-unlike-similar-motives-in-those-who-commit-genocide-by-israel-w-charny/. The same theme and much of the same material appear in the following chapter in a book: Israel W. Charny, "The Integri-ty and Courage to Recognize all the Victims of a Genocide," in *The Genocide of the Ottoman Greeks: Studies on the State–Sponsored Campaign of Extermination of the Christians of Asia Minor, 1912–1922 and Its Aftermath: History, Law, Memory*, ed. Tessa Hofmann, Matthias Bjørnlund, and Vasileios Meichanetsidis (New York and Athens: Aristide D. Caratzas, 2011), 21–38.

Overall, even given appreciations of the possible constructive intentions of the Israeli government to protect Jewish interests, Israel went much too far in the process of exercising ugly government power, set off dangerous rumors, damaged many people who were legitimately at work creating an innovative and important conference, did damage to any number of Jewish leaders or organizations, and of course executed inexcusable censorship of academic freedom and truth.

For the humor of it all, now the newly discovered Foreign Ministry documents also show that once the conference nonetheless was underway, Israel lied to the Turks repeatedly that there were absurdly small numbers of attendees at the conference. In one memorandum to Ankara—apparently when we held five pre-conference seminars, each with twenty participants—they reported a participation of four people; and when the larger full conference assembled with 300 participants, they reported to Ankara in one communication twenty-three participants and in another memo a hundred participants. What do you know? Liars (Turkey) can't even trust fellow liars (Israel).

For the further humor of this pageant of "fake news" by the IMFA, they, of course, could not resist attributing to me and Shamai Davidson a bit of monetary shenanigans. After all, all's fair in love and *realpolitik* lying.

IMMEDIATE

Date: June 17, 1982

To: Middle East Desk, Israel Foreign Ministry Jerusalem

From: Ankara

Document No. 906   [our page number 149]

[*Israel Ministry employee*] reported that participation of all institutions and Israeli officials has been prevented as a result of the Turkish government's request in response to the subject of the Armenian minority coming up in the conference.

[*Israel Ministry official*] expressed his thanks to the government of Turkey on its attitude towards the Jewish community and said that the Armenian problem is different from the Jewish tragedy and they should not be discussed together. He then accused Prof. Israel Charny and Dr. Shamai Davidson of receiving monies from Armenian sources in order to develop a discussion of the two topics together.[15]

---

15   Israel Ministry of Foreign Affairs, June 17, 1982, ISA-mfa-mfa-000367, 57.

CLASSIFIED/IMMEDIATE
Date: June 21, 1982
To: Ankara, Istanbul
From: Israel Ministry of Foreign Affairs Jerusalem
Document No. 1613   [our page number 156]

The number of participants in the opening was about twenty-three people. The organizers of the conference were forced to cancel halls that had been ordered for the opening and a cocktail hour and made do with a small room. Armenian people did not speak.[16]

TO CONCLUDE ONCE AGAIN WITH THE FACTS

The number of participants was around 300. The opening session took place in the ballroom of the Tel Aviv Hilton where rooms had been reserved originally for the remainder of the conference. No Armenian speakers had been scheduled for this session. The keynote speaker was Member of Knesset Ora Namir (who in subsequent years became Secretary of Welfare). Ora responded nobly to the emergency of our previous keynoters having withdrawn under government pressure.

The second half of the program was devoted to a round table with me with the entire audience in the course of which the history of the pressures of the conference were fully detailed. An almost funny situation developed when two people in the audience who had been scheduled to speak at the conference arose and spoke at some length about how and why they could not participate. In the one case of Rabbi Marc Tanenbaum, he cancelled his participation on order from his home office of the American Jewish Committee, in the other, participation was cancelled in response to intense Israeli government pressure that was delivered personally by Wiesel. Jack Eisner, President of the Holocaust Survivor's Memorial Foundation, cancelled the check for $10,000 he had already given us. In his remarks, he summarized clearly his sense of indebtedness to the Jewish/Israeli establishment and how his cancellation of his financial gift and participation "satisfied me as a Jew," but it did not sit well with him "as a member of the human race."

---

16   Israel Ministry of Foreign Affairs, June 21, 1982, ISA-mfa-mfa-000368i, 19.

A PERSPECTIVE: THE UNITED STATES IS NOT THAT DIFFERENT FROM ISRAEL IN THE WAYS IT DOESN'T RECOGNIZE THE ARMENIAN GENOCIDE FULLY

The Foreign Ministry of Israel is hardly alone in its style of manipulation and deception. It doesn't hurt to have that perspective in mind if one is to cultivate a mature perspective on these matters—though I do not mean that it is *kosher* because there is more than one foreign ministry busy with out-and-out falsehoods in order to achieve its policy objectives.

In an editorial in the prestigious Armenian-American newspaper the *California Courier*, publisher Harut Sassounian, an outstanding world Armenian leader who for many years was also president of the United Armenian Fund, reports on a Secret Document of the United States State Department. In the process, Sassounian reviews authoritatively the history of past official recognitions of the Armenian Genocides by the United States government, and it becomes clear that none of these positive steps of some recognition by the United States, however important in their own right, went on to constitute a full and historically lasting recognition by the United States. Each time, some degree of recognition was offered by the United States, whether by the President or a House of Congress, but other arms of American leadership denied the validity of the recognition.

On October 29, 2019, the US House of Representatives voted to recognize the Armenian Genocide, and this was followed by an unprecedented unanimous vote in the US Senate on December 21, 2019 also to recognize. What could be more meaningful? Certainly this constitutes official recognition of the Armenian Genocide by the United States. But it does not. There is no complete recognition because the White House promptly followed suit and made it clear that President Donald Trump would not endorse the recognition. This is what always happens (to date). One arm of the US government votes recognition and then another arm refuses to concur.

Sassounian reviews two earlier instances, in 1975 and 1984, in which the House of Representatives adopted resolutions just as the House of Representatives in October 2019 has done but the Senate did not follow through and in both cases were also accompanied by presidential refuses to recognize. He also reviews the Presidential Proclamation issued by President Ronald Reagan in 1981 on the day of the anniversary of the Armenian Genocide, April 22, but this proclamation was never followed by Congressional rulings let alone was pushed off by subsequent presidents, Republicans and Democrats.

Repeatedly, one presidential administration after another has opposed efforts at resolutions recognizing the Armenian Genocide either in the House or in the Senate. In each case the administration utilized its channels for political influence and control and instructed the US State Department to back its position. This was true of Republican administrations such as those of George H. W. Bush and then George W. Bush, and this was true of the Democratic administrations under Bill Clinton and Barack Obama.

The Secret State Department Document Sassounian reviews exposes data from the Clinton administration when Madeleine Albright was Secretary of State. It is particularly interesting because here the opposition to the recognition of the Armenian Genocide is linked to what may well have been genuinely good intentions to support a process that was underway which established a Truth and Reconciliation process on the subject entitled "Turkish Armenian Reconciliation Commission" (TARC).

The members of the commission included six Turks and four Armenians. In 2002 the Commission appointed an independent legal think tank, the International Center for Transitional Justice in New York, to conduct a study of whether the mass murders of the Armenians by the Turks constituted genocide. As is well known, the concept and legal basis for prosecuting genocide was pioneered by Jewish Holocaust survivor, Raphael Lemkin, beginning with his brilliant 1944 book, *Axis Rule in Occupied Europe: Laws of Occupation, Analysis of Government, Proposals for Redress*. The legal opinion of the International Center for Transitional Justice was that the Ottoman massacres of Armenians in 1915–1918 "include all the elements of the crime of genocide as defined in the [Genocide] Convention, and legal scholars as well as historians, politicians, journalists and other people would be justified in continuing to so describe them."[17]

So the US government all along had been supporting the TARC effort at reconciliation, and it was hardly a simple matter because there was tremendous resistance to the very construction of the commission and cooperation with it including from many—but not all—Armenian sources who felt that the Turks were pulling a Trojan Horse deception. The US State Department was busy squelching efforts to legislate resolutions recognizing the Armenian Genocide

---

17 "The Applicability of the United Nations Convention on the Prevention and Punishment of the Crime of Genocide to the Events Which Occurred during the Early Twentieth Century," International Center for Transitional Justice, 2002, https://www.ictj.org/publication/applicability-un-convention-prevention-and-punishment-crime-genocide-events-which.

on the grounds that these resolutions might impede the good work of reconciliation that was being advanced. So they were working for a good cause, and yet the political tactics they employed were the same tactics that the State Department had been using for years to defeat recognition of the Armenian Genocide on behalf of Turkish interests and not on behalf of reconciliation.

It seems that there is very good reason to doubt that there is a Santa Claus in this world and very good reason to doubt that a Ministry of Foreign Affairs/ State Department are operating with a basic integrity when they head out to achieve a given policy goal.

Here is Sassounian's editorial:

Secret Document Reveals State Dept's Interference in Genocide Recognition

by Harut Sassounian, publisher, *California Courier*, October 30, 2019

The United States government has recognized the Armenian Genocide multiple times in the past. In an official document submitted by the US government to the World Court in 1951, the Armenian Genocide was acknowledged for the first time as an example of Genocide. The House of Representatives adopted two resolutions in 1975 and 1984, acknowledging the Armenian Genocide. Furthermore, Pres. Ronald Reagan issued a Presidential Proclamation on April 22, 1981 referencing the Armenian Genocide.

Nevertheless, recent US Administrations have made repeated attempts to block the acknowledgement of the Armenian Genocide by the US Congress and successive American Presidents have avoided using the term Genocide in their April 24 commemorative statements.

For example, the Reagan Administration, after Pres. Reagan issued a Presidential Proclamation in 1981 acknowledging the Armenian Genocide, opposed Congressional resolutions recognizing the Armenian Genocide.

The George H. W. Bush Administration opposed Senate Majority Leader Bob Dole's efforts to have the US Senate recognize the Armenian Genocide Resolution in 1990.

The Clinton Administration blocked the passage of the Armenian Genocide Resolution in 2000, moments before the House was to vote on it.

The George W. Bush Administration objected to the adoption of the Armenian Genocide Resolution by the House of Representatives in 2007.

The Obama Administration opposed the Armenian Genocide Resolution in 2010, preventing it from reaching a full House vote.

An unclassified "secret" State Department document, dated October 2, 2000, discloses the length to which the US government went to block the passage of House Resolution 596 in the year 2000, while Bill Clinton was President and Madeleine Albright was Secretary of State. Resolution 596 was approved by the House International Relations Committee on 24 yes, 11 no and 2 present votes on October 3, 2000, but not put to a vote in the House of Representatives.

The "secret" document contains two letters: the first from Secretary of State Albright to Foreign Minister of Armenia Vartan Oskanian and Turkish Foreign Minister Ismail Ipekci; the second letter is from Tom Pickering, Under Secretary of State for Political Affairs, to Dick Solomon, President of the US Institute of Peace. In an introductory note, Steven Sestanovich, Special Adviser to the Secretary of State for the new independent states of the former Soviet Union, tells US Ambassador to Armenia Michael Lemmon that both Pickering and Solomon "are obviously part of the deal we are trying to put in place to head off the Genocide Resolution. I discussed them today with VO [Foreign Minister Vartan Oskanian] and Van Krikorian [co-chair of the Armenian Assembly of America] did the same. VO was positively disposed but said he could not speak for RK [president Robert Kocharyan], who had already gone home sick. VO will speak with him tomorrow and get his reaction. ..."

Secretary of State Albright, in her letter to the Foreign Ministers of Armenia and Turkey states: "The US Administration has strongly opposed this resolution, believing that it offers a completely counterproductive approach to the goal of improving relations between Turkey and Armenia and promoting reconciliation between the Turkish and Armenian peoples. I am hopeful that we will proceed in getting this resolution put aside, because we are strongly committed to what we believe could be a more promising approach. ... I will be writing in due course with some ideas about how to make this effort a success."

In the second letter, Under Secretary of State Pickering wrote to Solomon, President of the US Institute of Peace, an independent institution founded by Congress: "... Recently, the Congress has been deliberating a resolution, HR 596 on 'Commemoration of the Armenian Genocide.' As you know, the Administration has opposed this resolution, but we firmly believe that a Truth and Reconciliation process on this subject is needed. ... The Secretary [of State] has asked me to write to propose that the US Institute of Peace begin developing ideas for such a Truth and Reconciliation process with the goal of launching it in the near future. ... As a first step, we hope you will consider convening a group of credible and recognized Turks, Armenians and others. These should include the representatives of public groups, scholars, archivists, government or former government officials and others. Our hope is that an initial meeting could be held as early as December in Washington, DC. This initial planning group would review the historical and political contexts and generate a consensus on the scope and timetable of subsequent activities, including creation of a commission to prepare a report."

The initiative proposed by the Department of State was finally launched in July 2001 when the "Turkish Armenian Reconciliation Commission" (TARC) was founded with the participation of six Turks and four Armenians which included Van Krikorian from the Armenian Assembly of America, Antranik Migranian from Moscow, and two Armenian foreign ministry officials.

In the months succeeding the formation of TARC, I wrote several editorials opposing it because it was clear that TARC was a ploy by the State Department to block the proposed congressional resolution to recognize the Armenian Genocide. Even without the knowledge of the "secret" document disclosed in this article, most observers suspected that TARC was created and funded by the State Department in conjunction with the Turkish government to undermine the pursuit of the Armenian Cause.

Unfortunately, certain Armenian groups and individuals were deceived by this American-Turkish ploy which was naively supported by the Armenian Foreign Ministry. It took a considerable effort on the part of many Diaspora Armenians to convince the Armenian government to drop its support of TARC.

Armenians need to remain vigilant not to fall in the trap of those who pursue their own interests at the expense of the Armenian nation.[18]

---

18 Harut Sassounian, "California Courier Secret Document Reveals State Dept.'s Interference in Genocide Recognition," *California Courier*, October 30, 2019, http://www.thecaliforniacourier.com/secret-document-reveals-state-dept-s-interference-in-genocide-recognition/.

The "Now She Loves Me, Now She Doesn't" endless contradictions of the United States are quite similar to what has taken place in Israel and continues today. On the level of Israeli culture there is no doubt that the people recognize the Armenian Genocide, and public media such as newspapers and TV regularly produce stories and features that recognize the event. On the governmental level, the president of Israel, Reuven Rivlin, speaks personally of the Armenian Genocide, including his recalling as a youngster growing up in Jerusalem the arrival of Armenian refugees from the genocide who settled in the Armenian Quarter of the city. It is true that once he became president Rivlin *attempted* not to use the word "genocide" about the Armenians because, he explained, as president he was foresworn to carry out the decisions of the government even when he disagreed. However, I had the distinct pleasure of participating in a meeting with Rivlin at the presidential residence following the conclusion of a very meaningful conference on genocide at the Open University of Israel, and in the process he became so emotional that he blurted out charmingly, "OK, OK, I'm going to use the word I'm not supposed to use, the Armenian Genocide!" Previous to his presidency, Rivlin had served as Chair of the Knesset and there too he had fought for and supported efforts at legislation to recognize the Armenian Genocide. The same was true of Rivlin's successor in the Knesset, Yuli Edelstein. In the membership of the Knesset any number of times there was clearly majority support for such recognition. In July 2016, the process moved successfully from the Knesset plenary to the Education Committee which held a proper full hearing for all sides (including opposition to recognition of the Armenian Genocide by representatives of the Azeri-Israeli community and by a designated representative of the Foreign Ministry) and went on to vote decisively for recognition! We had won! Israel recognized the Armenian Genocide! But then again, just like the script says, the government stepped in and announced its unforgiving opposition to any such recognition, and the further process that would have taken place in the Knesset was aborted.

Conclusion: Democracies obviously can be very undemocratic.

SUPPLEMENT: LETTERS CONFRONTING PRIME MINISTER SHIMON PERES WHO OPPOSED THE CONFERENCE, AND IN LATER YEARS CONTINUED OPPOSITION TO RECOGNIZING THE ARMENIAN GENOCIDE

[To the tune of "When Israel Was in Egypt Land ..."] "When Israel Learned of the Armenian Genocide, Let the Truth Be Known"

The following are three letters sent in 2001, 2002, and 2004 to the famed Shimon Peres [1923–2016], alternately Prime Minister or the Foreign Minister or member of Israel's Knesset since the establishment of the State of Israel. He was an indisputable key leader of the country. Among other things, Peres was the key person in recruiting, setting, and organizing Israel's policy of nuclear defense.

Although he never scored a current political victory as the fully elected leader of the country, there is no question that by virtue of his "Founding Father" status, though he was obviously different from that of the national founding father, David Ben Gurion, amazingly he was nonetheless not at all far removed from a similar significance.

In 1982, during the months preceding the First International Conference on the Holocaust and Genocide where we were struggling with Israel's attempts to a) remove the subject of the Armenian Genocide; b) remove the Armenian scholars scheduled to lecture; c) (ostensibly) move the Conference to a venue outside of Israel; d) cancel the conference in entirety, there were any number of moments when my conversations would revolve around these various choices. On one such occasion, I believe in May 1982, Elie Wiesel instructed me to contact Shimon Peres—there really was an element of his ordering me, since, after all, as president he was the titular chief of our conference, and in general he was clearly the world-famous personage and the confidant of Prime Minister Peres.

Wiesel armed me with a private telephone number that would put me through directly to Peres. Peres was expecting my call, I was told. I was instructed to ask him directly should the Armenian lectures be dropped.

[*Conversation is in Hebrew*]

"Mr. Peres?"

"Yes."

"I am Israel Charny and Elie Wiesel asked me to ask your judgment whether the lectures on the Armenian Genocide should be removed from our conference."

"Yes. Cancel those lectures."

"Thank you. Shalom."

End of telephone conversation

Should I have argued or attempted to discuss Peres's ruling? I now think, "Yes." Should I at least have told him I did not agree and would not abide? Of course. But the atmosphere was one in which I had been granted the enviable privilege of a direct contact with the leader, my allotted time was used up, and more to the point I have been instructed clearly what I had to do—so go do it, period. Moreover, as a much younger man at the time, I confess that I hardly felt empowered to try to speak further. (Oh well, I'll do it differently next time.)

Nonetheless, when all was said and done, I had zero doubts about my course of action.

SEVERAL YEARS LATER AND FURTHER COMMUNICATION WITH PERES

Of course, Shimon Peres continued to play seriously major roles in the Israeli government, so that over and over again he was involved in setting the tone and direction of Israel's policy about the Armenian Genocide. There were a number of occasions when again I did attempt to communicate with him, though I never received a direct reply. There was one occasion when he was Foreign Minister that I was formally invited to participate in a welcoming luncheon at the Laromme Hotel in Jerusalem for the Armenian Foreign Minister who came to Jerusalem. I sat through what was a delicious esthetic occasion but was absolutely shocked by the endless double talk references to the "tragedy" or "massacre" of the Armenians by the Turks and the ada-mant—and I felt deeply insulting—avoidance of more powerful and accurate language about the murders of the Armenians, let alone the full-blown nature of the Armenian Genocide.

In the early 2000s there were at least three occasions when I wrote directly and publicly to Peres as will be seen in the letters that follow. Obviously, these letters had no impact whatsoever on Israeli policy, but I must say they aroused a tremendous emotional response from many Armenians in Armenia and every-where in the world, also Assyrians and Greeks, as well as from Israelis and car-ing people everywhere. Thus, the Armenian, Assyrian and Hellenic Genocide News website published the April 2001 letter with some further comments on how" denial of genocide has become a major sub-field of its own in the overall field of genocide studies.[19] So that if these letters only elevated the morale of many good people, I am very pleased that I wrote them.

In a larger frame, speaking up to a revered Israeli leader was part of our continuing efforts for Israel's recognition of the Armenian Genocide. Israeli public opinion has been favorable to recognition for many years, and in recent years there were definite evidences of growing support in the Knesset as well as including a major vote by a key committee for recognition, but throughout the government has repeatedly exercised its overriding political power to stop the Knesset from asserting formal recognition.

THREE LETTERS TO SHIMON PERES

1.

> Institute on the Holocaust and Genocide, Jerusalem
> *Toward Understanding, Intervention, and Prevention of Genocide*
>
> Founded in 1979 by:
>
> Israel W. Charny
> Shamai Davidson
> Elie Wiesel
>
> April 11, 2001
>
> The Honorable Shimon Peres, Foreign Minister
> Ministry of Foreign Affairs, State of Israel
> Jerusalem, Israel
>
> Re: Report in *Turkish Daily News*, Ankara, April 10, 2001

---

19 "Holocaust Scholar Israel Charny Responds to Shimon Peres Statements in the Turkish Press," *Armenian, Assyrian and Hellenic Genocide News*, April 12, 2001, http://www.atour. com/-aaghn/news/200104131.html.

Dear Mr. Peres,

I offer you my deepest respects for your enormous contributions to the security and development of Israel, and to peace.

Nonetheless, it is my privilege since many years ago not to agree with your position regarding the Armenian Genocide. It seems that because of your wishes to advance very important relations with Turkey, you have been prepared to circumvent the subject of the Armenian Genocide in 1915–1920. (Thus, you advised me in a telephone conversation in 1982 not to insist on including the subject of the Armenians in the First International Conference on the Holocaust and Genocide that we convened in Tel Aviv, and I then made the decision not to give in to pressures of the Foreign Ministry to cancel the lectures on the Armenian Genocide or to cancel the entire conference.)

It seems to me according to yesterday's report in the Ankara newspaper that you have gone beyond a moral boundary that no Jew should allow himself to trespass. You are quoted as follows: "We reject attempts to create a similarity between the Holocaust and the Armenian allegations. Nothing similar to the Holocaust occurred. It is a tragedy what the Armenians went through but not a genocide."

For the record, in 2000, at a Conference on the Holocaust in Philadelphia, a large number of researchers of the Holocaust, including Israeli historians, signed a public declaration that the Armenian Genocide was factual.

Also for the record, in 1997 at the meeting of the Association of Genocide Scholars, the Association as a whole officially voted a resolution that the Armenians had been subject to full-scale genocide.

Even as I disagree with you, it may be that in your broad perspective of the needs of the State of Israel it is your obligation to circumvent and desist from bringing up the subject with Turkey, but as a Jew and an Israeli I am ashamed of the extent to which you have now entered into the range of actual denial of the Armenian Genocide, comparable to denials of the Holocaust.

Respectfully,

Prof. Israel Charny
Executive Director, Institute on the Holocaust and Genocide, Jerusalem
Editor-in-Chief, *Encyclopedia of Genocide* (ABC-Clio Publishers, UK & USA, 1999)

2.

Institute on the Holocaust and Genocide, Jerusalem
Toward Understanding, Intervention, and Prevention of Genocide

Founded in 1979 by:

Israel W. Charny
Shamai Davidson
Elie Wiesel

March 4, 2002

Ministry of Foreign Affairs, State of Israel
Shimon Peres, Foreign Minister
Michael Melchior, Deputy Foreign Minister
Rivka Cohen, Ambassador to Armenia
Armenian Desk

Dear Honored Minister, Deputy Minister, Ambassador, and Professional Staff at Ministry of Foreign Affairs,

As a Jew and Israeli, I am deeply ashamed of the position taken by our Ambassador and Ministry to deny that the genocide of the Armenian people in 1915 was in fact genocide. That is the equivalent of denials of the Holocaust of our people.

Even in these very serious days of our national history, when the support of other countries such as neighboring Turkey is of great practical importance, I do not believe that historical/moral issues of recognizing respectfully and honorably the genocidal mass extermination of any people should be bypassed by any people, and in particular by our Jewish people.

I am enclosing with great concern for your attention an editorial in a leading US-Armenian newspaper calling on Armenia to expel the Israeli Ambassador. For your further information, the author of this editorial, who is the head of the Armenian United Fund in the United States—comparable to our United Jewish Appeal—was for many years a delegate to the UN Human Rights Commission in Geneva.

I am also enclosing for you a report dated February 28 that the European Union voted a second time urging Turkey to recognize the Armenian Genocide.

And I am enclosing for you a copy of a statement signed by 126 Holocaust scholars in 2000 recognizing the Armenian Genocide. Signators include a leader in Israeli Holocaust scholarship, our Prof. Yehuda Bauer; and Nobel Peace Prize Laureate, Holocaust survivor, Elie Wiesel.

Will not the values of Zion weep at our *realpolitik* shaming of another people who, like us, carry everyday grief and outrage of their memory of the mass genocidal murders of their people?

With prayers for the strength of our people and country in such grave times, when we are fighting in self-defense against a deadly and even genocidal terrorism that attacks indiscriminately including unarmed youths in cafes, and families of men, women, and children gathered to celebrate weddings and bar-mitzvahs, I am

Respectfully yours,
Prof. Israel W. Charny

3.

[Translated from the original letter in Hebrew which was written on stationery of the Marriott Hotel, in Yerevan, Armenia]

May 7, 2004
To: Ministry of Foreign Affairs, Israel: Foreign Minister, Sylvan Shalom, and the official responsible for the "Armenia Desk"
To: Member of Knesset Shimon Peres:
Copy to: *Haaretz* daily newspaper, Letters to the Editor
Copies in English to: Foreign Ministry of Armenia, Newsletter of the Association of Genocide Scholars, and to internet website *H-Genocide*

How ashamed I felt in one interview after the other for the media of Armenia in its capital, Yerevan, where I was participating in an international forum on maintaining the memory of the Armenian Genocide in the face of realistic political and economic interests, such as the need for more normal relations with Armenia's giant neighbor, Turkey.

Over and over again I was asked in pain and sadness and amazement how Israel, the homeland of the Jews, could possibly consent to denials of the Armenian Genocide! The interviewers said, entirely correctly, that our two nations should be standing shoulder to shoulder in a just war against the genocides *of any and all peoples* in our world.

It worried me very much, in an era of increasing anti-Semitism/anti-Israeli views, to hear through the pain of the interviewers, and notwithstanding the personal respect they conveyed to me, the accusation that perhaps Israel's denial of the Armenian Genocide confirms "what they say" that we are a people who seek excessive power over others and are overly brutal.

We dare not collaborate with ignorance, indifference or denial of the genocide of any other people, even if it will apparently "cost us" practically in some way. Cynicism and manipulativeness only eat away at our real strength.

Sincerely,

Prof. Israel W. Charny, PhD
Editor-in-Chief, *Encyclopedia of Genocide*
Executive Director, Institute on the Holocaust and Genocide, Jerusalem

What Was Elie Wiesel's Real Position about the Armenians, and about Addressing the Genocides of Many Non-Jewish Peoples Alongside the Holocaust?

O ver the years many people translated Elie Wiesel's withdrawal from heading the conference as a surrender/choice to go along with the intention of removing the subject of the Armenian Genocide.

Although I was very unhappy about his withdrawal from the role of president of the conference, at the time he did so, and as far as I thought I knew at the time also continuing after his resignation, I always defended him that he stood firmly with us against the Turkish/Israeli governments' efforts to censor any presentations on the Armenian Genocide. He definitely did stand with me and Shamai Davidson in the first rounds of the drama. When the Israel Foreign Ministry (IMFA) first approached me with a combination of a seductive request for loyalty to the state's needs and wishes, and then progressively orders and pressures to obey their commands, Wiesel's initial gut-level response to the Israeli government was that he would not agree to exclude the topic.

However, now with the newly released documents, I am less sure that he was not carried away later to a degree of collusion with the Israeli government officials who continued to want to solve their problem with Turkey by eliminating lectures on the Armenian Genocide and even by removing the Armenian speakers. The indications that we have found in IMFA records are that, before resigning, Wiesel may have given the Foreign Minister reason to believe that he would work to remove the subject of the Armenian Genocide from the conference. This information, which has reached me only recently, shocked me very much.

Again, however, I would add that just as we have seen IMFA misinterpreting me at times and believing that I might go along with them, and their periodic assessments that the conference was likely to break down and not take place, one must be respectfully careful in assessing IMFA records of their statements that they had Elie Wiesel fully "in their pockets."

Nonetheless, it is now entirely clear that after resigning as president of the conference, Wiesel did embark on a highly intensive destructive course of trying to block people from attending and/or speaking at the conference along with decisively injurious steps to bring about cancellation of our financial support.

My basic understanding of Wiesel's motives to this day is, first of all, that he was totally devoted to the State of Israel and believed entirely—naively, and, one might say, messianically—in the virtue, decency and integrity of the miraculous State of Israel that was redeeming our people following centuries of oppression of the Jewish people and most recently the indescribable hells of the Holocaust. Furthermore, and most understandably, when the Foreign Ministry conveyed to him that actual lives of Jews were at risk, his necessary choice of action was absolutely clear to him—in no way would he be a party to any risking of Jewish lives. I totally understand him in this respect and in general his trust and dedication to our Israel.

In addition, Wiesel lived with what I shall call a deep ambivalence about recognizing too strongly the genocides of other peoples in comparison to the Holocaust. He was particularly upset when one dared attribute to another genocide the word "holocaust." He also frequently even bridled at the thought that there were other events identified as "genocides" in the world other than the Holocaust. Thus, following the whole drama of our conference in 1982 I had written Wiesel to invite him to participate in what was then a conference being planned in Hiroshima, Japan, and he did agree!, but in the same voice he had to warn and order me: "Please do not use genocide in plural ..." and he indeed then goes on to assert his "philosophical beliefs in the uniqueness of the Shoah." [1,2] This letter by Wiesel on Boston University letterhead dated August 3, 1983 is reproduced in the texts of the "Gallery of Correspondence with Elie Wiesel" at the end of this chapter.

Nonetheless, it is very painful to become aware that after resigning as president Wiesel went on to exercise truly major roles in opposing the conference. Among other things, he advised a number of our most distinguished participants as well as the leadership of key American Jewish organizations and at least one senior foreign diplomat (from Sweden) not to attend. Moreover, he cancelled his own pledge of a contribution of $10,000, and as we also saw he recommended to sources of major financial support of the conference that they withdraw their support. In the case we cited earlier where we received a check for $10,000 from a Holocaust memorial organization and deposited it in our Israeli bank to the conference account only to find two weeks later that the check had been cancelled by the organization, we had assumed this was in response to IMFA pressures and had suspected Wiesel was also involved, but we now know for sure that this was done in response to Wiesel's personal intervention.

It is only fair to reemphasize that Wiesel was under enormous pressure not only internally in respect of his total loyalty to the State of Israel, but that he was also receiving repeated messages from the IMFA that the Prime Minister and

---

1   We were not the initiators or planners of this conference. The moving force was a Japanese architect who was a long-term resident of Israel, Fumikatsu Inoue, who felt very deeply about the Holocaust and who over some years attempted unsuccessfully to promote architectural drawings for building of a new Holocaust memorial museum, which, sadly, he never succeeded in bringing to fruition. Unfortunately, in the end, Inoue also did not succeed in convening such a conference in Hiroshima.

    At the time I invited him, Wiesel did indeed respond positively to my invitation. Yet, even in this context, where he obviously was going to pay a profoundly moving human tribute to the victims of Hiroshima, and make some meaningful linkages between the Holocaust and the nuclear deaths, Wiesel, nonetheless, needed to add explicitly, "Israel: please do not use genocide in plural. ..." He then went on further to spell out that he is asking me to "accept" his "philosophical beliefs about the uniqueness of the Shoah." (This letter by Wiesel on Boston University letterhead dated August 3, 1983 is reproduced in the texts of the "Gallery of Correspondence with Elie Wiesel.")

2   One of the rare publications that has conveyed publicly an appraisal of Elie Wiesel's inconsistency and "two-sidedness" was written by Max Blumenthal, a very controversial but also very serious and well-published writer: Max Blumenthal, "Elie Wiesel's Two Sides: The Holocaust Survivor Gave Voice to Jewish Victims while Ignoring Others' Suffering," *Salon*, July 6, 2016, https://www.salon.com/2016/07/06/remembering_elie_wiesel_ the_holocaust_survivor_gave_voice_to_jewish_victims_while_ignoring_others_suffering_partner/.

the Foreign Minister were also very involved in favor of cancelling the conference! Thus, according to Secret Document no. 6207, May 17, 1982, the General Consul in New York is instructed to inform Wiesel of the Prime Minister
and Foreign Minister's positions. "Please inform Wiesel that the Prime Minister
[Peres] is for cancellation of the conference—I repeat cancellation—and he is
in agreement with the Foreign Minister [Eban] on the subject."

Wow! Peres and Eban—two true greats of Israeli history! The message
continues that Wiesel is to be instructed further that he is to "instruct Charny
by telephone of same immediately" and that he should report back to Jerusalem
to the head of the Diaspora Desk as soon as he has done so—the tone is close
to one of a command to Wiesel to command me in turn to follow orders as any
loyal Jew must do when our State of Israel commands us—except, of course,
that I was, nonetheless, a citizen who was free not to be commanded.

URGENT/SECRET
Date: May 17, 1982
To: Israeli General Consul New York
From: Israel Ministry Foreign Affairs Jerusalem
Document No. 6207   [our page number 62]

1. Please convey to Wiesel that the Prime Minister is in favor of cancelling
    Repeat cancelling the conference and he is of the same opinion as the
    Foreign Minister on this subject.
2. We will ask you very strongly to make every effort that Wiesel will in-
    struct Dr. Charny by telephone immediately accordingly.
3. We will appreciate your reporting to us after your conversations with
    Wiesel and Charny. Thank you—Director, Diaspora Desk[3]

In the next cable the Consul in New York reports to Jerusalem that he
conveyed their message, including the positions of the Prime Minister and
Foreign Minister, and Wiesel replied that Charny left him a message that he
is reaching an agreement with the IMFA where "he hints at the possibility
of holding the conference after canceling the invitations to the Armenians."
The consul then says—more than correctly—that he told Wiesel he didn't
think this could be the case and again asks Wiesel to tell Charny that he must
yield to cancellation of the entire conference. "Wiesel agreed with me that he

---

3   Israel Ministry of Foreign Affairs May 17, 1982, ISA-mfa-mfa-000368i, 116.

would inform Charny that he must respect every decision of yours [Jerusalem] just as Wiesel accepts your decision as an absolute directive." The following is the fuller text:

SECRET/URGENT
Date: May 17, 1982
To: Director Diaspora Desk, Israel Ministry Foreign Affairs Jerusalem
From: Israel General Consul New York
Document No. 492   [our page number 63]

I contacted Wiesel just now and conveyed your position, including that of the Prime Minister and the Foreign Minister for cancelling the conference. He told me that Charny contacted him today and left a message according to which he is nearing an agreement with the Foreign Ministry in Jerusalem, and he [Charny] hints at the possibility of holding the conference after canceling the invitations to the Armenians. I told him that it didn't make sense to me, and asked him to inform Charny that he must reconcile himself to go along with your decision to cancel the conference in entirety. Wiesel agreed with me that he would inform Charny that he must respect every decision by you, just as he, Wiesel, accepts your decision as an absolute directive.[4]

SECRET/URGENT
Date: May 21, 1982
To: Director, Diaspora Desk, Israel Ministry Foreign Affairs Jerusalem
From: Israel General Consul New York
Document No. 664   [our page number 71]

URGENT! Wiesel repeats his position that he accepts and respects any decision we make with regard to the conference and that he has conveyed this to Charny. In his opinion if we are convinced that one must cancel the conference then it is best to cancel it. On the other hand, there is concern that if the damage from cancelling the conference will be too great and instead of this

---

4   Israel Ministry of Foreign Affairs, May 17, 1982, ISA-mfa-mfa-000368i, 122.

the alternative is to remove the controversial subject (meaning Armenian Genocide) and thus give the topic a much lower profile, it would be worth considering this option. In any case, he will abide by Jerusalem's verdict such as it will be.[5]

On May 21, the Consul informs Jerusalem that Wiesel has told him that if the damage from cancelling the conference will be too great, then "the alternative is to remove the controversial subject [Armenian Genocide—Ed.] and thus give the topic a much lower profile."

Notwithstanding all of the above, I am still left remembering most clearly the many times that Wiesel adamantly agreed with me that we would stand up against the pressures and never give in to censorship of the Armenian Genocide. I treasure the memory of these moments of solidarity between me, Shamai Davidson, and Elie Wiesel, and our unambiguous convictions that the story of the Armenian Genocide must be told and honored, and that the realpolitik of Israel's failures to recognize the Armenian Genocide and thus technically to engage in denial, just as so many people sought to deny the Holocaust, must be opposed.

Unfortunately, however, there is now further decisive evidence that in the following years too as the United States Holocaust Memorial Museum was being created (here, too, Wiesel was the presiding chair of the Commission, which was established by President Jimmy Carter, to create the Museum, and was slated to continue as the leader of the Museum when it was constructed, and here too he resigned from his post), Wiesel played an active role in the decisions that were ultimately taken by the Board of Directors not to include information about the genocides of other people. The discussions on this subject were protracted and intense with considerable emotionalism, and they certainly included, perhaps as the main topic, the subject of the Armenian Genocide.[6]

I learned directly about the climactic meeting of the Museum's Board of Directors on the subject from Michael Berenbaum. Berenbaum, a brilliant philosopher and Holocaust scholar (see his chapter shortly in this book, and see, among others, his works on non-Jewish victims in the Holocaust,[7] and

---

5   Israel Ministry of Foreign Affairs, May 21, 1982, ISA-mfa-mfa-000368i, document no. 664, 109.

6   One good source for viewing the intense controversies in the Museum in the late 1980's into 1990 is an article by veteran New York Times reporter, Judith Miller, "Holocaust Museum: A Troubled Start," New York Times Magazine, April 22, 1990, https://www.nytimes.com/1990/04/22/magazine/holocaust-museum-a-troubled-start.html.

7   Michael Berenbaum, ed., A Mosaic of Victims: Non-Jews Persecuted and Murdered by the Nazis (New York: New York University Press, 1990). Published simultaneously in the United Kingdom by I.B. Tauris.

about the question whether the Allies should have bombed Auschwitz),[8] who served as Deputy Director of the President's Commission on the Holocaust (1979–1980), Project Director of the Museum (1988–1993), and finally as Research Director of the Museum (1993–1997). It was he who led the enormously meaningful project of selecting and organizing that information that was to be displayed in the Museum, and he was very strongly in favor of a significant presentation on the Armenian Genocide, including the context that this genocide preceded the Holocaust and in many ways was a template from which the Holocaust issued and continued—not to speak of the many German officers who participated in the Armenian Genocide and went on as "experienced professionals" to preside over murders in the Holocaust such as the T4 murders of children and the Einsatzgruppen mobile killing squads who decimated the Jewish communities in the Soviet Union.

I happened to be in Washington, DC at the time and Berenbaum and I had planned a meeting one evening only for him to turn up several hours late, quite late at night, looking utterly beaten and distraught, and he told me that he had just come from a meeting of the Board of Directors of the Museum where the proposal about the Armenian Genocide was defeated by an obstinate refusal to recognize significantly any other genocide.[9]

It was also clear throughout our collaborative work with Wiesel that periodically he would express concern about our not keeping the Holocaust at the absolute center of our planning—an almost "Holocaust is uniquely unique" position—but then Wiesel would return to his wonderful universalist sympathetic position for all peoples who suffered genocide. Still, the record that has now become even clearer than we suspected is that after resigning as president of the conference, Wiesel put so much energy into reducing and/or cancelling the conference that altogether, today I must conclude that it is true Wiesel caved in.

As I have said, I know and respect the fact that the State of Israel was holy to Wiesel, and that he as a survivor of the hell of the Holocaust, and a deeply committed Jew, was fully committed to obey the demands of the State of Israel. In addition, as I also already have commented, I know personally that Wiesel delighted in being an honored persona with top leaders of Israel, including the Prime Minister, and it is very understandable that he would obey their dictates.

---

8   Michael Neufeld and Michael Berenbaum, *The Bombing of Auschwitz: Should the Allies Have Attempted It?* (New York: St. Martin's Press, 2000).

9   Michael Berenbaum, personal communication.

I can also add to this account that Elie Wiesel was a complex man—perhaps as we all are, but given his more than poignant life history, his great artistry and his record of outstanding inspiration and leadership, for all of which I also continue to love him, the whole story is more than touching even when one is seriously critical of him. I have spoken to a good number of people who, like myself, enjoyed periods of considerable closeness to him only eventually to come away disappointed by his pattern of inconsistency and failure to follow through on commitments and promises. Ultimately, as I will describe shortly, I became too disappointed in him to continue our relationship.

Altogether, I am indeed hurt by Elie Wiesel and angry at him, and yet, I say with no effort that I also continue to salute Elie Wiesel with all my heart for the true encouragement he gave to memorial of the Holocaust and to a memorable extent also to applying the meaning of the Holocaust to an impassioned concern for the welfare of other peoples.

In connection with the 1982 conference drama I would like to remember him in particular on two occasions. The first was when I turned to him to invite him to be the president of the conference that he agreed to do so without any fee; and he replied with Wiesel charm, "I am in need of a *mitzvah* [a good deed] these days." (See "Gallery of Correspondence with Elie Wiesel.")

The second was a year after the conference when there had been a good deal of newspaper response to the conference, virtually all very complimentary to us and in some cases including strong criticisms of Wiesel for his withdrawal. Elie Wiesel was a very sensitive man who did not take criticism very well and he was hurt and angry at me—at one point he wrote me explicitly that we were never to be in contact again. (See "Gallery of Correspondence with Elie Wiesel.") But we were, and a year later he agreed to my coming once again to his home in New York, and when he opened the door for me he threw his arms warmly around me in a very strong embrace.

Sadly, however, even so Wiesel's in-and-out pattern of connection and disconnection continued, and finally we reached a point of no return in our relationship. It was some years later as the monumental *Encyclopedia of Genocide*[10]

10 Israel Charny's *Encyclopedia of Genocide* was awarded "Outstanding Academic Book of the Year" by the American Library Association. Associate Editors: Rouben Paul Adalian, Steven Jacobs, Eric Markusen, and Samuel Totten. Bibliographic Editor: Marc I Sherman. Forewords by Bishop Desmond M. Tutu and Simon Wiesenthal: "Why Is It Important to Learn about the Holocaust and the Genocides of All Peoples?" 2nd ed., 2000. Partial French edition, *Le livre noir de l'humanité: Encyclopédie mondiale des genocides*, forewords by Bishop Desmond M. Tutu and Simon Wiesenthal, trans. Janice Valls-Russell (Toulouse: Éditions Privat, 2001). 3rd ed., 2002. Internet e-book ed., 2003.

was, under my initiative and editing, ready to appear, Wiesel had agreed to write the Foreword and had also promised that he would personally write a major review of the book for the *New York Times*. In fact Wiesel's Foreword was already being publicized prominently by the publisher in expensive promotional materials and was already listed formally in the Library of Congress citation of the forthcoming book, but at the very last moment Wiesel pulled out without any explanation at all and rejected all our appeals for an explanation. Fortuitously, he came to speak at the Academy of Science in Jerusalem at the time and I arranged to meet with him personally to appeal to him to retract his cancellation of his Foreword, but he had obviously came to a firm, even angry decision and virtually had nothing to say to me other than that he was not changing his decision. My own guess was that after seeing the publisher's final proofs of the encyclopedia, he regretted giving his name to a work that related so extensively to so many cases of genocide other than the Holocaust. We will never know.

Happily and meaningfully, Wiesel's intended Foreword was replaced by two memorable Forewords by survivor/Nazi hunter Simon Wiesenthal and South Africa's legendary champion of human rights, Bishop Desmond Tutu—both of whom independently expressed great delight at being linked with one another. They correctly experienced their sharing the roles of writers of the Forewords as an expression of the fact that the encyclopedia was aiming at the subject of genocide to *all* peoples everywhere on our planet, past, present and future. I will never forget my delight at receiving, from each one, separately, without either one knowing of the other's letter, a warm letter of greetings to be sent to the other and a powerful statement of a conviction that we—all human beings—were dealing with a shared universal problem for *all* of our species.

In respect of Elie Wiesel, that became the final nail in our relationship. I now felt assaulted by him too many times, and too capriciously, without possibilities for dialogue, clarification, and reconciliation, and there was no point in remaining in touch. But it was and remains sad for me, a real loss of connection to a very special person who, when all is said and done, had given all of us a great, great deal that was indeed Nobel-worthy.

In the following pages I have assembled a running diary of correspondence with Wiesel beginning with his response to the invitation to be president of the First International Conference on the Holocaust and Genocide, continuing through the unfolding of the conference crisis, then including his "Don't ever talk to me again or use my name" messages, but culminating with what I report was our seeming reconciliation and then my new invitation to him to play a role in a conference in Hiroshima and his positive response while nonetheless reaffirming his true ideological commitment—the Holocaust is never to be treated as anything but uniquely unique.

SUPPLEMENT: GALLERY OF CORRESPONDENCE WITH ELIE WIESEL

1. Wiesel Accepts Presidency of Conference

When I wrote to Elie Wiesel asking him to undertake being President of the 1982 conference that I was planning, under its title of First International Conference on the Holocaust and Genocide, he wrote back charmingly that the idea appealed to him and that he accepted the role and with no fee because he was in need of *mitzvoth* (the Hebrew word for good deeds) at this time. If one understands the incredible tension that surrounded the notion and insistence that the Holocaust was totally unique and truly incomparable to any other event of human tragedy and evil, the fact that he accepted such a role of a conference whose title linked the Holocaust with genocide as a broader process, and obviously involved other peoples than the Jews, was very dramatic, let alone heartwarming.

1.01 My Invitation to Elie Wiesel to be President of Conference

Elie Wiesel
239 Central Park West
New York 10024

September 18, 1979

Dear Elie,

I have decided to organize an International Congress on the Holocaust and Genocide in Israel in 1982.

To the best of my knowledge, there has been no international congress which has linked the Holocaust of our people with the genocides of other peoples. I can think of no more appropriate place for such a congress than Israel.

The goal of this Conference throughout is to project genocide as a universal problem in the history and futures of all peoples; to honor the national and historic concerns of each people who have been fated to suffer a tragedy of mass destruction; and at the same time to correlate these concerns with one another so that every event of genocide also reflects and articulates a concern for destruction of all peoples.

The Conference will be organized around several working tracks:

1. Reports of Ongoing Genocide in the World Today
2. International Law and Statesmanship
3. International Human Rights and Threats of Future Genocide
4. The Role of the Media in Informing the World
5. Teaching Genocide of One's Own People and Internationally
6. Treating Survivors and their Families
7. The Psychology and Sociology of Genocide
8. Ecocide and Omnicide: the New Faces of Genocide

Elie, there is no person in the world more suited to be the central figure in this Conference than you, and I would like to invite you to take on several roles.

First of all, I would like to ask you to be the President of the Conference and in this capacity to appear on a number of occasions: at the opening session; a session at Yad Vashem; and a session where one or more international figures will address us.

Secondly, I would like to ask you to deliver a keynote address to the entire Conference.

Thirdly, I would like to ask you to be one of the twelve leader/teachers who will offer an intensive two-day Workshop preceding the Conference (a full Thursday and half-day Friday), to a limited registration of thirty people. These will be serious working sessions for interested professionals. (The larger Conference will convene on Sunday night and run through Thursday.)

The Conference will be organized technically by Kenes, an excellent firm whose work you probably have seen in Israel, and travel arrangements will be by Peltours, Tel Aviv and their worldwide affiliates. I can assure you that the Congress will be conducted in the finest taste. But most of all, Elie, I assure you that I intend to do everything for this Conference to become a real event—for all of us who want to learn from one another, and be strengthened by one another in our awareness of the epidemic of genocide, and efforts to contain this epidemic.

Sincerely,
Israel W. Charny, PhD

Elie Wiesel Responds Accepting Presidency of Conference (photo of original)

Boston University

College of Liberal Arts
745 Commonwealth Avenue
Boston, Massachusetts 02215

Elie Wiesel
Andrew W. Mellon Professor of Humanities

October 11, 1979

Dear Israel:

Thank you for your letter. The idea appeals to me.
But we need to think about mechanics: who will do
what? Or, as we used to say in the Yeshiva: Mi vami
haholkhim?

As for your my fees: forget it. If I feel apt to
prepare something worthwhile, I will do it free. I am
short of Mitzvot lately...

We should meet and have a lengthy talk.

When? Where?

Be well, Israel. With every good wish,

Figure 8. [Mitzvot *is Hebrew and refers to good deeds in Jewish tradition. Above his*
signature Wiesel has written, warmly, in Hebrew, shelcha, *or "yours"—Ed.*]

2. Following Wiesel's Interview in Paris to the *New York Times*, Revealing the Turkish Threat and Resigning as President, Israel Charny and Shamai Davidson Reply to Wiesel, June 6, 1982

Shamai Davidson and I now cabled Wiesel trying to reengage him in the conference. We now had a new momentum for our case in that two major Israeli

newspapers had come out strongly supporting our position of not accepting dictates of IMFA. We also felt and hoped that the comparison of denial of the AG to denials of the Holocaust would impact on him.

2.01 Shamai Davidson and I Appeal to Elie Wiesel Not to Resign

Kenes Tours
06-06-1982
Outgoing

341171 Kens IL
Elie Wiesel
Hotel Belle Chasse
Rue Belle Chasse
Paris
France

Dear Elie,

Your story to the N.Y. Times in Paris telling of the Turkish pressure on Israel foreign ministry has created a new momentum and involvement in the very goals of the conference STOP you have removed the coercive power of secrecy stop israel and world public opinion may create a climate of support which will free the conference to its full work. STOP *Davar*, Friday, page one, says: "for years we spoke of the silence that the world kept about the holocaust for reasons of convenience or political expediency now we know it can also happen to us." The conference will convene under any circumstances even for a proverbial 10 participants. The price of killing truth and history is ultimately more human lives stop ironically without any connection to our conference. *Haaretz* on 27/5 ran a five-column article on the Armenian Genocide STOP. I see no reason why government may not interfere with a free press but can press for cancellation of a scholarly scientific congress. You are the only person with the stature to have brought the truth out in the open along with your own statement of conscience STOP. I pray—the public clarification you have brought about will both protect life and enable you to preside and contribute your genius and heart to the conference we have built together for 3 years. We urgently plead you come from Paris to Israel to help us deal with this situation STOP.

Israel Charny
Shamai Davidson
341171 Kens IL

[Davar *refers to a prominent daily Hebrew newspaper of the Labor Zionists—it is no longer published. The "proverbial 10 participants" refers to the Jewish concept of a* minyan, *which is the requirement that at least ten men participate in a prayer service for it to qualify as a "full" service.—Ed.*]

3. Elie Wiesel Replies in a Letter on June 8, 1982 to the Directors of Kenes—the Congress Events Company Organizing the Conference— Reaffirming that He Still is Withdrawing

Wiesel now responded to our plea that he continue as president of the Conference by reaffirming to the congress events company that we had engaged with a copy of a telegram he sent to Israel Charny in which he explains his repeated pleas to postpone or relocate the conference. The notion of such postponement and relocation had been introduced to us by the Israel Ministry of Foreign Affairs which also promised that it would cover all expenses associated with the delay of the immediately scheduled conference in June and its transfer to a location probably somewhere in Europe. It was my judgement that the Ministry was making this offer manipulatively and that one could not rely on it. Wiesel reconfirms that if we do not postpone, he is out.

3.01 Elie Wiesel Makes a Last Bid to Me to Accept Government Postponement

June 8, 1982

To: Kenes Congress CO., Tel Aviv
Dear Madam/Sir,

This is a copy of a telegram I felt I had to send to Dr. Israel W. Charny. I sent it with pain and you understand why:

For weeks and weeks, since early May, I have been urging you and your colleagues in the name of conscience, to postpone or relocate our important conference, as asked by highest officials of the Israel government, who fear conference at this moment could jeopardize vital interests of the Jewish people.

I am urging you again to do so. I know that you and your friends have invested years of work in this project, but there are other and higher priorities.

However, should you decide to disregard these profound concerns, i shall feel compelled to withdraw from the conference altogether and give up all responsibilities related to it—but it is not yet too late.

With deep regrets and hope
Elie Wiesel

4. A Telegram Jointly Signed by Wiesel, Charny, and Davidson, Designed to be Sent to Participants on June 13, 1982—but It Was Never Sent— Announcing to Registrants that the Conference was Postponed

These continued to be heady days of intense back-and-forth between us and Wiesel and between the organizers and professionals managing the conference, news media from all around the world, registrants who were asking about the fate of the conference, and of course the Israel Ministry of Foreign Affairs. Proposals and tentative decisions came and went in breathtaking rapidity.

Along with the considerable collaboration of Shamai Davidson, I was the person primarily responsible for decisions. There was no question that we did not in any way want to see any damage done by the Turks to any Jewish person, whether in Turkey itself or among those escaping from other Arab countries to Israel. So that even at this late date we even entertained the possibility of accepting the Foreign Ministry's offer of a postponed conference in another venue outside of Israel, to the point where Wiesel joined with Davidson and myself in formulating what to me was a terrifying announcement to be sent to registrants announcing the last-minute postponement of the conference. On this basis, Wiesel now agreed to continue as President and indeed to participate in a limited Workshop that we would hold for all those who had or will have arrived already in Israel. However, before long, it became clear, as I had anticipated much earlier, that the IMFA would not commit itself genuinely to funding a postponed conference and our cancellation was cancelled. This letter never went out.

4.01 We were Giving Every Consideration to Cooperating with IMFA, but ...

Figure 9.

International Conference on the Holocaust and Genocide
Towards Understanding, Intervention, and Prevention of Genocide

Intensive Dialogue Workshops June 17–18, 1982;
Conference June 20–24, 1982, Tel Aviv

Conference President Elie Wiesel	Telegram to be dispatched June 13, 1982 to all Conference registrants [*the telegram was never sent*]
Executive Director Prof. Israel W. Charny	Cable approved 12.6.82 by Elie Wiesel, I. Charny, and S. Davidson
Co-Directors Yocheved Howard, MS Ephraim Howard, PhD Shamai Davidson, MD	Due to recent events in Israel the conference is postponed to a later date. Elie Wiesel will continue to serve as president of the conference. Full information follows. However, a preparatory workshop seminar will take place at Tel Aviv Hilton at scheduled time for all conference participants already in Israel including Elie Wiesel.
In affiliation with: Holocaust Survivors Memorial Foundation New York, USA	Israel Charny, Shamai Davidson, Elie Wiesel

5. After the conference took place very successfully despite Wiesel's absence and despite the many pressures to cancel the conference, Elie Wiesel went on to resign on June 29, 1982 from the Institute on the Holocaust and Genocide, which he had founded together with Israel Charny and Shamai Davidson

He was angry! For the longest time, Elie Wiesel conveyed an outright blame of me as having conveyed to the world that he had agreed to eliminate the Armenians and the subject of the Armenian Genocide from the conference—which was not at all the case. In all public communications, I had scrupulously emphasized that Wiesel was fully with us in turning down the Ministry's adamant demands to satisfy the Turkish government's insistence that there be no recognition of the Armenian Genocide.

Wiesel's final brush-off is telltale. He writes the letter of resignation both directly to me and to the attorney for our new Institute, Israel Braude. He concluded with a knock-out punch: **"Please inform Dr. Charny** [*this after many years of first-person communication*] **that he may not use my name in any way in the future."**

5.01 Wiesel to our Attorney Resigning from Conference and the Institute as Well! Plus a Memorable Injunction: Don't Use My Name Again!

Boston University
University Professors
745 Commonwealth Avenue
Boston, Massachusetts 02215
617/353–4566

Elie Wiesel, *Andrew W. Mellon Professor in the Humanities*

June 29, 1982

The Hon. Mr. Israel Braude
(Counsel to Dr. I. Charny)
P.O.B. 29784
Tel-Aviv, Israel

Dear Israel:

I resign forthwith from the Institute and the Foundation both as Founder and member.

Please inform Dr. Charny that he may not use my name in any way in the future.

Sincerely,
Elie Wiesel

5.02 The Above Loving Letter of Resignation and Injunction Addressed Directly to Me. I Have Now Become a "Dear Dr. Charny" after Years of Intimacy

Boston University
University Professors
745 Commonwealth Avenue
Boston, Massachusetts 02215
617/353-4566

Elie Wiesel, *Andrew W. Mellon Professor in the Humanities*

June 29, 1982

Dr. Israel Charny
P.O. Box 29784
Tel-Aviv, Israel

Dear Dr. Charny:

I heard you misrepresented my views at the Conference.

I hereby resign from the Institute and the Foundation both as founder and member.

You may not use my name in any way in the future [*my bold—Ed.*].

Sincerely,
Elie Wiesel

6. On July 25, 1982, I Write to Wiesel in Return that I have been Protecting His Reputation and that I am Both Hurt and Angry at His Personal Accusations and Responses to Me

6.01 *"Dear Elie, I have been Protecting You"*

July 25, 1982

Elie Wiesel
Boston University

745 Commonwealth Ave.
Boston, Mass. 02215
USA.

Dear Elie,

In reply to your "Dear Dr. Charny" letter of June 29, you fail to mention how, you heard and believe, that I "misrepresented" your views at the Conference.

The record of my remarks about you is on tape as a matter of fact.

If anything, I would say I was told by several people that in their judgment I was "protecting" you, and they wondered why I continued to express respect for you when, understandably, so many of the participants had reactions of anger at your not being present with us.

Is it possible in the intense play of emotions around the value decisions this Conference generated that you were drawn to finding personal faults with me because we differed in the one policy decision as to whether or not to postpone the Conference? Is it possible that you are being unkind and hurting to me personally?

It is my judgment that I conducted the Conference, under the very difficult circumstances, in an entirely dignified, respectful and positive manner in which your difference of opinion was respected, your absence so regretted, and your contribution to the development of the Conference of three years fully honored.

Combined with the severe pressure you have produced for me as a leader and for my own personal financial situation by withdrawing the Foundation's $10,000 days before the Conference opened, the withdrawal from colleagueship and friendship and the future purposes of the Institute we created are making me feel angry for the first time. For I see you going way beyond the integrity of taking the position you did about the Conference out of your deep caring and concern about the Jewish people.

I told you in Jerusalem at our last meeting that if it must be that we will never speak again, I know that I have been deeply in your heart and you know the place you have had in mine.

It will be up to you whether or not to renew our serious work together and lovely friendship—as we should.

Sincerely,
Israel W. Charny, PhD
Executive Director

[*"The Foundation's $10,000"* refers to the pledge Wiesel had made that his— Wiesel's Foundation—would contribute $10,000 to the costs of the Conference. This amount is separate from the check for $10,000 from the Holocaust Survivors Memorial Foundation that was cancelled at Wiesel's behest to the donor after we had deposited it.—Ed.]

7. A Year Later I Invite Elie Wiesel to Join the Organizing Committee for a Conference in Hiroshima, Japan

Although the scars of 1982 never really healed fully, it did not take very long before a large degree of reconciliation was played out between Wiesel and myself. For example, we had an unforgettable physical reunion at his home in New York, after he agreed to my request to visit him. When Wiesel greeted me at the door, he threw his arms around me and I around him in a warm embrace.

In June 1983 I wrote to Wiesel once again inviting him to play a role in another conference that clearly bespoke our linking the Holocaust with an enormous event of mass death of another people that, for all of its justification in the military terms of World War II is considered by many, many thinkers an unnecessary act of genocidal murder—if not Hiroshima, then certainly Nagasaki—and which in any case represented the enormous threat of a weapon for the genocides of the future. Note in my invitation that I remind Wiesel of "our special history of pioneering in linking the Holocaust with the genocides of all peoples."

7.01 Hiroshima is Calling, Elie. Will You—and Our Holocaust—Join?

June 26, 1983

Elie Wiesel
239 Central Park West
New York
USA.

Dear Elie,

You will have heard that the town of Kurose in Hiroshima Province, Japan has embarked on the building of an Auschwitz Memorial Pavillion. The architect in charge and who is now the Executive Director of the entire project is our dear Jerusalemite, Fumikatsu Inoue.

Because of our special history of pioneering in linking the Holocaust with the genocides of all peoples, the Auschwitz Memorial Pavillion has asked our Institute to undertake the creation of an international scientific conference which will take place on the remarkable occasion of the dedication of their museum and center.

With all my heart, I would like to ask you to join the Organizing Committee for this conference. I do so for all the reasons of my wanting you associated with such a conference, and also out of my continuing conviction that it is good for all of our people—I mean Holocaust and genocide scholars—to know of the healing and coming together between us and our mutual dedication both to the memory of the Holocaust and to the understanding and prevention of genocide in the future.

You will note, Elie, that I have not asked you to be President, Vice President, or even shamosh. Someday, perhaps, we can undertake to lead a project together again, while at this stage I think we will do well to re-connect in this major symbolic way. At a later stage, I would leave it to you to let me know to what extent and in what ways you would be prepared to appear on the unique program we will design for the occasion.

Sincerely,
Israel W. Charny, PhD
Executive Director

[Shamosh *refers to a role of a designated organizer in a synagogue who is responsible for equipment being ready, selecting members of the congregation for roles and honors, and more—Ed.*]

8. Elie Wiesel Accepts the Invitation! But He Chastises Me in the Process and Orders Me Explicitly, "Israel: Please Do Not Use Genocide in Plural"

8.01 Elie Wiesel Accepts the Invitation to Hiroshima, but Enjoins, "Please Do Not Use Genocide in Plural" [photo of original]

 Boston University

College of Liberal Arts
745 Commonwealth Avenue
Boston, Massachusetts 02215

Elie Wiesel
Andrew W. Mellon Professor of Humanities

August 3, 1983

Dear Israel:

    In haste--thank you for your letter. You may include me in the Hiroshima conference. I am ready to deliver the keynote address. However, Israel: please do not use genocide in plural...

    I need dates: when will the conference take place? who else has been invited to participate? If you accept my philosophical beliefs about the uniqueness of the Shoa, I am ready to serve not only as speaker but as anything we would find useful.

    Kol habrachot,

Figure 10. [Kol habrachot *are Hebrew words meaning "all blessings" ("best wishes")—Ed.*]

CHAPTER 4

Critique: How Should We Have Handled the Threats to Jewish Lives?

Let us return to the situation where we are being told that Jewish lives were actually threatened by the Turks. The cardinal question is: did we or did we not conduct ourselves wisely, morally, with the requisite caring for actual human life, let alone for our fellow Jews?

As will be seen in the forthcoming chapter by Michael Berenbaum, soon after our conference another such threat by Turkey appeared—in this case as a threat against including the Armenian Genocide in the United States Holocaust Memorial Museum. It is true that here again it is the Israelis who are conveying the Turkish threats so that now one can wonder if once again it was Israel that really was behind the threats, although it is also a fact that a *New York Times* story reported at the time in the name of a staff member of the museum that he had received the threat *directly* from a Turkish spokesman—who later vehemently denied doing so. "The counsel for the United States Holocaust Memorial Council said that a Turkish diplomat had threatened retaliation if the fate of Turkish Armenians was included in a proposed Washington museum on the German death camps of Worlf War II." The American official was named Monroe H. Freedman and he identified the Turkish diplomat as Mithat Balkan who was then quoted by the *Times* as saying, "I never said such a thing. No man in his right mind would even think such a thing."[1]

Whatever the truth of this Turkish threat, the question we want to explore now is whether, in the context of the information we had at the time, we acted soundly in response to the threats against Jewish lives.

---

1 Special to the *New York Times*, "Genocide Seminar, Opposed by Israel, Open," *New York Times*, June 22, 1982. The story on the Museum is a section of the above entitled, "Turkish Threats to US Reported."

As noted, the first message to us of threats to the lives of Jews in Turkey was in general terms, and in the days that followed, particularly after Elie Wiesel held a press conference in Paris to announce his resignation as president of the conference because of these threats, this is what was cited in the *New York Times* and elsewhere. However, as I have. reported, before long the IMFA communicated to me in no uncertain terms that there was a more serious and more probable threat that the Turks would cut off the escape route of Jewish refugees fleeing from Iran and Syria through Turkey. I was ordered in the greatest seriousness *never* to mention the nature of this threat to anyone, but then slowly but surely as the imbroglio unfolded, the Ministry itself ended up explicitly invoking the threat to the Jewish refugees such as when they called scheduled conference participants in the name of the State of Israel virtually to order them not to attend.

This was also the very explicit message that I received from the self-described head of the Turkish Jewish community, Jak Veissid, when he descended unannounced on my clinic apartment in Tel Aviv. He emphasized in every possible way my responsibility as a Jew and as a human being not to endanger the lives of these refugees.

Of course, I and we took these threats seriously! We would not dare to dismiss them. They deserved and required the most extensive research and analysis. As I will report shortly, among other things I turned to the US State Department and asked for their help in assessing the seriousness of the threats.

We knew our basic positions at all times were, first of all, to do everything to protect human lives—even if it cost us—and, secondly, in no way ever to give in to government censorship and dictate, nor in my case to professional pressures from my university. By its very nature the process had buffeted us about like a sailboat on high seas with mixed and changing winds, as contradictory developments and contradictory opinions of different colleagues poured in.

It is therefore not surprising that, in fact, at various times we did express our readiness to compromise with IMFA by reducing the visibility of the Armenian subject at the conference, though we never ceased to maintain, without any possible reservation, that we would never have the Armenians turned back from attending, and we would never agree to remove the subject of the Armenian Genocide entirely from deliberations. However, we were willing to reduce the broad public exposure of the subject given the serious requests of the government. For example, we proposed that the titles of the lectures of the Armenian Genocide would not be printed in the official program, but that the lectures would be announced and take place at the conference. For another example, we would enter in the program "Special Session—To Be Announced at Conference: For diplomatic reasons the details of this important session are not being posted but will be given to conference participants." We might well have had a much larger attendance at these sessions as a result! We also agreed—and because the logistics had already been set in motion this actually happened in part—to remove some films about the Armenian Genocide from the official conference program (but others were shown).

The Ministry refused our compromises, and once they knew we would not remove the Armenians or the subject in entirety they moved into a high gear of demanding cancellation of the entire conference.

Because of the presumed seriousness of the threats to Jewish lives, we still continued naively to search for effective solutions though without compromising our basic non-negotiable principle that the subject of the Armenian Genocide would not be censored out of our conference process. Along the torturous path, we also did make ourselves open to some extent to explore with the Ministry the possibility they had raised of granting us funds to cover some of our expenses to that date and their funding the conference as a whole in another venue outside of Israel at a later date. In the real world we were now in quite immediate need for money. After all we had employed a congress travel organization and had made extensive reservations for rooms at the Tel Aviv Hilton, in addition to considerable secretarial and printing expenses. We were so pressed financially that a key member of our Organizing Committee, the Armenian Archbishop, Shahé Ajamian, personally volunteered some $5000 to keep us afloat; the owner-director of the Kenes congress agency in Tel Aviv, Gideon Rivlin, extended to us every conceivable courtesy of continuing the intense work of his staff on our conference without any assurance of future income; and I dipped into my personal finances to keep us going. Yet, here too it became clear that although the Ministry spoke of giving us funds, it was manipulative "blah blah" and they were not really going to do any such thing.

However, still, to the best of our knowledge at the time the issue of threats to Jewish lives remained. This was not the kind of issue that could be resolved on the basis of financial considerations alone.

As the originator of the vision of the conference and the prime person responsible for its organization, it was primarily my personal responsibility to decide what we would do. I thought a lot about it. First I found myself guided by my knowledge that Turkey was an old, old hand at making bombastic far ranging threats such as cutting off major commercial deals or withdrawing/denying political recognition from any country where whatever recognition of the Armenian Genocide was developing, including as noted earlier in talks, museums, films, and publications. It was my conviction that threats of this sort should never be honored to any extent whatsoever, let alone I had also come to understand that in these respects Turkey was a blowhard that rarely followed through in the months after the brouhaha.

My second source for my judgment was no less than the US State Department whom I contacted directly with a request for consultative advice about the Turkish threats. The State Department representative was fully responsive and after looking into the matter assured me, almost without any reservation or uncertainty, that they did not believe the Turks were a real threat to Jewish lives.

I am also sure that underneath it all I wanted to reach the decision to continue the conference. I wanted to stand up both to the ugliness of Turkey's longstanding denial of the Armenian Genocide and their brazen political efforts to control the historical and intellectual record all over the world, and to the terribly disappointing—even heartbreaking—betrayal of basic moral values by my own beloved State of Israel.

In retrospect, I know we made the right decisions, and I am proud of how we went about arriving at them.

A POSTSCRIPT

I believe the whole *imbroglio* could have been avoided simply by Israel telling Turkey that there was no way whatsoever to interfere with academic freedom.

My further conclusion is that all those who were prepared to be liars in their professional and public roles are ones who, then and today, are deeply dangerous threats to democracy. More than sadly, it is obvious that there are a lot of them all around, including at the highest levels of government in one country after another, including the strong-man-led Turkey where thousands suffer in jails because they speak unacceptable truths; and including the ostensibly and certainly more democratic Israel where, despite principles of free speech and a largely effective judicial system, state employees are seduced by the sirens of power and a philosophy that the end justifies the means into becoming manipulators and dictators of thoughts and actions, strong-arm *realpoliticians*, and purveyors of lies of very fake history and news.

With great sadness I also add the conclusion that it is now clear that the People of the Holocaust, and they of course are the original People of the Book, to whom a frightened and demoralized humanity has looked hopefully through the centuries for moral inspiration and guidance, has proven to be the purveyor of much "fake news" and *realpolitik* machinations over many years.

In my judgment it is not surprising that, slowly but surely, much of American Jewry and decent people everywhere are showing signs of losing interest and becoming less loyal to Israel. To my mind the moral of the ridiculous 1982 soap opera, along with many other historical issues since, is a wakeup call to our beloved Israel to return to a policy of purity of arms and to seeking justice to all peoples alongside our primary and distinctly holy purpose of effective self-defense.

CHAPTER 5

Israel's Tragically Immoral Denials of, and Indifference to, the Genocides of Other Peoples

DENIAL OF THE ARMENIAN GENOCIDE, MORE RECENTLY THE YAZIDI GENOCIDE, AND INDIFFERENCE TO MANY OTHER EVEN ONGOING GENOCIDES

For many years up until recently, I had understood—while disagreeing with it intensely—Israel's avoidance of recognizing the Armenian Genocide as intended to protect its vital relationship with neighboring Turkey. In addition, but to a much smaller extent, I understood that denying recognition of the Armenian Genocide also fit a common Israeli misconception—with which I also disagree intensely—that no other event of genocide can/should possibly compare to the terrible Shoah of our people.[1]

But now, after seeing previously secret and classified documents of Israel's Foreign Ministry that detail Israel's policy efforts with regard to the inclusion of information about the Armenian Genocide—and for that matter the inclusion of information about *any other people's genocide*—also in the influential US Holocaust Memorial Museum in Washington, DC, I am shocked to the core by the realization that much of our policy is indeed generated and backed up not only by a misunderstanding of the significance of the Holocaust in relation to other genocides. It is also more generally a powerful entree into understanding much more deeply the construction of genocidal thinking and practice in the

---

1 Alan S. Rosenbaum, ed., *Is the Holocaust Unique? Perspectives on Comparative Genocide* (Boulder, CO: Westview Press, 1996, 3rd ed., New York: Routledge, 2009).

human mind and behavior, where we identify open and shut arrogance, disregard for historical truths, and, frankly, ugly efforts to achieve a national/cultural superiority over other peoples.

Is the Holocaust unique? Of course it is—very much so. But so are other cases of genocide unique in other ways, each in its own story of development and execution and aftermath. But there is also a basic and horrendous commonality: *In all genocides, people are being cruelly tortured and murdered en masse.* For me, this commonality is the largest fact, and no intellectualization whatsoever—what I have called "definitionalism" or an endless obsessive controversy about the proper definition of *genocide*—can be allowed to obscure these masses of dead bodies or fail to give them a meaningful category name.[2]

It is, of course, entirely human and so very legitimate for an individual survivor and also a given survivor group to becry *their* tragedy as the worst suffering and evil that ever took place, but it is wrong to translate these understandable human feelings as if into historic facts that one genocide is to be placed at the ultimate untouchable apex of a hierarchy of genocidal suffering.

At the level of the individual, I never argue with a survivor, say a Jewish survivor of the Holocaust or an Armenian survivor of the Armenian Genocide, or with any child of theirs, when they cry out and say in pain and anger that the cruelty of *their* genocide was the greatest evil ever seen in human history.

At the same time, on an intellectual level I dare say that a collective effort by any people to place their own unbearable cataclysmic tragedy *above* the cataclysmic tragedies of other peoples is, even if only unconsciously, inherently a continued expression of the same rotten intentions to lord it over and dominate other people that the hateful perpetrators of genocides expressed and translated into their deadly policies. In other words—however much it is both paradoxical and sad—when a victim people claims to be the top or ultimate victims above all others, they are playing with the same nasty seeking of power and superiority that is intrinsic to the horrors executed by perpetrators—who are certainly out to be above all others.

Moreover, although we will not enter into a fuller discussion of these kinds of events in this chapter, the same issue applies when a victim people withhold recognition of co-victims who perished alongside them—such as the Russian POWs, Roma and Sinti, homosexuals, Jehovah's Witnesses, and others in the

---

2   Israel W. Charny, "Toward a Generic Definition of Genocide," in *Genocide: Conceptual and Historical Dimensions*, ed. George Andreapolous (Philadelphia, PA: University of Pennsylvania Press, 1994), 64–94.

Holocaust, and the Assyrians, Yazidis, and Greeks in the Armenian Genocide. Too often the "main victim" has ignored the others.

When the International Association of Genocide Scholars (IAGS) was first founded in 1994, I was happy to play a role in our passing, what I think was the first resolution of the association, to recognize the Armenian Genocide. Some years later when I was president of the association in 2005–2007, I proposed a resolution to add to the above recognition of the Armenian Genocide, the genocides of the Greeks and Assyrians, who in fact were in very large part co-victims of the Armenians though they also 'enjoy' several separate chapters of their own. I expected the resolution to be confirmed without question by our Board, but to my horror there was enormous resistance that was led in particular by a colleague with whom I had worked warmly and closely for many years in a large number of our battles against denials of the Armenian Genocide, and whom I had just recently invited to present a very moving reading on the Armenian Genocide when we assembled for a unique genocide seminar no less than on the grounds of Auschwitz.[3]

Armenian Genocide Resolution Unanimously Passed by the Association of Genocide Scholars of North America, June 13, 1997

The Armenian Genocide Resolution was unanimously passed at the Association of Genocide Scholars' conference in Montreal on June 13, 1997.

Resolution: That this assembly of the Association of Genocide Scholars in its conference held in Montreal, June 11–13, 1997, reaffirms that the mass murder of over a million Armenians in Turkey in 1915 is a case of genocide which conforms to the statutes of the United Nations Convention on the Prevention and Punishment of Genocide.

---

3   In the same year that we are talking about the IAGS Board considering recognition of the Greek and Assyrian Genocides I had organized a three day Genocide Seminar at Auschwitz-Birkenau where we had the privilege of being guided both by Deborah Lipstadt, the famed scholar of the Holocaust who stood up successfully to a dangerous legal suit against her by arch-Holocaust denier, David Irving, and Michael Berenbaum, who had been the second in command building the superb US Holocaust Memorial Museum and had been in charge of the selection of all the exhibits in the museum. It was in this auspicious and deeply moving setting that we were also made privy to the heartfelt reading about the Armenian Genocide. We then flew from Krakow to Sarajevo for the full international conference of the IAGS, and now the colleague who had spoken about the Armenian Genocide at Auschwitz—a site obviously devoted to the fate of the Jewish people—turned lividly opposed to recognition of other victim peoples along with the Armenians.

It further condemns the denial of the Armenian Genocide by the Turkish government and its official and unofficial agents and supporters.

Background: Among the prominent scholars who supported the resolution were: Roger W. Smith (College of William and Mary; President of AGS); Israel Charny (Hebrew University, Jerusalem); Helen Fein, Past President AGS); Frank Chalk (Concordia University, Montreal); Ben Kiernan (Yale University); Anthony Oberschall (University of North Carolina, Chapel Hill); Mark Levene (Warwick University, UK); Rhoda Howard (McMaster University, Canada); Michael Freeman (Essex University, United Kingdom); Gunnar Heinsohn (Bremen University, Germany).

The Association of Genocide Scholars is an international, interdisciplinary, non-partisan organization dedicated to the understanding and prevention of genocide. The Association is an affiliate of the Institute for the Study of Genocide, New York

Dr. Helen Fein, executive director

Second Resolution by the International Association of Genocide Scholars (IAGS), 2007, Affirming Genocides of Assyrians, Pontian and Anatolian Greeks

Resolution: WHEREAS the denial of genocide is widely recognized as the final stage of genocide, enshrining impunity for the perpetrators of genocide, and demonstrably paving the way for future genocides;

WHEREAS the Ottoman genocide against minority populations during and following the First World War is usually depicted as a genocide against Armenians alone, with little recognition of the qualitatively similar genocides against other Christian minorities of the Ottoman Empire;

BE IT RESOLVED that it is the conviction of the International Association of Genocide Scholars that the Ottoman campaign against Christian minorities of the Empire between 1914 and 1923 constituted a genocide against Armenians, Assyrians, and Pontian and Anatolian Greeks.

BE IT FURTHER resolved that the Association calls upon the government of Turkey to acknowledge the genocides against these populations, to issue a formal apology, and to take prompt and meaningful steps towards restitution.

Background: The Resolution recognizing other Christian people as victims of the Turks in what is known largely as the Armenian Genocide was initiated by the Executive Board of the Association during the presidency of Israel Charny. The Resolution failed to gain a majority vote of the Board and therefore was referred to a membership-wide vote in the following months under the presidency of Gregory Stanton and was now resoundingly passed.

True authenticity calls for once victim peoples to acknowledge and care about other peoples who were killed alongside them.[4] Simon Wiesenthal, for example, very much identified the Roma (Gypsies), whom he had personally seen being taken to the gas chambers in Auschwitz, as co-victims, but no few Holocaust survivors expressed displeasure at his concern for this other victim people.

True authenticity also requires once-victim peoples to face an even more difficult task of acknowledging honestly any of their own lapses into genocidal massacres of others. For example, in the case of Israel there are a number of incidents of genocidal massacres of Arab Palestinians in the course of the entirely just War of Independence that had been foisted on Israel. Of course, it was the Palestinians who refused to accept the UN creation of an Arab state and a Jewish state in Palestine and who were joined immediately by the invasion of multiple Arab armies including the British-led Jordanian army. In a number of locales such as Deir Yassin, Lod, Zichron Yaakov, Israelis behaved in wanton cruelty and engaged in what are definitely acts of genocidal massacres, and there were any number of forced evacuations of civilians, even as overall there was also a prevailing sense and intent of decency on the part of many Israeli fighters in many zones of the war.[5]

It is an understatement that most peoples or nations do not at all like to look at the histories of their being perpetrators of genocidal events (the Germans have been an outstandingly admirable exception in their forthright acknowledgment of their World War II ugliness). Thus, Japan has notoriously

---

4   Israel W. Charny, "The Integrity and Courage to Recognize All the Victims of a Genocide," 21–38. See also http://www.ihgjm.com/the-psychology-of denying-other-victims-of-a-genocide-a-quest-for-exclusivity--and   superiority-not-unlike-similar-motives-in-those who-commit-genocide.

5   The scholar who can be credited with being the outstanding source of information about these events is Benny Morris. See his two eminent works: Benny Morris, *The Birth of the Palestinian Refugee Problem, 1947–1949* (Cambridge: Cambridge University Press, 1989); and Benny Morris, *1948: A History of the First Arab-Israeli War* (New Haven: Yale University Press, 2009).

avoided taking responsibility for its invasion and far-reaching cruelties including Mengele-like experiments in Manchuria in the 1930s, and then again it has
never acknowledged its legendary cruelty to Allied prisoners or the sexual slavery it imposed on thousands of Korean women. Poland has recently set in force
new legislation, which makes it a criminal violation to refer in any way to the
participation of Poles and Poland in the murders of the Holocaust and subsequently in the aftermath of World War II when Jews sought to return to their
homes and a great many were murdered by their Polish neighbors.[6]

In what was for me an intriguing study of Jewish Israelis who really cared
to know a lot more about the Holocaust—our research students met the subjects at the box office of a theatre in Tel Aviv when they were purchasing tickets
to spend more than nine hours of their lives viewing Claude Lanzmann's historic film, *Shoah*—my colleague Daphna Fromer and I sought to understand
the degrees of acknowledgment and empathy these same people had for a terribly unjust genocidal massacre of some forty-nine Arab men, women, and children in the village of Kfar Kassem in 1956. This was the first day of the Sinai
War and an area commander had declared an early curfew for the evening, but it
was obvious that information about this curfew had not reached Arab workers
who had set out early in the morning to their agricultural tasks. Now, returning
home from work as the sun was setting, these innocent unarmed Arab men,
women, and children in Kfar Kassem—a village near the Jewish city of Petach
Tikva—were literally mowed down by one of the platoons in the area responsible for enforcing the curfew. The commanders of all the other platoons in the
area were wise enough to ignore the vague and unduly provocative order to
which the Kfar Kassem commander responded with extreme brutality.

We now asked the people getting tickets to Lanzmann's film the following
four questions.

1. In your opinion, are the people who committed the murders in the
    Holocaust capable of living out the remainder of their lives quietly
    and without regrets after what they have done?
2. Do you believe that Jews are capable of killing members of a minority
    group, including old people, women and children who are not carry-
    ing arms, if they are ordered to do so?

---

6   Jan T. Gross, *Neighbors, The Discussion of the Jewish Community in Jedwabne, Poland*
    (Princeton, NJ: Princeton University Press, 2001); Jan T. Gross, *Fear: Anti-Semitism in
    Poland after Auschwitz* (New York: Random House, 2009).

3. (a) Do you know what happened at Kfar Kassem?
   (b) Had you known what happened at Kfar Kassem before the recent media coverage on the occasion of the thirtieth anniversary of that event?
4. Recently a number of the soldiers who had been tried for the slaughter of the Arab residents at Kfar Kassem were interviewed, and one of them expressed himself thus: "Regrets? No regrets. I did what was expected of me. I know that I am a soldier who serves his country, and that is what was expected of me." What is your opinion?

On the completion of the responses to the four study items, the interviewees were asked a brief series of demographic questions: age, education, country of origin, age of immigration to Israel, their relation to the Holocaust—specifically whether they themselves were survivors, or children of survivors, were there other losses in their family, or did they generally feel close to those who were lost in the Holocaust.

In analyzing the data we concentrated on question 4. The results were that 62% of the research subjects did oppose the justification of the slaughter by the soldier, while 38% either justified or rationalized the soldier's position on the slaughter. Although in conventional research parlance the clear majority of 62% permits a conclusion that Israeli society is predominantly against genocidal actions, the 38% result negates a more idealistic view of Israeli society as much more dedicated to an intense opposition to crimes against other human beings.

It will come as no surprise that when I presented the results of this study to a Faculty Colloquium at Tel Aviv University, I was in effect booed out of town to the familiar sounds of ostensible professional criticism that the methodology of the study was somehow defective—when in fact the study was methodologically legitimate and earned publication in a fine peer-reviewed journal.[7]

The suffering of all the victims of all genocides is ineffable. The deaths of all victims in all genocides are equally tragic and criminal events. At the same time comparisons of different genocides remain necessary and is legitimate academic work to search for understanding how such disastrous events can be brought about both in a variety of ways, yet also with a great resemblance to one another, and in the view of many genocide scholars how a shared generic

---

7   Israel W. Charny and Daphna Fromer, "A Study of Attitudes of Viewers of the Film, 'Shoah,' towards an Incident of Mass Murder by Israeli Soldiers (Kfar Kassem, 1956)," *Journal of Traumatic Stress* 5, no. 2 (1992): 303–318.

or basic process leads and enables human beings to be so bastardly destructive to their fellow man.[8,9,10,11]

In sum, it is more than ironically absurd that victim peoples can be found utilizing the same mindsets as perpetrators in seeking to be superior to others, the latter by unbearable and untouchable force, the former by elevating their victim experience to establish their superiority. It is hard, and on the surface seemingly disrespectful and irreverent, to associate the concept of fascism with the victim experience, but when any people seeks to place itself in a superior position to others it is in truth on a fascist path. It is further disillusioning to learn that a victim people will deny other victim peoples who perished alongside them. And it is outrageously upsetting and painful to face the facts that victim peoples can carry within their histories various degrees of complicity also as genociders.

As victims through the centuries, our Jewish people certainly know the grave dangers of claiming privilege, power, and ultimate significance over and above others. Yet now we have to face the disillusioning truth that we too are susceptible to making ourselves superior to others—beginning with our claims of utter uniqueness as victims, and continuing with various overuse and excesses of power by our beloved State of Israel even as it fights often so bravely in legitimate self-defense.

MY CRITICISMS OF ISRAEL AS AN ACTOR IN GENOCIDAL KILLING AND DENIAL ARE DEEPLY PAINED

Needless to say, as a Jew and as a human being, the memory and limitless significance of the Holocaust are, and always have been, uppermost in my heart and mind. At the same time, I have no need at all to apologize to Holocaust survivors, scholars or confirmed loyalists of our Jewish cause for my caring about the victims of other genocides and my concern for all co-victims of any genocide, nor for my participating in critiques of Israel's errors in overuse of strength. Basically and unreservedly, I continue wholly my identification with and love for our Jewish people and Zionism.

---

8 Israel W. Charny and Chanan Rapaport, *How Can We Commit the Unthinkable*, later republished as *Genocide: The Human Cancer*.

9 Ervin Staub, *The Roots of Evil: The Origins of Genocide and Other Group Violence* (Cambridge: Cambridge University Press, 1989).

10 Steven Baum, *Psychology of Genocide* (Boston: Cambridge University Press, 2008).

11 James E. Waller, *Becoming Evil: How Ordinary People Commit Genocide and Mass Killing* (Oxford: Oxford University Press, 2007).

Indeed, it was my very deep caring about the Holocaust that propelled me into my lifelong efforts as a genocide scholar to understand and to attempt to bring about some reduction of our "species ugliness" as mass torturers and murderers. I always loved the concept that "from Zion there would issue Torah" ("Torah" here means "wisdom") and hoped that our Jewish people would be true leaders in genocide scholarship and in meaningful reduction of genocide in our world. Now I am disheartened and deeply ashamed by what I have found out about my beloved people's official leaders doing one dirty thing after another to ignore, silence and even erase the memory and significance of a variety of genocidal events.

I am going to emphasize here Israel's denials of the genocides of other victims peoples. Israel has hardly stood up as a champion against Holocaust-like disasters to other peoples. Thus, recently in November 2018 the Israeli government rejected an effort to have the Knesset recognize the still ongoing Yazidi genocide. There is also an endless list of major persecutions and genocides ongoing in our world in many countries in which we are silent—as the world was to us in our Holocaust.

The still larger truth is that we—our Israeli government—not only throw off efforts to have a given genocide such as the Armenian Genocide or the Yazidi Genocide recognized by the Knesset, but that we Israelis often sit it out as if unknowingly without expressing opinions about any number of ongoing genocides. Thus, we basically have not taken a stand in Myanmar on the murders and forced expulsion of the Rohingya;[12] in Africa in long-suffering Sudan the continued murders and starvation of the people in the Nuba Mountains;[13] and the never-ending genocidal actions in the Democratic Republic of Congo;[14] or

---

12 "Myanmar Rohingya: What You Need to Know about the Crisis," *BBC News*, January 23, 2020, https://www.bbc.com/news/world-asia-41566561; Erin Blakemore, "Who are the Rohingya people? Called the Most Persecuted Minority in the World, the Rohingya have a Millennial-Long History in Myanmar, the Country that's Excluding Them," *National Geographic*, February 9, 2019, https://www.nationalgeographic.com/culture/people/reference/rohingya-people.

13 Samuel Totten, *Genocide by Attrition: The Nuba Mountains of Sudan* (New Brunswick, NJ: Transaction Publishers, 2012, reprinted, New York: Routledge, 2017); Samuel Totten, ed., *Sudan's Nuba Mountains People under Siege: Accounts by Humanitarians in the Battle Zone*, foreword by Caroline Cox, afterword by Israel W. Charny (Jefferson, NC: McFarland Publishing, 2017).

14 "Violence in the Democratic Republic of Congo," Global Conflict Tracker (cfr), *Center for Protective Action*, April 2, 2020, https://www.cfr.org/interactive/global-conflict-tracker/conflict/violence-democratic-republic-con; "Democratic Republic of Congo: Events of 2018," *Human Rights Watch*, https://www.hrw.org/world-report/2019/country-chapters/democratic-republic-congo, accessed April 4, 2020.

the ongoing genocidal orgy in the course of war in Yemen;[15] in response to the clear-cut persecution of Uighurs in China; or about periodic reports of blatant genocidal facilities in mysterious North Korea;[16] and, perhaps most paradoxically, after so many centuries of our complaints of persecution and genocidal pogroms by Christians, where are our voices about the deadly persecution of Christians today in an endless number of countries?[17]

Where are we, moreover, with regard to arms sales to nations where there are gathering storms of potential genocide? Very notably are Israel's massive arms sales to Azerbaijan who represent a standing threat against the Armenians in Nagorno-Karabakh. Now since late 2019 the world is faced with a new titanic threat gathering in India where Prime Minister Narendra Modi[18] has embarked on a vicious campaign of cancelling basic rights, including actual citizenship, of Muslim residents of Kashmir.

It is obvious that these strange and for the most part non-white and otherwise racially and culturally so-different people do not set off intuitively emotional and spiritual caring in us. But what is less clear is that politically, Israel, the refugee of the Jewish people after generations of persecution and after the overwhelming Holocaust, has made it a matter of political policy *not* to be even a moral watchdog over the comparable deadly fates of masses of other human beings. For many of us this is downright shameful in its essence as well as a betrayal of basic Jewish tradition.

In our reactions of indifference and a failure to identify with 'other' peoples who are strange to us, *we are like they were to us.* The Jews were an

---

15   "Humanitarian Crisis in Yemen Remains the Worst in the World, Warns UN," *UN News*, February 14, 2019, https://news.un.org/en/story/2019/02/1032811.

16   Lydia Smith, "Life in the North Korea Labor Camp: 'We were Forced to Throw Rocks at a Man being Hanged:' Defector Confined in Yodok Concentration Camp for 10 Years," *London Independent*, September 28, 2017, https://www.independent.co.uk/news/world/asia/ north-korea-forced-labour-survivor-camp-15-hermit-kingdom-kim-jong-un-a7971926. html; Willa Frej, "North Korean Prisons are Worse than Nazi Concentration Camps, Says Holocaust Survivor," *Huffington Post*, December 18, 2017, https://www.huffpost.com/en-try/north-korean-prisons-nazi-camps_n_5a2fad6ce4b0461754330e3d.

17   "Christian Persecution 'at Near Genocide Levels,'" *BBC News*, May 3, 2019, https://www. bbc.com/news/uk-48146305; Ewelina U. Ochab, "Recognizing the Phenomenon of Persecution of Christians Globally," *Forbes*, November 30, 2019, https://www.forbes.com/sites/ ewelinaochab/2019/11/30/recognizing-the-phenomenon-of-the-persecution-of-christians-globally/#69f75f6d3935.

18   Narendra Modi, "The Observer View on India's Divisive Citizenship Law," *Guardian*, December 22, 2019, https://www.theguardian.com/commentisfree/2019/dec/22/observer-view-of-india-citizenship-law-narendra-modi.

unattractive other who naturally evoked disdain and repugnance, so to many Europeans and Americans it hardly felt necessary to react to their persecution. Isn't this the way we Israelis and Jews feel toward Rohingya (who are also a Muslim people), Sudanese, Congolese, and a host of other peoples who are at various stages of being persecuted, such as Eritreans, Egyptian Copts, Nigerian Christians, and endless more? Do we as a society even know about them—the first level of caring—and if so, are we drawn to any empathetic caring for them? We took it for granted that this is what the world owed our Jewish people in response to our Holocaust and utterly failed to deliver, and now we are failing others.

Of course, it is hardly the responsibility of Israel to resolve all these tragedies, but our voice and concern and readiness to join in collective international efforts should be prominent. And as Jews, with an epic legacy of leadership in respecting the holiness of human life, we should be among the moral leaders. How often have we criticized and hated the world for remaining ignorant and ignoring the Holocaust of our people? And now it is we too who are ignorant, ignore, and deny.

THE CASE OF THE DENIAL OF THE GENOCIDE OF THE YAZIDIS

The Yazidi case is a good one to look at more closely, since there was the wholesome effort in the Knesset to recognize the genocide and it was defeated not so much by the people but by the government which ordered a halt to its adoption. The Yazidis (sometimes spelled Yezidis) are a people centered in Iraq, Kurdistan, Syria, and Turkey. They are described by fundamentalist Muslims as "devil-worshipers." The Yazidi faith is a complex amalgam linked to Zoroastrianism with a light/dark duality and sun worship and also shares many elements with Christianity and Islam. We referred to them earlier as co-victims of the Armenians. It is little known that in the Armenian Genocide between 300,000–500,000 Yazidis also were slaughtered by Turks and by Kurds.[19] Now, in our time, the Yazidis have been singled out by ISIS (Da'esh) for genocidal murder and sexual enslavement of Yazidi women.

---

19 "The Virtually Unknown Genocide of Yazidis by the Turks along with the Armenians, Assyrians and Greeks," *Genocide Prevention Now* 5 (2011). As noted earlier, *GPN* is no longer accessible on the Internet, but many of its articles are posted on the website of the Institute on the Holocaust and Genocide. The above article can be found at http://www.ihgjlm.com/the-virtually-unknown-genocide-of-yezidis-by-the-turks-along-with-the-armenians-assyrians-and-greeks/.

The resolution introduced in November 2018 to the Knesset to recognize this recent and actually still ongoing genocide of the Yazidi people by ISIS was rejected: Fifty-eight members of the Knesset voted against the resolution and thirty-eight were in favor. The member of Knesset who sponsored the legislation, Ksenia Svetlova, wrote in a thoughtful and emotional article in the *Jerusalem Post*:

> Should Israel, the state that arose from the ashes of the Holocaust recognize and acknowledge a genocide when it happens to other people? Or should it just concentrate on its own survival and let go of moral principles such as "Never again?" Not so long ago, I thought I knew the answer. After my bill that called to recognize the genocide of the Yazidi people was rejected by the coalition [*the government led by Prime Minister Netanyahu and the Likud party—Ed.*], I am no longer certain of that.[20]

The "excuse" given by Israel's Deputy Foreign Minister was that the government was opposed to the law so long as the United Nations has not recognized the genocide—although she acknowledged that "there is no question that there is no basic disagreement with the fact that this is an historical event that has to be recognized."[21]

Note, of course, the hypocrisy: when it comes to the Armenian Genocide which Israel has stubbornly and shamefully refused to recognize, the United

---

20 Ksenia Svetlova, "MK Svetlova in 'Post': Failing to Recognize Yazidi Genocide is Like World Ignoring Holocaust," *Jerusalem Post*, November 26, 2018, https://www.jpost.com/Opinion/Recognizing-the-genocide-of-the-Yazidis-or-looking-the-other-way-572884. (Not long afterwards MK Svetlova announced that she would not be a candidate for the Knesset in the next elections.)

21 Jonathan Lis, "The Knesset Rejected a Proposed Bill to Recognize the Genocide of the Yazidis: Deputy Foreign Minister Tzipi Hotovely Said that the Government is Opposed to Recognition as Long as the UN has not Taken a Position on the Subject. The Author of the Proposed Legislation, MK Svetlova: 'The State of Israel was Created from the Ashes of the Shoah. What about the Shoah of Others?'" [Hebrew], *Haaretz* (Hebrew Edition), November 22, 2018, https://www.haaretz.co.il/misc/article-print-page/1.6677525; see also report in *Haaretz* (English Edition): Jonathan Lis, "Israel Votes Down Recognition of Yazidi Genocide, Citing U.N.: The Yazidis, a Kurdish Religious Minority in Iraq and Syria, Became Subject to Persecution by ISIS when It Captured Territory where the Group Lives," *Haaretz* (English Edition), November 22, 2018, https://www.haaretz.com/israel-news/.premium-israel-votes-down-recognition-of-yazidi-genocide-citing-un-1.6677742.

Nations long ago *did* recognize the genocide in 1985,[22] but that has never made any difference to Israel.

The Deputy Foreign Minister added about the Yazidi Genocide, "We need to investigate the subject much more deeply."[23]

Bah!

In the Hebrew edition of *Haaretz*, the Deputy Foreign Minister is quoted further,

> I want to say from the podium of the Knesset that it will take further time to complete a fundamental and deep investigation in which we will be able to formulate a policy on such a matter. I am saying here, from this podium, that we, as a government, cannot agree to the proposal of this legislation so long as international processes are going on and so long as there is no decision of the United Nations on the subject.[24]

Bah! Bah! Bah!

In fact, the same *Haaretz* report of the rejection of the recognition and the "explanation" of the Deputy Foreign Minister reports, "UN experts had warned in June 2016 that ISIS was committing genocide against the Yazidis in Syria

---

22 "UN Report on Genocide. Armenian Genocide," United Nations Human Rights Commission, 38 session, Geneva, Switzerland, August 5–30, 1985, https://genocideeducation.org/wp-content/uploads/2014/08/UN-Report-on-Genocide-excerpts.pdf. For full detail and analysis, see the Special Issue of the *Internet on the Holocaust and Genocide* 3/4 (January 1986): *Revised and Updated Report on the Question of the Prevention and Punishment of the Crime of Genocide*, prepared by Ben Whittaker for the United Nations Economic and Social Council in Geneva.

The *Internet on the Holocaust and Genocide* was published by the Institute on the Holocaust and Genocide in Jerusalem in 1985–1995. The original issues are available to researchers on request to the Institute, encygeno@gmail.com, or in the libraries of selected institutions, which maintain copies of the newsletters. The following libraries are listed in Worldcat.org as carrying the above: National Library of Israel; Ben Gurion University Library; TU Berlin Universitatsbibliothek; Universitats- und Landesbibliothek Sachsen-Anhalt/Zentrale Germany; National Library Board, Singapore; Brandeis University Library; HCL Technical Services; Harvard University; College of the Holy Cross; University of Connecticut; New York Public Library System; Syracuse University; YIVO Institute for Jewish Research; Swarthmore College Peace Collection, Westchester University; United States Holocaust Memorial Museum; Hebrew Union College—JIR, Cincinnati; University of Florida; University of Arkansas–Fayetteville; University of British Columbia Library; Stanford University Libraries; University of California, Los Angeles.

23 Jonathan Lis, "The Knesset Rejected a Proposed Bill."

24 Ibid.

and Iraq to destroy the minority religious community through killings, sexual slavery and other crimes."[25]

Ben Cohen wrote in *Jewishpress.com* about the rejection of the resolution to recognize the Yazidi genocide:

> This was a bad, bad day for Israel's parliament. The Knesset's decision has disappointed many Israeli voters, along with Jews abroad who would like Israel to show the same leadership on the issue of genocide-prevention that it displays in its responses to humanitarian disasters around the world.[26]

THE DEADLY ROLE OF ISRAEL AS A PROMISCUOUS MAJOR ARMS DEALER, EVEN TO COUNTRIES ACTIVELY COMMITTING GENOCIDE

I want to return here to the subject that was introduced above notwithstanding a degree of repetition. I believe the subject is a crucial one and that it is virtually neglected in Israeli society even among liberal thinkers, and that it is generally ignored in the world at large as well. It is hardly a secret that Israel has been an active and major arms dealer in the world for quite a number of years. Personally, I have always been opposed to having arms dealings as a major economic and security goal of the Israeli nation. In general, I would want to see a utopian world where arms development everywhere was strictly controlled by international law, and countries would be limited to development projects aimed only at the integrity of their self-defense. Obviously, such a world is far away from possible reality, but in the meantime it has seemed to me essential that decent peace-seeking nations would absolutely refrain from selling arms to *any* other nation or group who were known or even believed by qualified intelligence experts to be involved in open and shut crimes against humanity and genocide against any of their own people, and/or in attack and destruction of other peoples.

In the case of Israel, shocking allegations have been made that Israel has sold arms in the past even to countries actively engaged in genocidal campaigns

25 "ISIS is Committing Genocide against the Yazidis," United Nations Commission of Inquiry on Syria, 2016, https://www.ohchr.org/en/NewsEvents/Pages/DisplayNews.aspx?NewsID=20113.

26 Ben Cohen, "Knesset Confused on Yazidi Genocide," *Jewish Press*, November 27, 2018, http://www.jewishpress.com/indepth/opinions/knesset-confused-on-yazidi-genocide/2018/11/27/.

at the time such as to Guatemala in what is referred to as the Mayan Genocide or even as the Silent Holocaust (and which, one reviewer of this book for the publisher could not help pointing out, was taking place at the time of our conference on genocide in 1981–1983); the Hutu in Rwanda; the Serbs in Serbia who massacred Bosnians; the Sudanese government that continued murder and starvation in the Nuba Mountains; and, most recently and currently, to Myanmar which has been persecuting the Rohingya; also that Israel has sold arms to countries that are perceived to be potential aggressors or genociders such as the substantial sales that were noted to Azerbaijan and which at least on one previous occasion had demonstrated firing an Israeli missile against the Armenians in Nagorno-Karabakh, and indeed, when a new war came in 2020, Israeli weapons were decisive in defeating the Armenians.

In a powerful article in *Haaretz* entitled, "Israel, Partner in Genocides: Sending weapons to a government that is guilty of genocide is very similar to sending weapons to Germany during the Holocaust," Yair Auron, the Associate Director of the Institute on the Holocaust and Genocide in Jerusalem, wrote that Israel "knowingly desecrated the memory of the Holocaust in the process." Together with Tel Aviv attorney, Itay Mack, he has attempted on a number of occasions to demand of the courts access to government records about deliveries of arms to Rwanda, Serbia, and Myanmar, and in each case has been stymied by the court's acceptance of the argument of the Ministry of Defense that exposing records "would undermine state security and the state security exports."[27]

Speaking about the sales of arms to Myanmar, Attorney Itay Mack has said, "Even if Israel has some [security] interest in being involved in selling arms there, which I don't believe it has, we haven't heard any words of condemnation from senior officials about what's happening there. ... When Israel remains silent, it is the equivalent of endorsing what is going on."[28] (We will return to the work of Auron and Mack in the next chapter.)

One orthodox forty-year-old Jewish woman in Israel has taken on a personal mission of challenging government officials about arms sales. According to *Haaretz,* this lady insists that "the duty to save human life overrides almost all obligations in Jewish religious law." She is quoted directly as telling the *Haaretz*

---

27 Yair Auron, "Israel, Partner in Genocides," *Haaretz* (English Edition), October 2, 2017, https://www.haaretz.com/opinion/.premium-1.81516.

28 Judy Maltz, "Campaign to End Israeli Arms Exports to Rogue Regimes Gets Knesset Push," *Haaretz* (English Edition), December 26, 2017, https://www.haaretz.com/israel-news/.premium-campaign-to-end-israeli-arms-exports-to-rogue-regimes-gets-knesset-push-1.5629731.

interviewer, "For me there is no Torah at all and no believing in God at all—this is worthless if you are doing such a crime."[29]

To sum up. I emphasize that an important key to what is the "payoff" for denials of another people's genocide is a quest for exclusivity and superiority for one's own people. When we deny, belittle, or are indifferent to the torture and killings of other in favor of promoting our own histories of suffering and being virtuous, it is as if we are saying:

> *We are unprecedented/*
> *incomparable/*
> *unique and exclusive/*
> *superior/*
> *the ultimate people*

The more shamed and shocked are we when we realize that we are seeing such hateful arrogance in people who themselves have experienced fiendish genocidal destruction, where we would rather have expected heightened sensitivity and caring for others who became victims.

In other words, we have made the startling discovery that hateful perpetrators of genocide and victim peoples who deny the genocides of others are in some critical ways mirror images of one another—for, indeed, we are all of the same "god-given" human species. The shared characteristic is a pursuit and an insistence on attributing to one's selves uniquely superior status over others. It is amazing how through the years of our claim to be the most important and chosen victim people, and our denials and unknowing of the genocidal tragedies of many other peoples, most of us have not caught on to how claims for superiority and power over others are at work in us much as had been the case in the people who had destroyed us in genocide.

I once witnessed a senior Yad Vashem staff member explode angrily at a lecture by an outstanding Armenian scholar, Prof. Richard Hovannisian, "How dare he come here (to Yad Vashem) and compare what happened to the Armenians to the murders of the Jews in the Holocaust?"

---

29 Patty Nieberg, "The Religious Activists Waging a 'Holy War' against Israel's Arms Exports," *Haaretz* (English Edition), September 11, 2019, https://www.haaretz.com/israel-news/.premium-the-religious-activists-waging-a-holy-war-against-israel-s-arms-exports-1.7831957.

ISRAEL AND THE ARMENIAN GENOCIDE

The nonsense of Israel denial—meaning its failure—to recognize the Armenian Genocide in particular deserves to be highlighted. It has been going on for the longest time.[30,31] There have been so many instances of erasure and censorship of the known facts of the Armenian Genocide. Many years ago an issue of the beautiful magazine, *Ariel,* that was published by Israel's Ministry of Foreign Affairs was literally withdrawn, despite enormous cost, when it was discovered that a folksy tourist-attracting article about the Armenian Quarter in Jerusalem included a very brief reference to the Armenian Genocide as a source of the influx of survivors of the Armenian Genocide into Israel.[32]

The reader of this book obviously knows how in 1982 a huge brouhaha exploded around the scheduled First International Conference on the Holocaust and Genocide which I began organizing in 1979. Over many years the government forbade Israel's television to refer to the Armenian Genocide and certainly not to air any of the films that were beginning to appear about that event. In approximately May 1992 an intrepid TV announcer (I don't know his name nor have I ever learned the background story for the event) informed the public that a week later a film, *An Armenian Journey,* would be shown about the Armenian Genocide, and when the government ordered the cancellation of the filming a huge controversy erupted.

A heated meeting then ensued of the government commission that is responsible for broadcasting policy (Reshut Hashidur). The meeting brought in two expert witnesses, one this writer as a scholar of genocide who certainly recognizes the validity of the Armenian Genocide, and the other a Jewish scholar of Turkish origin who held to the Turkish party line that there had been no such systematic murders. The commission voted overwhelmingly "yes" to screen the film, only for the prime minister, Yitzchak Shamir, to exercise his

---

30 Yair Auron, *The Banality of Indifference: The Attitude of the Yishuv and the Zionist Movement to the Armenian Genocide* [Hebrew] (Tel Aviv: Dvir with Kibbutzim College of Education, 1995). An English edition of this book was also published: *The Banality of Indifference: Zionism and the Armenian Genocide* (New Brunswick, NJ: Transaction Publishers, 2000).

31 Yair Auron, *The Banality of Denial: Israel and the Armenian Genocide* (New Brunswick, NJ: Transaction Publishers, 2003).

32 I know about this incident first-hand because my late brother, T. Carmi, a celebrated Israeli poet and translator, was editor of *Ariel.* Living as many did at that time in a bare, cold Jerusalem apartment, with the most minimal appliances, he was aghast at the expense of recalling thousands of bound copies of the luxurious publication on expensive glossy paper, let alone at the undemocratic censorship of a legitimate historical fact that was not even being emphasized in the article.

authority the next morning to override the commission's decision. What we did in turn at the Institute of the Holocaust and Genocide in Jerusalem is we screened the film to a full house at the Cinemateque in Jerusalem with the participation among others of the legendary mayor of Jerusalem, Teddy Kollek, the Armenian Patriarch, and the wife of the well-known Russian human rights warrior, Andrei Sakharov.[33]

In April 1994, on the occasion of the Memorial Day of the Armenian Genocide, Deputy Foreign Minister Yossi Beilin announced Israel's recognition of the genocide. Hooray! We were all overjoyed, but unfortunately, true to form, the government then disassociated from Beilin's statement as if it were only his personal view and returned to its denialist position.

Sometime later, also in April 1994, an intrepid senior broadcaster, who remained a leading and deeply respected newscaster until his recent retirement, Yaakov Achimeir, took it upon himself bravely to violate the horrible censorship law and for the first time spoke of the Armenian Genocide on Israeli media, following which the taboo was broken and many programs have since been aired.[34] In 2015, the 100th anniversary of the Armenian Genocide, Achimeier traveled to Yerevan and brought back to Israel a meaningful review of the occasion—which included an interview with this writer as one of the lecturers in Yerevan and climaxed with a touching spontaneous encounter with an elderly survivor of the genocide who "simply" wandered into our camera scene and captured both of us with the pathos of his memory.[35]

The Israeli juggernaut against recognition of the Armenian Genocide has not been limited to activity in Israel itself. Over the years, at various times serious efforts were made by Israel's diplomatic representatives to influence and cajole members of the United States Congress not to vote for legislation that was being proposed in the US to recognize more fully the Armenian Genocide. President Ronald Reagan had expressed such recognition but, like in Israel, the US Congress was blocked by the administration from doing so more fully

33 "Historic Vote of Israel Broadcasting Authority to Show Cancelled Armenian Genocide Film," *Internet on the Holocaust and Genocide* 27, no. 3 (June 1990).

34 "Armenian Genocide Recognized for the First Time by Israel," *Internet on the Holocaust and Genocide* 48, no. 3 (April 1994). This story also reports on the first official recognition of the Armenian Genocide by a senior Israeli government official, Deputy Foreign Minister Yossi Beilin. Unfortunately, the government then dissociated itself from Beilin's recognition and returned to its longstanding denial of recognition of the Armenian Genocide.

35 Yaakov Achimeier, film segment on 100th anniversary of Armenian Genocide, *Roim Olam* TV program (May 2015), Channel Khan 11, Israel. Filmed in Yerevan.

on subsequent occasions. And Israel played a huge role, behind the scenes, in overcoming plans to exhibit a display about the Armenian Genocide at the United States Holocaust Memorial Museum.

In Israel there have now been several periods in which official recognition of the Armenian Genocide seemed imminent. Thus, we have seen such recognition has been forcefully and touchingly supported by leaders at the level of the current president of Israel, Reuven Rivlin, also when he was the Chair of the Knesset, and then by his successor as Chair, Yuli Edelstein. As I reported earlier, in at least one round of processing proposed recognition in the Knesset, there was an instance where the proposal did receive the overwhelming vote of the Knesset Education Committee yes to recognize the genocide, and another incident where there was a unanimous vote of the Knesset to bring the bill before a committee, but in both cases the government prevented further developments.

It is clear that overall the people of Israel know about the Armenian Genocide and want our government to recognize it officially, but such recognition has never been forthcoming. Recognition of the Armenian Genocide has always been trapped by direct pressures and orders from the government to the Knesset.

Again I will point out that we have now also learned from Ministry of Foreign Affairs documents that even as these political games have been played out ostensibly in the name of political and security issues vis-à-vis Turkey (and in recent years one adds Azerbaijan to Turkey, with whom Israel is carrying on a booming multimillion arms trade) is that a central and dominating issue in the minds of significant leaders in the Ministry is also a resolute insistence to banish consideration of any genocide from being compared to the Holocaust. They believe, what for Yad Vashem and many others for years has been virtually axiomatic and as if a critical test of one's loyalty to Israel, that the Holocaust must remain unquestionably the most uniquely unique event of genocide that has ever descended on humanity since Creation.

In a report that I published in the *Jerusalem Post* in 1982, I described how

... one serious historian (name supplied to editor) decided to contact US government officials to evaluate for himself the risks of the Turkish threat. He then told the Israeli Consul he did not believe Turkish pressures justified cancelling an historic conference on the Holocaust and genocide in Israel, whereupon the Consul told him frankly: "I can tell you that the real reason we wanted to cancel the conference is because the inclusion of other genocides dwarfs the Holocaust and reduces its significance."[36]

CONCLUSION

Notwithstanding my own truly never-ending agony and rage at the Holocaust that befell our Jewish people, to the claims of uber-uniqueness I reply, as I said earlier, that the moral of the story is that this is a quest to make one's self superior to all other people. It derives from the same tragic quality that has descended on humanity ever since Creation of our world. This is a *tikkun* (correction of a moral fault) that we owe *ourselves* as well as the Armenian people and the world. The denial of another people's genocide leaves us deeply flawed and seriously weakens the integrity of our demands that governments and peoples around the world banish denials of the Holocaust. Our stand needs to be resolute and clear: Israel and the Jewish people oppose mass killing unconditionally—and damn the lucrative trade deals (let alone there are many of us who painfully wish Israel were not so heavily into the arms business).[37] Protecting the continuation of the so-lucrative arms trade is, of course, a major goal of successive Israeli governments on both sides of the political map; and thus specific huge trade of arms with the Azerbaijanis—a Turkic-speaking people who joined Turkey in threats against the Armenian people—and a major dynamic and motivation for not recognizing the Armenian Genocide.

A further word. One expression of Israeli claims of exclusivity and of the ultimate and unique importance of the Holocaust has been the literal rage directed against anyone who has committed the "worst sin of all" by referring to the Armenian Genocide, or to any other genocide, also as a "holocaust." Let it be known for the record that the Armenian Genocide was called the "Armenian holocaust" as far back already in the 1920s—or way before the Nazi murders of the Jewish people.[38] Moreover, in Israel, several scholars, including a professor

---

36 Israel W. Charny, "Pressures on Genocide Conference. Letter to the Editor," *Jerusalem Post*, August 29, 1982.

37 Harut Sassounian, "Jewish Professor Requests Information from Israeli Government fon Armenian Genocide," *California Courier*, January 11, 2018, reprinted on website of Institute on the Holocaust and Genocide, March 21, 2018, http://www.ihgjlm.com/.

38 Israel W. Charny, with contributions by Rouben Paul Adalian and Steven Jacobs, "Holocaust: The Word 'Holocaust' and Its Usage," in *Encyclopedia of Genocide*, ed. Israel W. Charny (Santa Barbara, CA: ABC-Clio, 1999), 40–43. Note also that as Colin Tatz pointed out in

of history at Bar Ilan University years ago, have written in Hebrew of the *Shoah Haarmenit*—"the Armenian shoah (holocaust)."[39]

For the fun of it, in 2012 an intriguing conference on Turkish-Armenian relationships took place in Venice. In the course of my remarks, I proposed to my Turkish colleagues in the audience, that henceforth they might use the Hebrew words *rezach am* for "genocide" and *shoah* for the "holocaust" when they refer to the Armenian Genocide/holocaust, and back in Israel I would be using their Turkish words *soykirim* or *genosit* for "genocide" and *soykırım* for "holocaust" when discussing the fate of the Armenians, so that in both cases we could escape much of the distasteful criticism and repugnance that we otherwise encounter from the true-blood scholars in our respective societies (let alone the jail sentence that Turkish colleagues might face). From the podium I could see half the audience bursting into laughter while half were frozen in discomfort.

We, the Armenians, the Greeks, the Yazidis, and a whole world of peoples deserve far better from us Israelis. Correcting such immorality will also help restore some of the original image of Israel as a leader in justice-seeking democracy and help repair the growing disconnection between American Jewry and caring people from Israel which is now seen as more and more callous and aggressive.

POSTSCRIPT OF INTEREST

As this book headed into production, two articles appeared in Israel's most prestigious newspaper, *Haaretz*, which bring home how widespread denials of the Armenian Genocide have been for too many influential Jewish leaders when they believed their first interest was in curtsying up to and pandering to Turkey. And also how the myth of Holocaust uniqueness was adopted by Yad Vashem staff as a kind of mandatory even religious requirement.

The one is about Shimon Peres—and, along with him, other respected Israeli and Jewish leaders—who, in *Haaretz* headline terms, became no less than "genocide deniers." This is important to understand for many people who

---

his book, *With Intent to Destroy* (London: Verso, 2003), the term "holocaust" appears even earlier with reference to an earlier genocide—which, many of us believe, really should be taken as the beginning period of what we call the Armenian Genocide which then flares into its known fullness in 1915—by Sultan Abdul Hamid in the late 1890s.

39 Pinchas Lapid, "The Dress Rehearsal for the Holocaust" [Hebrew], *Bar Ilan University Bulletin* (Summer 1974): 14–20.

simply respect leaders like Peres and Wiesel, who did so very much good for Israel, and are suspicious of possible extremism or an anti-Israel bias when a major aspect of the work of these good leaders is treated critically. The *Haaretz* article also goes on to identify two other scholars who are treated as big-time deniers in our text, Stanford Shaw and Bernard Lewis.

> The most influential leaders within Turkey—chief rabbis David Asseo and Ishak Haleva, the editors-in-chief of the Jewish Weekly, Salom, and lay leaders such as industrialists Jak Kamhi and former Jewish community president, Bensiyon Pinto—opposed recognition of the Armenian Genocide. They were joined by supporters in Israel (including Presidents Shimon Peres and Moshe Katsav as well as the Foreign Ministry and the Union of Turkish immigrants in Israel) and almost every major American Jewish organization including the AntiDefamation League, the American Jewish Committee and the Jewish Council for Public Affairs, and the most influential Jewish historians of the Ottoman Empire, Bernard Lewis and Stanford Shaw.[40]

The second is a touching human story of a person (today an *Haaretz* reporter) with Jewish and Armenian parentage, who identifies and addresses constructively the core issue for so many Israelis and Jews, and certainly for official Israel and Yad Vashem, whether recognizing another people's genocide reduces the monumental significance of our Holocaust. As the article states, "When our Yad Vashem guide asked, rhetorically, if we'd ever heard of 'any other Holocausts,' I immediately replied: 'The Armenian Genocide.' It took me years to unpack why she dismissed my answer so brusquely.[41]

---

40 Marc David Baer, "The Jews Who Befriended Turkey and Became Genocide Deniers: Prominent Jews, from Turkish Chief Rabbis to Israel's President to US Lay Leaders, have Propped Up Turkey's Armenian Genocide Denial. That's Only Just Begun to Change," *Haaretz* (English Edition), April 23, 2020, https://www.haaretz.com/middie-east-news/.premium-the-jews-whobefriended-turkey-and-became-genocide-deniers-1.8792672.

41 Sivan Gaides, "Recognizing the Trauma of the Armenian Genocide Doesn't Diminish the Holocaust," *Haaretz* (English Edition), April 16, 2020, https://www.haaretz.com/middle-east-news/.premium-recognizing-the-armenian-genocide-doesn-t-diminish-the-holocaust-1.8769665.

CHAPTER 6

Israel's Denial-Concealment of Cruelty, Genocidal Expulsion, and Massacres of Arabs in the Nonetheless Entirely Just War of Independence

A STRIKING CHAPTER OF THE UNIVERSAL CHALLENGE TO ALL PEOPLES TO RESPECT AND PROTECT LIFE

Israel's Systematic Cover-up of Documentations of Its Excesses of Destructiveness

The subjects of various unethical and strong-arm behaviors of the Israeli government over the years, and the denials of such actions, are painful for all of us who treasure Israel as the fulfillment of a centuries-old need for greater protection of the Jewish people and a return to the greater safety of our ancient homeland rather than being a weak dispersed minority. As is entirely known but too often forgotten, the Jewish people have suffered for hundreds of years as objects of discrimination, persecution, forced expulsion, murders, massacres, and pogroms, culminating in the Holocaust.

Israel is the brilliant "therapy" of the Jewish people restoring powers of self-defense and a dignity of strength and independence. At the same time, the natural expectation has been that a people who had suffered so deeply intrinsically would be all the more sensitive and care to protect and help other peoples not be oppressed.

Moreover, rich traditions of Jewish culture and religion are dedicated to the holiness of human life and to injunctions not to kill others, and indeed to do well unto others including the minorities living as the strangers in one's midst. So that Jewish/Israeli transgressions and blatant violations of basic rules to honor human life naturally arouse a heightened disappointment and disillusionment, as well as a triumphant revengeful anger at the People of the Book for betraying humanistic values.

The drama of the play of human evil in Jews/Israelis reached its height in the very inspiring and heroic successes of the Zionist movement in establishing a safe-haven country for Jews, and the remarkable skill of the Jewish *yishuv* (Jewish community) in Palestine and then the new State of Israel in protecting Jews against many forces opposing the existence of Israel and seeking its literal destruction—just as Jews have always been objects for destruction.

Israel's War of Independence was an entirely legitimate and Just War of self-defense. Moreover, Israel Defense Forces were characterized by a great deal of concern with the ethics of military actions (the policy of "purity of arms"), but at the same time many serious unethical excesses did take place.

When we take a penetrating look at the play of destructive forces in Israelis/Jews in the course of the magnificent overcoming of weakness in the War of Independence, we also gain a perspective on the capacity of Israel to deny its wrongdoings, as do so many countries. We have otherwise singled out Turkey in this book because our basic focus in this book is on the attempts by Turkey to deny the Armenian Genocide—Armenians and other co-victims such as the Greeks, Assyrians, and Yazidis. But the book is also very much about the full complicity and knowing leadership of Israel in promoting such Turkish denial.

From here we are also led on to confront the upsetting but undeniable truths that at various times, beginning especially with the War of Independence, Israel has engaged in acts of wanton cruelty and genocidal destruction, and has often adopted a policy of rank untruth and denial.

A major exposé by reporter Hagar Shezaf in *Haaretz* (Hebrew and English editions), on July 5, 2019, reveals that the Israeli government has been systematically removing the availability of historical documents of considerable cruelty and genocidal expulsion and murder of Arab inhabitants of Palestine in the 1948 War of Independence.[1]

For many years the official Israeli version of events and the prevailing beliefs of committed Zionists, like myself, was to minimize the extent of such actions, and to emphasize the understanding that when regrettable cruelty and

---

1 Hagar Shezaf, "Burying the Nakba: How Israel Systematically Hides Evidence of 1948 Expulsion of Arabs," *Haaretz* (English Edition), July 5, 2019, https://www.haaretz.com/israel-news/.premium.MAGAZINE-how-israel-systematically-hides-evidence-of-1948-expulsion-of-arabs-1.7435103.

massacres by Israelis did take place they were after all exceptions to an overall policy of "purity of arms" (a prevailing saying for many years in early Israel) and ethical warfare.

The War of Independence after all was an entirely just war in legitimate self-defense in response to the refusal of the Arabs to agree to the UN Declaration of two states in Palestine for the Jews and the Arabs, and the immediate attacks on the *yishuv* by several Arab countries, including by the most advanced army in the Middle East at the time, the British-led army of Transjordan, "the Arab Legion."

Nonetheless, over the years a solid trail of information about Israel's reprehensible actions has developed by a variety of historians and researchers, with special credit due to Professor Benny Morris of Ben Gurion University in Beer Sheva beginning with his seminal book, *1948: A History of the First Arab-Israeli War*,[2] and continuing with a variety of works including *The Birth of the Palestinian Refugee Problem 1947–1949*[3] and others.

In recent years Morris became aware that any number of documents that had been released and made available to him in past years by the censorship authority of the Israeli government have subsequently been removed from public access. He learned that the Defense Ministry's secretive security department, *Malmab*, whose activities and budget are classified, is the responsible agency that has been pursuing a relentless campaign to remove information about Israeli atrocities from public access. *Malmab* is a Hebrew acronym for "director of security of the defense establishment."

Thus, Shezaf tells us that in 2014 the agency arrived at the Harry Truman Research Institute of Hebrew University and insisted on having access to the papers of Israel's legendary Foreign Minister Abba Eban and Shlomo Gazit, an outstanding former major general in the Israel Defense Forces who headed Israel's military intelligence service. The initial reaction of Professor Menahem Blondheim, then director of the Truman Institute, was to refuse access. He told the Malmab team that he could not possibly imagine that there was any security issue that would justify denying access to researchers to those archives. Blondheim reports that they said to him in turn, "What if we were to discover that there are evidences that we poisoned wells [of the Arabs] in the War of Independence?" Blondheim answered, "Excellent, so then the people who did it should be put on trial." Nonetheless, it is reported that the Malmab agents

---

2   Benny Morris, *The Birth of the Palestinian Refugee Problem*.
3   Benny Morris, *A History of the First Arab-Israeli War*.

persisted and that explicit threats were made by them, and here the reporter becomes vague and says that a settlement was reached but she does not describe its terms.

The more left-wing parties in Israel are reported to have protested many times against the atrocities that were being committed in the 1948 war. Shezaf reports that the archive of Kibbutz Givat Haviva, which for many years was the educational center of the left-wing *Mapam* political party, included a document that reported the following:

> Safsaf [former Palestinian village near Safed]—52 men were caught, tied them to one another, dug a pit and shot them. 10 were still twitching. Women came, begged for mercy. Found bodies of 6 elderly men. There were 61 bodies. 3 cases of rape, one east of Safed, a girl of 14, 4 men shot and killed. From one they cut off his fingers with a knife to take the ring.[4]

The historian Tamar Novick first called attention to this document which had also been reported by Benny Morris. But at a later date, when Novick returned to examine the document once more, she discovered that it was no longer there because it had been removed by the teams of censors that had been at work. Shezaf reports further:

> An investigative report by *Haaretz* found that Malmab has concealed testimony from IDF generals about the killing of civilians and the demolition of villages, as well as documentation of the expulsion of Bedouins during the first decade of statehood. Conversations conducted by *Haaretz* with directors of public and private archives alike revealed that staff of the security department had treated the archives as their property, in some cases threatening the directors themselves.

TURKEY'S DENIAL OF THE ARMENIAN GENOCIDE IS A STAR, BUT ISRAEL'S DENIAL-CONCEALMENT OF GENOCIDAL ACTIONS MOVES IT ALSO INTO THE 'LEAGUE OF DENIERS'

For me, after so many years of being a leader in the battle against Turkey's malignant denials of the Armenian Genocide (I was honored as the first non-Armenian to

---

4   Hagar Shezaf, "Burying the Nakba."

be awarded the Presidential Gold Medal by Armenia), including many instances of their removing vital documents from government archives as well as periods of closing off the archives and at other times denying access to the archives to known scholars, the increasing exposure of Israeli suppression and concealment of historical records comes as a shock and deep disappointment.

However, this is hardly the first time that I have encountered Israeli censorship. As the reader of this book already knows quite well, in 1979 I initiated, entirely on my own, without an organization backing, the plan for a First International Conference on the Holocaust and Genocide, which did indeed take place in Tel Aviv in 1982, but only after a powerful concerted effort by Turkey and Israel to cancel the conference. Turkey demanded of Israel to remove any discussion of the Armenian Genocide. First, the Israeli government insisted that we remove the subject of the Armenian Genocide, and then it "advanced" to a demand that all Armenian professionals who had agreed to lecture to the conference be removed. When I and my colleagues adamantly refused, the government proceeded to devote enormous efforts to block funding for the conference, pressure me professionally at Tel Aviv University where I was a professor, contact professionals who were committed to lecture at the conference in the name of the government of Israel to request of them not to attend, and even call participants who did arrive in Israel for the conference at their hotels to tell them that the conference had been cancelled when it was in fact going ahead despite all the pressures.

At the same time, under its authority to censor newspaper reports that endangered security, the government arranged that no report whatsoever of the conference appear in the press in the days prior to the conference (this also left many attendees to believe that our opening ceremony would take place at Yad Vashem in Jerusalem as planned without their knowing that the government had caused cancellation of Yad Vashem's participation and that we had to move the opening to Tel Aviv). Again, a tribute to the democratic foundations of Israel is called for in that once word of the conference reached people and there was also wide exposure of the story in the international press, including five stories in the *New York Times*, the Israeli press truly rallied to cover the conference, and any number of newspaper columnists praised our initiative and also expressed their deep critique of the government (as well as of my university—and that ended up causing me plenty of career trouble, though in the larger picture of my life I do not regret the choices I made).

Now as the reader of this book knows, there is even more to this story of Israeli government conspiracy that has become clear to us only this last year when we gained access to many previously classified government records.

Israel is a "funny" mixed bag of quite democratic safeguards and procedures together with a disturbing patchwork of what even deserve to be called
totalitarian measures of control and denial of basic rights of citizens in a lawful
democracy. Fortunately, overall free speech very much prevails in Israel. And
with respect to records of its own destructive action, it is still not at all fair or
correct to say that Israel is "the same as Turkey." I do not know for a fact that the
Turkish government censorship has led to the actual destruction of the original
documents but this appears to be the consensus of any number of researchers
over the years, while in the case of the Israeli government the news that we are
apparently being given is that the documents that are being withdrawn from
public access are locked up in securely in accessible archives but have not been
destroyed. Further, the Turkish denial of the Armenian Genocide is backed by
law, and although exact numbers are not available to us, we know of hundreds
who have been jailed in Turkey for their speaking and writing openly about
the Armenian Genocide, major newspapers have been closed down, and people
have lost their jobs. In addition, brutish Turkish intrusions into international
conferences all over the world have been matters of routine (and reached a
point where, for all of their seriousness became a matter of almost comic routine for many of us).

Even more to the point, for all that Israeli brutality, expulsions and murders of civilians in the War of Independence were tragic and criminal, and
far more of them took place than were previously acknowledged, the scope
and numbers of murdered Palestinians in no way compares to the systematic Turkish killings in the Armenian Genocide that are estimated to include
1,500,000 Armenians and 1,500,000 Assyrians, Turks, Greeks, Yazidis, and
others.[5]

Finally, one is absolutely obligated to recognize that the context of the
Israeli brutality was a war of defense against annihilation that Israel did

---

5   One has to differentiate between murders and expulsion. There has always been a great deal
of controversy about the number of Arabs who were expelled. According to the Jewish Virtual Library, "Many Arabs claim that 800,000 to 1,000,000 Palestinians became refugees in
1947–1949. The last census was taken by the British in 1945. It found approximately 1.2
million permanent Arab residents in all of Palestine. A 1949 Government of Israel census
counted 160,000 Arabs living in the country after the war. In 1947, a total of 809,100 Arabs
lived in the same area. This meant no more than 650,000 Palestinian Arabs could have become refugees. A report by the UN Mediator on Palestine arrived at an even lower figure,
472,000, and calculated that only about 360,000 Arab refugees required aid." "Myths and
Facts—The Refugees," *Jewish Virtual Library*, 1998, https://www.jewishvirtuallibrary.org/
myths-and-facts-the-refugees#a.

not initiate in any way. As has been noted clearly, Israel was attacked from within by parts of its Arab population along with a bevy of surrounding Arab nations, all of whom refused to accept the United Nations decision to partition Palestine into Jewish and Arab states—a decision Israel celebrated and accepted. Further, the Arab warfare rang with cries and symbols of eradicating the Jews. Such threats were also naturally contextualized with the actual events of mass slaughter that had occurred in Hebron in 1925, and now also characterized Arab attacks such as at Kfar Etzion, and then of a medical convoy to Hadassah Hospital on Mount Scopus in Jerusalem. Moreover, this war took place barely a few years after knowledge of the catastrophic Holocaust overwhelmed Jewish and Israeli consciousness with news of the deaths of so many relatives as well as colleagues in Zionist movements. In fact, this was the direct personal experience of many of the Israeli fighters in the War of Independence who were themselves newly arrived immigrants from the Nazi hells, and one can easily identify with their and other Israelis' rage and inclinations to revenge.

We now also know that it is true of all peoples that war by definition releases potentials for sadism and cruelty beyond the excesses in warfare that are in themselves structurally inevitable. No less important, the propaganda of Israeli purity of arms was not entirely contrived because there were in fact many fighters and commanders who did hold themselves to an edict of "just war" and decency in their fighting and in their treatment of fleeing refugees.

I think it also has to be acknowledged that battles for ascendancy in national relations are also a built-in natural aspect of our inherent human psychological makeup. Even if idealistically questionable, it is hardly surprising and certainly not unnatural, especially in a war of self-defense against aggression that was launched against it, for a nation to take advantage of an opportunity to expand its territory and dominance—and in the case of Israel it is also to territory to which it has distinct historical claims.

I personally have given up my childlike naiveté and trust in an incontestable decency of our Jewish people—then and today, but I still honor fully the victory in the War of Independence, our survival of the enormous threats to destroy us, and our continuing battle to achieve a secure country that is basically still largely democratic and life affirming for all its inhabitants although it is riddled with fascist trends and humiliation and discrimination against many non-Jewish people, including fully entitled citizens of Israel.

ISRAEL'S ARMS TRADE ALSO CONTRADICTS AN ETHOS OF PEACE AND LEADS TO COLLABORATION WITH GENOCIDAL GOVERNMENTS

Another very major issue that we know is subject to profound Israeli denial-concealment is the sale of weapons to other countries that we have discussed earlier. Together with many other people, my naive hopes for a better world include effective international regulation of such sales, with particular emphasis on forbidding or stopping sales to any country that uses weapons for purposes of persecution and commission of atrocities. In the absence of such international machinery there is an expectation and wish that countries committed to democracy, such as Israel and the United States, would adopt such a policy for themselves.

In the case of Israel, the horrendous information we have received in recent years has implicated Israel in the sales of arms not only to certain strong-man regimes but to countries that were actively engaged in genocidal campaigns even at the time of the sale, such as in the past in Rwanda and Serbia, and more currently in Myanmar—though it has just been announced that military officials from Myanmar coming to examine available Israeli arms would be denied entry. There have been several courageous efforts by Professor Yair Auron, associate director of the Institute on the Holocaust and Genocide Jerusalem (who became the second non-Armenian to win the Presidential Gold Medal for his research contributions to recognizing the Armenian Genocide), and his colleague, Attorney Itay Mack, to access government records of sales using the Israeli laws of access to government information, but in each case the "passion play" that is enacted in the courtroom is that the government representative asks to speak to the judge in closed quarters, pleads that Israeli security concerns are at stake, and the court refuses to rule for release of the records.

Attorney Itay Mack writes pithily in *Haaretz*:

> With the agreement of the US, Israel developed rapidly into the central arms provider for a series of murderous regimes in central and south America, Africa and southeast Asia. Thus, for example, Israel's important assistance in the preparation of the U.N. General Convention that went into effect in 1951, has been replaced with support for the military regimes of Guatemala, and the genocide of the aboriginals has been done with Israeli arms.

In addition, Mack castigates Israel's Yad Vashem, the more so in its comparison to the US Holocaust Memorial Museum (USHMM) in Washington, DC, that

> ... in the course of the years has attributed universal meanings to the implications of the Shoah, and has documented genocidal destruction and crimes against humanity that have also been executed against other peoples and even has constructed and organized a research institute for the prevention of genocide. [In contrast] Yad Vashem (with the exceptions of some individual staff members) avoids any engagement with events that do not directly affect Jews.

Mack concludes bitterly and powerfully:

> Yad Vashem indeed for tens of years serves as an obligatory ceremonial stop for dictators, murderers, bigots, and fascists who have come to Israel in order to finalize arms deals and to gain legitimacy and a "certificate of kashrut" from Israel's ally, the United States.[6]

Mack, who has been an intrepid fighter against Israel's arms sales, is actually touching on a broader topic of the role of Yad Vashem in Israel and for the world. Personally, I have always accepted that Yad Vashem more than legitimately devotes the overwhelming majority of its resources to the memorial and research of the Holocaust, but I also believe that it also should link the Holocaust and its profound meanings to the tragedies and dangers of genocides all through history and all over the world. For example, I proposed many times that Yad Vashem and other Holocaust museums should include what I call a "World Genocide Situation Room" where up-to-date information about ongoing genocides and threats of imminent genocide are made available to museum visitors. Only recently has there been the development of a "Genocide Gallery" in a newly opened Holocaust museum in Dallas, Texas.[7] To the best of my knowledge, this is the first serious inclusion of other peoples' genocides in a Holocaust museum.

---

6   Itay Mack, "The Yad Vashem Laundry" [Hebrew], *Haaretz* (Hebrew edition), January 22, 2020.

7   "Dallas Holocaust and Human Rights Museum Includes a 'Genocide Gallery,'" Institute on the Holocaust and Genocide, March 5, 2020, http://www.ihgjlm.com/2020/03/05/the-dallas-holocaust-and-human-rights-museum/.

Unhappily, neither I nor others have ever succeeded in having this perspective adopted by Yad Vashem. Gideon Levy is a gifted writer for *Haaretz* whose work I dislike strongly because along with his powerful exposures of Israeli wrongdoing and evil, he never says a single word about the beauties and decency of Israel. However, I do yield to him when he put his finger on the core issue when he wrote beautifully:

> Yad Vashem could have become a global beacon of conscience. It could have used its prestige around the world to behave as a universal institution rather than as a provincial one, speaking out against crimes against humanity throughout the world, even when its victims aren't Jews, crying out against the injustices done to persecuted minorities everywhere.[8]

If we are not naïve, it is clear that governments do have legitimate needs to withhold certain records over periods of time, but in a democracy it is critical that such withholding of information be for limited periods of time only, which is very different from what fascist governments do.

EXPOSING FASCIST POLICIES IN "THE SOLE DEMOCRACY IN THE MIDDLE EAST"

I have a good number of colleagues whose work I respect who object strenuously to my use of the word "fascist." Something similar took place when I published my book *Fascism and Democracy in the Human Mind: A Bridge between Mind and Society.*[9]

For many colleagues, the concept of "fascism" has to refer to an ideological and structural codification of a formal known political movement and party that spells out clear cut and legally mandated policies of prejudice, discrimination and persecution. For me "fascist" is, first of all, the spirit of bigotry and a movement towards hierarchical discriminatory provisions in social practice and in law for treating any other people as less privileged and less entitled to full

---

8 Gideon Levy, "Yad Vashem Doesn't Have the Courage to Be a Global Beacon of Conscience," *Haaretz* (English Edition), November 24, 2019, https://www.haaretz.com/opinion/.premium-yad-vashem-doesn-t-have-the-courage-to-be-a-global-beacon-of-conscience-1.8166136.

9 Israel W. Charny, *Fascism and Democracy in the Human Mind* (Lincoln, NE: University of Nebraska Press, 2006). Awarded "Outstanding Academic Book of the Year" by the American Library Association.

measures of safeguard, protection, privilege and protection as are all other peoples. These discriminatory advantages are more often attributed to and assigned to the predominant national, ethnic, religious, or political identity of the local majority or politically powerful identity. I tend to use the word "fascism" interchangeably with the word "totalitarianism." I was very happy to see my book honored by the American Library Association as "Outstanding Academic Book of the Year," which carried the implication that my basic point of view about fascist thinking and a "fascist mind" had been accepted despite the intellectual objections that had been raised.

Obviously, the powerful exposure of such censorship by Shezaf in a major Israeli newspaper in itself is a tribute to the fundamental democratic policies and safeguards that continue in Israel. (It should be noted that by this time, 2020, the issue of increasing fascist (totalitarian)-type legislation and administrative procedures by the governing Likud party under the endless leadership of Benjamin Netanyahu became an increasingly serious issue in Israeli life.)

More and more Israel is refusing the right to enter the country to writers, intellectuals as well as diplomats who have opposed Israeli policies—a distinctly totalitarian policy to say the least. Legislation that has already been passed includes the removal of Arabic from the official languages of the Israeli government (which remain Hebrew and English). The Nation-State Law that has been passed emphasizes the predominance of Jewish identity in Israel, minimizes pluralism and inclusiveness of all people and the explicit inclusion of their democratic rights in the law—as was the inspiring anthem of the very original proclamation of the creation of the Jewish State of Israel. Nonetheless it should be clear that there is no legislation revoking specific democratic rights to date, but a smell of totalitarianism is in the air that is frightening, and a great many of us Israelis are objecting.

However, there is even a further painful bite to the suppression of the truth of our own actual destructive and murderous behaviors. These insult the essence of Israeli and Jewish values of democracy and justice no less than they are objectionable political restrictions on freedom of thought and expression.

Many caring Israelis will argue that because there is so much antagonism to Israeli in the world today, and that anti-Israeli attitudes have also become a major and perilous weapon of classic antisemitism which is now increasing dangerously in many parts of the world, including notably by liberals and their organizations such as we saw in Britain's Labour Party, that one should not expose Israel's record of atrocities. I have heard the argument before, often from my own family and friends and colleagues. Thus, after reading this essay my son wrote me happily, "Congratulations on a beautifully written, bold and enlightening article. I really admire your willingness to tackle rough issues." But then he added pointedly, "Would it be prudent to make these excellent, difficult points in a broader discussion about genocide and the protection of life? You might find that using Israel as one of several examples in a broad discussion would enable you to make these bold points without the perception of Israel bashing." He then reminded me, based on a recording by former US Ambassador to the UN, Nikki Haley, that from 2006–2016 the UN Human Rights Council condemned China zero times, Syria, six times, North Korea, nine times, and Israel, sixty-eight times.[10]

I recall again the study of the attitudes of Israelis toward the genocidal massacre of unarmed civilian Arabs in Kfar Kassem that we executed in 1956. We purposely chose as our subjects good people who came to purchase tickets to see Claude Lanzmann's nine-hour film, *Shoah*.[11] Was I ever cold-shouldered by my colleagues in the university's School of Social Work to whom we initially presented the study, as well as sadly remonstrated by family members, not simply for the results but for calling attention to our being terrible murderers at Kfar Kassem.

Yet I have a firm belief that a democracy cannot compromise with telling truth, and a firm belief that democracy cannot survive not telling truth. Writing recently about Malmab's suppression of truth, Benny Morris writes:

> In general, Malmab's actions regarding the documents on 1948 and the following years (such as material on the expulsion of Bedouin from the Negev in the '50s) is a foolish and malicious act typical of totalitarian regimes. The damage to Israel's image caused by Malmab's actions and their inevitable revelation is much greater than any damage that could have been caused by revelation of the actions from 1948 (most of which were already public knowledge before Malmab's purging operation began). What happened in 1948 happened 70 years ago in a difficult war that was forced upon the Jews. Malmab's actions, meanwhile, only attest to Israel's increasingly benighted character today.[12]

---

10 "Nikki Haley IAC Las Vegas Gala 2019," Israel American Council (IAC), April 4, 2019, https://www.youtube.com/watch?v=7m6r86eyEx0.

11 Israel W. Charny and Daphna Fromer, "A Study of Attitudes of Viewers." This article was later republished with a new introduction in *IDEA, A Journal of Social Issues* 9, no. 1 (September 25, 2004), http://www.ideajournal.com/articles.php?id=35.

12 Benny Morris, "Benny Morris: Israel's Concealing of Nakba Documents Is Totalitarian," *Haaretz* (English Edition), July 15, 2019, https://www.haaretz.com/opinion/.premium-is-rael-s-concealing-of-documents-on-the-nakba-is-totalitarian-1.7495203.

THE CORE ISSUES IN THE CURRENT EXPOSÉ

Altogether, several core issues are involved in the current exposé of massive Israeli censorship of atrocities in 1948. First and foremost is the basic principle of free access to all information which is critical in a democracy. Of course, all reasonable people will recognize that there are security issues which do justify periods of temporary blackouts and censorship, but these are absolutely not acceptable as justifications for massive denial and concealment of basic historical facts. Dr. Yaacov Lozowick, who had been the chief archivist of the State of Israel, wrote in his summary when he concluded his post, "A democracy must not conceal information because it is liable to embarrass the state. In practice, the security establishment in Israel, and to a certain extent that of foreign relations as well, are interfering with the public discussion."[13]

The second core issue that censorship of atrocities by a government brings up in a democracy is the fundamental question of whether a democratic nation and people are capable of and should be made to struggle with the truths of their failures, shortcomings, abuses, and evil actions. Most proponents and theorists of democratic government opt for the desirability of a genuine struggle with such truths as a more effective way of strengthening democracy than suppression of the information.

Finally, the even more underlying core issue that arises in the face of Israeli denial-concealment of its atrocities and genocidal behaviors is the understanding we are to have of the fundamental nature of man in Israelis too in relation to our understanding of the fundamental nature of all homo sapiens, an issue that we will now address in a fuller way.

THE POTENTIAL FOR GENOCIDAL ATROCITY IS PART OF THE HUMAN NATURE OF ISRAELIS JUST AS WE HAVE LEARNED IT IS IN THE NATURE OF HUMAN BEINGS EVERYWHERE

It took a good many years and a great deal of intellectual and spiritual pain for the behavioral sciences and mental health professions to come to the conclusion that the majority of killers are—very sad to say—essentially what are to be called "normal human beings." Following the Holocaust in particular, with

---

13 Yaacov Lozowick, July 5, 2019. Cited in Hagar Shezaf, "Burying the Nakba."

the availability of advancing tools for psychological investigation and research, we arrived at this painful conclusion slowly but surely.[14]

At the same time it was and remains a fact that different peoples—groups, organizations, institutions, political parties, religious faiths, nations—do develop different levels of commitment to democratic safeguards against violence and to spiritual ideals of forbidding the taking of human life (except in genuine self-defense, it always has to be noted). There are indeed many very strong foundations for a spiritual idealism of not taking human life in the Jewish tradition, and a strong foundation of respect for all human beings and an obligation to protect their safety in the basic Jewish traditions. Thus, the doyen of early genocide studies, Professor Leo Kuper of the University of California, did a comparative study of the traditions of violence in Judaism, Christianity, and Islam and credited Judaism with being the most positively oriented to the protection of life of the three religious traditions, though also with its component calls and legitimation of degrees of violence.[15]

In fulfillment of the value of transparency, my own disclosure is that I remained loyal to the upbringing I had enjoyed as an American-Jewish child in which we had been firmly imbued with a belief in Judaism and Zionism being deeply consistent with democratic ideals. As a young adult and continuing into my middle years of adulthood, I remained impressed and encouraged by the

---

14 See, for example, the reports by psychologist Gustave Gilbert and psychiatrist Douglas Kelly of the convicted prisoners at the Nuremburg Trials following World War II, or a study by British psychiatrist Anthony Storr of the Tavistock Clinic in London who went to visit and examine convicted Nazi criminals in Europe: Gustave M. Gilbert, *The Psychology of Dictatorship: Based on an Examination of the Leaders of Nazi Germany* (New Yok: Ronald Press, 1950); Douglas M. Kelley, *Two Cells in Nuremberg: A Psychiatrist Examines the Nazi Criminals* (New York: Greenberg, 1947, reprinted, New Yok: MacFadden, 1961); Anthony Storr, *Human Destructiveness: The Roots of Genocide and Human Cruelty* (New York: Routledge, 2014, original publication, 1991). See also my summary of a variety of studies on the normality of the killers in Israel W. Charny, *How Can We Commit the Unthinkable?*

Before moving to Israel, I presented a paper to the Israeli Psychological Association on the "normality" of the genociders, which was subsequently published as Israel W. Charny, "Normal man as Genocider: We Need a Psychology of Normal Man as Genocider, Accomplice or Indifferent Bystander to Mass Killing of Man," *Voices: The Art and Science of Psychotherapy* 7, no. 2 (1971): 68–79. I can still remember how my presentation was greeted by the total silence of a large audience. Little did I know this was standard practice in Israeli academia at the time. I thought and felt this was the reaction to the message I brought at that time, and to this day I'm not sure if that wasn't also true. Anyway, I had all of one verbal feedback afterwards and otherwise total silence.

15 Leo Kuper, "Theological Warrants for Genocide: Judaism, Islam and Christianity," *Terrorism and Political Violence* 2, no. 3 (1990): 351–379.

standard reports of the Zionist establishment and the young Israeli State that insisted that Israel for the largest part had not engaged in any atrocities nor in forced migration of Arabs in the War of Independence, but that migration of the Palestinians was essentially in response to the policies of their leader—which, for much of it, was indeed the case. Evidence for such that is given to this day is that in several communities such as Abu Gosh, a delightful village near my home today in the hills of Jerusalem, the population simply refused the order given by the Israeli military to leave the town and no harm at all was done to them—but harm was certainly done in a good number of other locations. While some expulsions of Arab civilians from their homes can be justified by the logistics of military strategy; and some expulsions can be understood—however regretfully—as examples of the natural horror of war that character-izes human society since time immemorial, the considerable extent of Israeli expulsions of Arab residents during a necessary and justified war does raise painful questions. Thus, to return to my neighboring village of Abu Gosh—where we like to eat and shop and very much enjoy the people and atmosphere of the village, which in a dramatic way stands for non-violence and fellowship with another ethnicity—should Israel, after all, have evacuated the village in the justifying context of the war? So, weren't there other villages where a future peaceful co-existence might have been possible?

I also remember how in the United States the Zionist Organization of America parroted Israeli declarations that no massacre had taken place in Deir Yassin, even though there is absolutely no doubt that in April, 1948 a massacre did take place of the villagers there—who we now know were largely peace-ful and that the population murdered was largely one of old people, women, and children. In 1981, I took a lead role at a meeting of the International Peace Research Association in Tokyo against charges that were being leveled of Israeli atrocities, and I portrayed in my remarks and later in a formal publication, how Israel's basic respect for Arabs and their culture was being developed in Israel in a shared pluralistic society.[16] In short, I was fully caught up in the propaganda of Israeli denial and I was very inaccurate in my defense.

What we now have to face in no way changes the critical conclusion that has been advanced by distinguished researchers such as Prof. R. J. Rummel of

---

16   Israel W. Charny, "One Very Simple Idea: A Possible Israeli Contribution to a Lasting Mid-dle East Peace (and also a Model for Other Ethnic Hubs on Planet Earth)," in *Peace and Justice in the Middle East* (Report of the International Peace Research Association Commis-sion on Termination of War in the Middle East), ed. Elise Boulding (Boulder, CO: Lynne Rienner Publishers, 1994), 287–294.

the University of Hawaii that the record is clear that cultures that adopt and live by democratic values have a far lesser potential for genocidal exterminations of others.[17] But we do have to face the no less critical conclusions that despite our pretentions, Jews and Israelis too are *not* far away from a potential to be cruel, beastly and murderous.

The roots of democratic and life-protecting values run deep in Judaic culture and millions of Jews/Israelis do live by them. But they do not automatically overcome what many of us now recognize is an instinctive predilection in the basic nature of homo sapiens to murder-- in self-defense, in a pursuit of power, and in seeking superiority over others, as well as a readiness as if to sacrifice others so one can live. Jews, too, need to work at cultivating ethical values to respect and protect human life as do all human beings from every ethnic, national, and whatever backgrounds.

As everybody knows, this of course is an enormous challenge especially for Islamic society in our world today, but intrinsically the challenge to respect and protect human life is one for **all** peoples with no exceptions.

Personally, I believe it is the ultimate challenge to our entire species. The pandemic of collective human murder can kill our very civilization.

---

17 R. J. Rummel, *Power Kills: Democracy as a Method of Nonviolence* (Brunswick, NJ: Transaction Publishers, 1997).

Three Contemporary Updates: The Voices of a Distinguished Contemporary Turk, an Armenian, and a Jew

CHAPTER 7

A Contemporary Turk: Ragip Zarakolu—The Banality of Denial

Figure 11. Ragip Zarakolu holding a book in Turkish entitled *The Armenian Genocide: Evidence from the German Foreign Office Archives, 1915–1916.* We are grateful to ANF English News Agency for permission to use the above photo and to quote from the news releases that follow.

EDITOR'S INTRODUCTION

The following chapter by Ragip Zarakolu succeeds in conveying that he is, outstandingly, and captivatingly, a brave, super-principled man who has stood up time and time again against Turkish government censorship and tough recriminations. The latest, as will be seen below, is the Turkish government moving to denude Zarakolu of all of his remaining assets in Turkey including his pension. Zarakolu has been in jail countless times. His late wife, who worked with him heroically in their publishing house, died of cancer in the course of a jail term, and their son Deniz was also jailed in 2011.

Zarakolu has never faltered. He published Truth about violations of fundamental human rights especially about the Kurds and about the Armenians. I also would like to add personally that as president of the International Association of Genocide Scholars, I was very proud to award Ragip Zarakolu one of his many well-deserved awards as a heroic champion of freedom.

Yet I confess that I found editing his chapter for our book an "impossible" job because it is so rich with information and analysis. His original text was two or three times longer than what we are able to publish. He reports and reviews an endless number of entanglements with the Turkish government, as well as efforts by him and his colleagues, together with many of us colleagues from around the world, to hold conferences in many different places. For many of us in genocide studies the recollection of some of the major conferences is professionally valuable and heartwarming, and fills much of the story of how the "forgotten" and "unknown" Armenian Genocide was pulled back from oblivion.

It would be a major work in its own right to tap the fuller range of Zarakolu's knowledge and his real insider's understanding of the complex dynamics of many of the events in the history of Turkish denial of the Armenian Genocide and related crimes against other peoples and Turkish retaliations against those who speak the truth. We have selected from his text a certain number of events that he describes from the beginning of the Turkish Republic until today. In the remainder of this Editor's Introduction we have also added information from some other sources such as the Committee to Protect Journalists in Turkey in an attempt to project a broad picture of the fascist shambles to which Erdoğan has brought Turkey. This information will then be followed by autobiographical information provided directly by Ragip Zarakolu.

CURRENT STATUS AND SOME PAST HISTORY OF TURKISH VIOLATIONS OF BASIC HUMAN RIGHTS

ANF News Agency Stockholm reported on December 22, 2019 that the Swedish Supreme Court rejected Turkey's extradition request against journalist and publisher Ragip Zarakolu.[1] The Turkish government had accused Zarakolu of

---

1   Ajansa Nûçeyan a Firatê, "Swedish Court Rejects Turkey's Demand for Zarakolu Extradition," *ANFNews*, December 22, 2019, https://anfenglish.com/news/turkey-confiscates-assets-of-ragip-zarakolu-in-kck-trial-40317.

"supporting terrorism" and demanded his extradition. Zarakolu said that Turkey wanted him extradited because he defended human and minority rights.

The Turks had issued a "Red Bulletin" for Zarakolu in September 2018 "for a speech he gave in a "Politics Academy held by the Peace and Democracy Party in 2011." Ragip Zarakolu is quoted as having responded, "It would seem that me continuing to defend human rights and minority rights, defending peace, expressing my ideas and writing articles disturbed some people. Let them be disturbed. I'm marching on."[2]

In 2017, ANF reported that the offices of Zarakolu's publishing company, Belge Publishers, had been raided by the police and 2000 books were confiscated. ANF commented that "Belge Publishing has been putting out opposition books for forty years and has suffered systemic pressure for it." It also noted that the publishing house had in fact been founded by Zarakolu's wife, the late Ayşe Nur Zarakolu, and they note that she "lost her life in 2002." As we already noted, Mrs. Zarakolu died of cancer—at a time that she was in jail and under threat of additional charges because of a book about Pontos.

According to *Balkan Insight*,[3] the agency in charge of the state advertising budget in Turkey has imposed a ban on two of the country's remaining independent media outlets, extending a crackdown on dissent that has seen dozens of newspapers and broadcasters shut down since a failed 2016 coup:

> Since a failed coup in 2016, authorities under Turkish President Recep Tayyip Erdoğan have closed 70 newspapers, 20 magazines, 34 radio stations and 33 television channels, accusing them of ties to terrorism. A handful of independent outlets remain, but now they too are feeling the squeeze from a ban on vital state advertising. International media watchdogs and critics of Erdoğan's increasingly authoritarian rule say the indefinite bans imposed by Turkey's Press Ad Agency, BIK, represent another tool to suppress dissent. We are a media outlet which only aims to tell the truth, but the government only wants to see its own version of the truth, said Berkant Gultekin, managing editor of the leftist Turkish daily *BirGün*. That is why we have huge pressure on us.

---

2   Ajansa Nûçeyan a Firatê, "Red Bulletin issued for Ragip Zarakolu," *ANFNews*, September 5, 2018, https://anfenglishmobile.com/freedom-of-the-press/red-bulletin-issued-for-ragip-zarakolu-2.

3   Hamdi Firat Buyuk, "Under Erdoğan, Independent Turkish Media Find Revenues Squeezed," *Balkan Insight*, March 3, 2020, https://balkaninsight.com/2020/03/03/under-erdogan-independent-turkish-media-find-revenues-squeezed/.

In September 2019, the Committee to Protect Journalists (CPJ) joined an international press freedom mission to Turkey that met with journalists, civil society, diplomats, the judiciary, and government officials. The visiting delegation voiced concern about the continued crackdown on journalists in the country and the need for the authorities to protect free press, address inconsistencies and flaws in the trials of journalists, and release those detained unfairly. Turkey is the world's worst jailer of journalists, with a least 68 in jail in direct relation to their work at the time of CPJ's 2018 prison census.[4] In December 2019, the CPJ concluded, "In Turkey reporting is a daily struggle."[5]

Middle East Eye News reported that the number of criminal investigations opened in Turkey against individuals who allegedly insulted President Recep Tayyip Erdoğan went up 30% in 2018, according to official statistics. The Turkish Justice Ministry's Judicial Statistics 2018 stated that 26,115 criminal investigations were conducted last year under Criminal Code Article 299. Of these cases, Turkish courts convicted 2,462 individuals, including 19 children and 12 foreigners.[6]

AUTOBIOGRAPHICAL INFORMATION

Ragıp Zarakolu, journalist, publisher, human rights defender, was born in 1948. He is the co-founder of *Demokrat* newspaper (1979), the Human Rights Association, (1986) History Foundation (1991), Belge Publishers (1977), *Alternative* (Turkish edition of *L'etat du monde* yearbook, 1982–1984), and Alan Publishing.

He was put on trial with his wife, Ayşe Nur Zarakolu, more than fifty times as editor and translator or because of their conferences and petitions. He was arrested after 1971 and in the 1980 military coup because of journalism. He was arrested in 2011 because of a conference. He is currently a Swedish citizen, married to Monica Elisabeth Åström Zarakolu.

---

4   "Press Freedom Situation in Turkey Remains Highly Restrictive, despite Some Room for Very Cautious Optimism, Joint Mission Finds," CPJ, September 13, 2019, https://cpj.org/blog/2019/09/press-freedom-situation-in-turkey-remains-highly-r.php.

5   "In Turkey, Reporting is a Daily Struggle," *CPJ*, December 26, 2019, https://cpj.org/blog/2019/12/turkey-reporting-police-harassed-detained-challenge.php.

6   Ragip Soylu, "Turkish Court Cases over 'Insulting' the President Up 30 Percent in 2018," *Middle East Eye News*, September 24, 2019, https://www.middleeasteye.net/news/26000-people-investigated-insulting-erdogan-2018.

He has received awards of Turkey Journalists and Publisher Associations, International Association of Genocide Scholars, the Norwegian Writers Association, Danish PL Freedom, Diyarbakır Chamber of Physicians, World Publishers Association, American Publishers Association and PEN, Dutch PEN, Abdi Ipekci Turkish-Greek Peace Prize, Armenian Presidential, Assirian Cultural Awards, and others. He was a 2012 Nobel Peace Prize nominee.

He currently writes voluntarily for dissident press such as *Arti-Gerçek* in Germany, *Evrensel, Yeni Yaşam,* and *Agos* in Turkey. He was also arrested in absentia in 2016 August and given a life sentence because of his solidarity with the Kurdish Newspaper, *Özgür Gündem* (with Aslı Erdoğan, Eren Keskin, Filiz Koçali, Necmiye Alpay, Bilge Akut, Kemal Sancılı, Zana Bilir, and İnal Kızılkaya). He is currently in the status of arrested in absentia in Turkey and de facto lives in exile in Sweden.

RAGIP ZARAKOLU'S BOOKS IN TURKISH

Democratic and National Revolutions, with Ayşe Nur Zarakolu (*Devrim ve Karşı Devrimler Ansiklopedisi,* Istanbul: Gelişim Publishing, 1975); *World Economy, Crises and the State* (Problems of the World Collection, Istanbul: Alan Publishing, 1983); *Crises, Neo-Liberalism and Reagan* (Problems of the World Collection, Istanbul: Alan Publishing, 1985); *State, Militarism and Democracy in Latin America* (Problems of the World Collection, Istanbul: Alan Publishing, 1985); *Globalism, European Left and Soviets* (Problems of the World collection, Istanbul: Alan Publishing, 1986); *Thatcherism and Authoritarian Populism* (Problems of the World Collection, Istanbul: Alan Publishing, 1986); *Middle East File/Israel and Philistine Rebellion, Iran and Iraq* (Problems of the World Collection, Istanbul: Alan Publishing, 1987); *1989 East Europe File* (Problems of the World Collection, Istanbul: Alan Publishing, 1990); *Elegy for a Woman/ Essays from 1992* (Istanbul: Belge Publishing, 2003); *Elegy for a Country/Essays during Dirty War, 1993* (Istanbul: Belge Publishing, 2003); *Albatros/Essays 2007–2011* (Istanbul: Evrensel Publishing, 2012); *Turkish-Armenian Dialogue in Civil Society* (İstanbul: Pencere Publishing, 2008).

TRANSLATIONS

He has translated books of K. Marx, Lukacs, Oscar Lange, Lothar Rathman, V. İ. Lenin, İsaac Babel, Janucz Korczak, Bertold Brecht, and George Andreadis, among others.

THE BANALITY OF DENIAL

Ragıp Zarakolu

Introduction

The Republic of Turkey denies not only the Armenian Genocide, but also the existence of the Kurdish people.

On one level, negationism has helped the advancement of genocide research a lot and it has helped public opinion and parliaments to be convinced about the truth of 1915 Genocide against Armenians, Greeks, Assyrians (but also the Yazidis and Jews of the region had to pay a high price during that period).

The 1915 genocide became the backbone of the nation and national state building in Turkey. Recognition of the Ottoman Genocide could do great damage to the myths of the state-founding nationalist ideology.

I defined another aspect of Turkish denialism as "Israel syndrome," that is: "One day the Armenians may come back to their homeland like the Jews." Turkish nationalism had this fear before the Israel Republic was born. One of the signers of the Lausanne Peace Threaty, Dr. Riza Nur, wrote in his memoirs, which were kept at the British Museum, "Topal Osman mobs were burning and destroying the churches and cemeteries in Pontos region, I approve this, to finish the hope of comeback."

A priest from Etjmiadzin told me once, "Genocide forced Armenians to be a nation and to build little Armenian Republic, with a survival instinct."

I call the fears of Turkish, Arabian, and Iranian nationalisms of a possible emergence of Kurdistan during last century, "Poland syndrome." Poland was divided between three strong empires. But after World War I it became possible to unite Poland. Kurdistan was divided between Iranian and Ottoman Empires, later between four states (like Armenia was divided between Russian and Ottoman Empires). One of the reasons for the 1915 genocide was to prevent a united Armenia. At the end, it could be possible to build an Armenian nation state only at Russian behest.

Actual Arab-İranian-Turkish nationalisms' struggle and big powers struggle in the Middle East make the Kurds a threat now, like Armenians and Assyrians during World War I.

The memory of the Armenian Genocide was forgotten not only in Turkey, but also in the world. It came back, with commemoration of the fiftieth anniversary of "Meds Yeghern" in Yerevan.[7]

Genocide scholarship helped a lot to make memory fresh against forgetfulness, also to illuminate the forgotten events, and to prevent new destruction.

During rare dialogue meetings between Armenians and Turks, some retired Turkish diplomats would ask, "We had to come back from Balkans to Turkey, we forgot, why don't you forget?"

Turkey gained time, for example, to prevent reparations like Germany did. Turkey gained time also for the Kurdish question with denial, accepting them as "Mountaineer Turks."

It is also an Ottoman tradition not to solve the problems, to leave them decomposing. At the end, the Ottoman Empire collapsed like Austrian Empire. If the Republic of Turkey goes on without solving the basic problems, I am afraid it will share the same fate.

BELGE PUBLISHING'S STRUGGLE FOR THE TRUTH AND CONSCIENCE 43 YEARS

Belge Publishing survived after the 1980 military coup d'etat and founded a "sister" publishing named Alan. Alan and Belge focused mostly on transition back to democracy and the alternative history and the literature of the "others" under the title of Marenostrum. Under this title we published forty books from Greek literature,[8] as well as Arab, Armenian, Jewish, Circassian, Assyrian writers.

We began with the Greek writer, Dido Sotiriyu. Her book, *Bloody Earth* (Ματωμένα Χώματα) is published by Alan Publishing in 1982 with the title *Farewell Anatolia*. Belge published an academic book by Mete Tunçay[9] in

---

7   Cf. Aris Nalcı and Serdar Korucu, *50 Years after 1915 and 50 Years before 2015* (first edition 1965, reprinted, Istanbul: Propaganda Publishing, 2015).

8   Osman Bleda translated many Greek books for the Marenostrum series. He was a Circassian, whose family left Caucasus during the Circassian genocide and relocated in Greece. His family came to Aegean region of Turkey after the population exchange in 1920s. Belge also published books about the Circasssians' role in the Ottoman Empire and the Turkish Republic, such as *Circassian Diaspora* by Dr. Arsen Avakian.

9   Prof Dr. Mete Tunçay worked a lot on political thought and methodology of history with translations and collections, he had a pioneering role for writing the history of the Turkish left. He focused also on Balkan nationalism and Armenian revolutionary movement very early. He became a part of the Turkish-Armenian dialog. He was fired from the university after every coup d'etat.

the same year about history of the Turkish left in the early 20s. When we published this book, a violent political cleansing against the left was going on. The political police commissaire shouted at Ayşe Nur Zarakolu, "We destroyed a generation, do you want to raise it again like a ghost!?" Both books were banned and these were in trials at martial law courts. Ayşe was put in Metris Military Jail, but both trials ended with acquittal. Dido Soiriyu won a Turkish and Greek Peace Prize in the same year. She was invited to İstanbul Book Fair as an honoured guest in 1987.

The military junta was also strongly anti-Armenian and created the definition of the "so-called" Armenian Genocide. It also banned the Kurdish language with a special law. Harold Pinter wrote a play about this ban on the mother tongue, with the title *Mountain Language*. The Junta also banned *Encyclopaedia Britannica* and *Encyclopédie Larousse*, because they contained parts about the history of Armenia.

In 1986 the Human Rights Association of Turkey was founded and the discussions about transition to democracy became popular at the end of the 80s. Alan Publishing published Dr. İsmail Beşikçi's[10] challenging book *Interstates Colony Kurdistan* and *Tunceli Law (1935) and Dersim Genoside* in 1990 in Turkish. The last one was the first book in Turkey that accepted the concept of genocide and used it for a fact. The books were immediately banned and the writer and the publisher put in trial at State Security Court. Sociologist Dr. Beşikçi was arrested. Ayşe used universal human rights documents and agreements during her defense. She said, "Genocide is a crime, not to talk about genocide is a crime! And genocide is a crime against the humanity."

Vedat Aydin spoke in Kurdish at the General Congress of HRA, first time in Turkey. He was arrested immediately on October 28, 1990. Vedat Aydın was kidnapped and murdered in July 1991. Tens of thousands of people attended the funeral. Security forces attacked to the people and 6 people died.

Alan Publishing was closed *de facto* after Beşikçi trials and Belge Publishing, which changed its name to Belge International Publishing, went on to publish Dr. Beşikçi's other books and other Kurdish writers with civil disobedience. All of them were banned and put on trial.

A short while later the government accepted the Anti-Terror Law (ATL). The first book banned under the Anti-Terror Law was Dr. Beşikçi's *Republican*

---

10 Ismail Beşikçi had a pioneering role, for the sociology and history of the Kurds. He was fired from the university after the 1971 coup and arrested by military. He was put in jail after 1980 coup and arrested by "civilian" government in the 90s.

Party's 1931 Program and Kurdish Question in July 1991. Ayşe would now be the first publisher who went to prison because of the Anti-Terror Law in 1994.

The government accepted a kind of reform in April 1991 and cancelled famous articles of Turkish Panel Code 141/42 banning the political parties based on class and ethnicity, and Code 163 banning political parties based on religion, particularly political Islam, and also a special law banning the Kurdish language. Eight banned books published by Belge were acquitted.

In 1992 we published the first book about the wealth tax after decades of silence: Ridvan Akar's research, *Wealth-Tax as an Example for Anti-Minorities Policy of One Party System.*

Belge Publishing decided in 1992 to open the curtain on the Armenian Taboo now that it was possible to talk and write about the Kurdish Question. Many Kurdish publishing houses were opened in 1991, though with many bans and trials.

We published Yves Ternon's *The Armenians: History of a Genocide* in 1993. The same year a Turkish scholar, Taner Akçam, published his first book about the "Armenian Question" with the cooperation of the Armenian scholar, Vahakn N. Dadrian. This was a beginning of Armenian-Turkish dialogue about the genocide issue. Taner Akçam has gone on to work thirty years on proofs of the Armenian Genocide based on official documents.

Ternon's book was immediately banned. We received threats and our publishing house was bombed on December 4, 1994. Ayşe was accused of propaganda for terror because of Ternon's book about Armenian Genocide and was convicted to two years in prison. She went to prison for the fourth time in 1996.

Belge published, as a kind of defense, a book by genocide scholar Vahakn N. Dadrian's, *Genocide as a Problem of National and International Law: 1915 Armenian Case and its Contemporary Legal Ramifications,* in 1995. It was also immediately banned with an accusation of agitating Armenians against Turks on a racial basis (Article 312 of the Turkish Panel Code). But we won this trial. The court decided for acquittal, "because there is no threat from Armenians, with their very little population." For us it was indirectly accepting the truth. After this acquittal, it became possible to use the "genocide" concept for the Armenian case, at least until 2004.

In 1994 Human Rights Association founded a special committee on minority rights (later it became the Committee against Racism and Discrimination) and opened the first exhibition about the Istanbul Pogrom of September 6–7, 1955. Belge Publishing published a book on this topic, also about the 1964 extradition of Istanbul Greeks.

ANZ published a report of HRW (in 1996), about the war crimes of the Turkish army during the *de facto* Kurdish War. It was an act against the militarism taboo in Turkey. She was convicted, with an accusation of "defaming the Turkish Army" in 1997, but she was acquitted after her death in 2002 in Strasbourg.

In the same year, German journalist Lissy Schmidt's book, *The Price of Freedom: Interviews from Kurdish Part of Iraq* was published by Belge and banned. She was killed in 1994 in a terror attack in Iraq.

In that same year Belge also decided to open the curtain on the Pontos genocide 1916 and later. We published Georgios Andreadis's books based on oral history. We invited him to Symirna Book Fair as an honorary guest, when the tension between Turkey and Greece was so high. He became very popular at the Black Sea region of Turkey. He was coming to attend a common concert of Greek and Turkish Pontiacs in December 1998, but was stopped at the airport, sent back, and declared persona non grata until his death in December 2015 in Thessaloniki. The officer, who stopped him, asked at the Istanbul airport: "What are you thinking about Abdullah Öcalan (leader of Kurdish Workers' Party)?" His reply was simple: "You must ask the Kurdish people, not me!"

In 1996 we published the books by feminist and minority rights activist Yelda (Özcan), *Diminishing in Istanbul and Diyarbakır* and later *Racism between the Majority Intellectuals* (1998) and *Dialogue is Possible Only after They Left!* (2003). Yelda was also a part of the Armenian-Turkish dialogue. Because of threats she had to leave Turkey and go into exile in 1998.

Belge published Haşim Kutlu's book about *Alewite Identity* in 1997. This book was banned because of a comparison of the 1915 massacre against Armenians and the1998 massacre against Alewiten in Marash region.

Ayşe's last trial was about *Pontos Culture and Dictionary*, prepared by Ömer Asan. She was acquitted in 2003 after her death, but she was convicted the same year because of "banned books" which were confiscated after a raid on the Human Rights Association center in Ankara.

Belge published Swedish scholar David Gaunt's book about the Assyrian Seyfo (Holocaust), *Massacres, Resistance, Protectors: Muslim-Christian Relations in Eastern Anatolia during World War I* in 2007 and was invited as the guest of honor to the Istanbul Book Fair.

Belge also published first books about mixed identities as a cultural heritage in the 1990s, such as *Sabatay Sevi Community* (1998), *Muslim Armenians* (1996), *Muslim Greeks* (1997), and *Muslim Bulgarian Pomaks* (1996) who were always under the pressure of nationalist circles.

Antisemitic trends became stronger during last decades. Belge published books also on Jews in Islam countries and Ottoman Empire (1999) and on the history of antisemitism (1999).

Sabatayist community is also a target of antisemitism in Turkey. For Islamist circles, the founder of Republic of Turkey, Kemal Atatürk was a *dönmeh*.[11] Belge challenged this, by publishing a book, defending this special Sabatayist identity as a part of Jewish identity, "Yes, I am Thessaloniki!" Islamist circles accepted this as a kind of confession and they said: "Look at this! They accepted, they are Jews!"

Our trials following the publication of *12th September Executions with Capital Punishment* (by Hayri Argav, 1997) and *Documents of Hannover Symbolic Tribune against the Junta Government* (ed. Dr. Gazi Çağlar, 2003) ended without any conviction, because of "Turkish Spring." It came to Turkey earlier than "Arab Spring," with the results of 2002 elections: Erdoğan's AKP founded the government. But Belge publishing had new trials just two years after the so called "reform" of the penal code.

Article 159 of the Turkish Penal Code (TPC) was always a problem for journalists and writers and publishers. With new "reformed" article 301, to talk and write about the Armenian Genocide became a problem again. To talk about genocide is accepted as defaming the Turkish nation.

Belge Publishing had to face the Anti-Terror laws, articles 7 and 8, because of the books about Kurdish Question and the Armenian Genocide. Later Belge had to face article 312 of TPC, with an accusation of "racial agitation." And we had to face TPC's article 159 for "defaming the government, president, army, parliament etc." **It became later article 301 with a supplement, "defaming Turkishness." Criticising or to talking about the truth were defined as "defaming." During Erdoğan's eighteen years, "defaming" trials set world records.**

Research based on linguistic rights was labelled "terror" propaganda. Accordingly, Gülçiçek Günel Tekin's book, *Our Language is Our Existence: Our Language is Our Identity* was banned and put on trial 2002. But she went on with new books based on oral history with Belge Publishing, such as *From Unionist Party Today One Polcy: Turkification* (2006); *The Tragedy of Muslimised*

---

11 *Dönmeh* in Turkish means "convert," but it is used only for converted Jews, not converted Christians. The *dönmehs* were believers in Shabtai Tzvi (Sabbatai Zevi), a leader in study of the Kabalah who declared himself a messiah to the Jewish people, but later accepted Islam as his religion when he was forced to a choice between conversion and death.

Armenian Women (2008), *Disappearences and Extrajudicial Killings Beginning from Unionist Party* (2011), and *Kurdish Testimonies about Armenian Genocide* (2013).

In 2004, a new wave of suppression began on the basis of TPC article 301. As responsible editor of Belge International Publishing House I was accused because of three different books. The first book was George Jerjian's *The Truth will Set Us Free: Armenians and Turks Reconciled,* and the second, Dora Sakayan's *An Armenian Doctor in Turkey/Garabed Hatcherian: My Smyrna Ordeal of 1922.* To the second book, another accusation was attached: "defaming the memory of the founder of the Turkish Republic, Kemal Atatürk." The third book was about the Kurdish and Assyrian villages, made empty and burned in 90s. Many of them had the same fate in 1915. This book was written by Zülküf Kışanak and edited by ex-mayor of Diyarbakir, Gülten Kışanak, who is in prison now.

In 2010 I was convicted together with writer N. Mehmet Güler because of a book I published *File of KCK.* Some thousands of Kurdish civil politicians were put in jail in waves of arrests after April 2009.

I think a trial for a book was not enough for growing authoritarianism. In 2011 October I was arrested with an accusation of helping "terror organizations" because I attended the opening ceremony of the Political Science Academy, Legal Peace and Democracy Party. I was released six months later, after international and national campaigns on my behalf, three months before the trial began and the court decided to free me to attend the trial.

In 2016, some months later after the coup attempt on July 15, the judges of the trial and the prosecutor, who wrote the indictment against me, were arrested. Normally this file should then be dismissed, but it was kept waiting under the carpet for possible use if it would be necessary.

Istanbul Heavy Crimes Court decided to arrest me again in June 2018 on the basis of the KCK 2012 trial. In October 2018, the same Court decided to arrest me through the Interpol Red Code just after my Free Word Exhibition about the basic taboos and the history of banned books in Turkey was closed at Frankfurt Book Fair.

On December 23, 2019, the High Court of Sweden refused the demand of Turkey to extradite me. On December 24, 2019 Istanbul Third Heavy Crimes Court decided to confiscate my property and to begin with my pension. I now have only my share of the publishing company of Belge. So next step of the Court might be to confiscate it.

Confiscations of property were a part of genocide and ongoing ethnic cleansing after 1915 in Turkey. Genocide scholar Sait Çetinoğlu defined the wealth/property tax during World War II as "economic genocide." Sait Çetinoğlu is a scholar focused on wealth tax, Pontos genocide, official ideology, and the role of (some) Kurdish tribes in connection with the Armenian Genocide. In 2014 he succeeded in organizing the first international conference about the Armenian Genocide in Ankara.[12]

Belge co-founder, Ayşe Nur Zarakolu, died on January 28, 2002 at the early age of fifty-six years because of cancer, as a result of her imprisonment at Metris Military Prison in 1982. There are some stones and trees planted in her memory in Padua, Milan, and Catania in Italy, at the Giardano Giusti (Garden of the Righteous).

All her life, she worked not only for the truth but also for righteousness. She stood in solidarity with the academics who were fired, writers and journalists in prison or exile, and the families of disappeared people and political prisoners. She helped them with their survival, opened her house, gave them jobs, helped them to leave the country, went voluntarily to help hopeless Kurdish refugees waiting at Iraqi border during the Gulf War. The municipality of Diyarbakır gave her name to a park. But it was cancelled by the government immediately. The Kurdish mayor of Beyazid gave her name to a women's culture and health center at the border of Armenia, looking over Mount Ararat, which was established with the help of Italian municipalities. Mayor Ms. Mukaddes Kubilay is in the prison now and Ayşe Nur Zarakolu Women Health and Culture Center is closed by the government.

FROM MONOLOGUE TO DIALOGUE, FROM DIALOGUE TO A SOLUTION: APOLOGY, FORGIVENESS, AND REPARATION

After a long oblivion, the Armenian Genocide was remembered with a mass rally in Yerevan in 1965 for the fiftieth anniversary of the genocide. It had seemed that events of 1915 already had been forgotten. In 1933, the government of Turkey banned *The Forty Days of Musa Dagh* by Franz Werfel after the book was published in Germany. Ankara achieved the same ban as Germany did by the new Nazi government. After that, in the USA, the film

---

12 Sait Çetinoğlu, Attila Tuygan, Yasemin Gedik, Ahmet Batmaz, Mehmet Ali Varış, Hayati Güngören, and Sena Adalı helped Belge Publishers with editing books about Armenian, Pontos, and Assirian genocides. We are grateful to our courageous translators, including the poet Emirhan Oğuz, Ali Çakıroğlu, Süheyla and Saliha Nazlı Kaya, Yavuz Alogan, Kudret Emiroğlu, Osman Akınhay, Nesrin Oral, Zafer Avşar, Naringül Tateosyan, Suzan Zengin, Diran Lokmagözyan, Zekiye Hasançebi, and others. I am grateful to all of them.

of the book was prevented from being developed as well. Moreover, entry of many books and magazines into peoples' homes had been banned. Clearly, the bans had an influence on obscuring the matter in a complete fog. Now a new stage had begun that banned not only the theme of genocide, but also foreign encyclopedias which mentioned historical Armenia and included maps of Armenia.

Considering there had not been much academic research on the Armenians tragedies until then, in the 1980s there was a wave of publications on what happened in 1915. In addition to the many memoirs of the survivors, the documents concerning the same period were the diaries of Morgenthau, Ambassador of the USA; the *Blue Book* by Toynbee as *The Treatment of Armenians in the Ottoman Empire* by the British Foreign Office; Lepsius, a German clergyman's collection of documents on the period from the archives of Germany Foreign Ministry; and the documents bought by Aram Andonian, an Armenian author and journalist who survived the genocide, from Naim Bey, an Ottoman civil servant at the end of the World War I.

Along with new editions of these works came significant scholarly works by the first generation of scholars, such as Richard G. Hovannisian, Vahakn N. Dadrian, and Arthur Beylerian, one after another. In 1967 the first scholarly work on the foundation of the Republic of Armenia, *Armenia on the Road to Independence*, by Richard Hovanniasin had been published, and in this connection we should also remember Hovannisian's, *Historical Armenian Cities and Territory* (2000–2007), a collection of papers from conferences he organized over the years at UCLA.

The History of the Armenian Genocide: Ethnic Conflict from the Balkans to Anatolia to the Caucasus by Vahakn N. Dadrian (1995) had pride of place as a magnum opus. In addition to his many academic papers, Dadrian's *The Armenian Genocide and the Evidence of German Involvement* (1996), and *Warrant for Genocide* (1999) could be listed as significant contributions.

Non-Armenian historians and historians of genocide, representatives of a new field, began to study that event. The results of their research include *History of the Armenian Genocide* by Yves Ternon (1977), published by Belge Uluslarası Yayincilik in 1993 as *Ermeni Taboosu* in Turkish; *Genocide: Its Political Use in the Twentieth Century* by Leo Kuper (1981), and *The Banality of Denial* by Yair Auron. Within two decades, the new studies that deal with the Armenian Genocide from different perspectives, collections of memoirs, and publication of archival documents led to the information explosion in genocide studies.

Many valuable works which dealt with different aspects have been published by a generation of men of letters, historians, critics, and thinkers such as Gregor Suny, Anahid Ter Minasian, Marc Nishanian, Raymond Kévorkian, Claire Muradian, Stephan Astourian, Ara Sarafian, Rubina Peroomian, Peter Balakian, Dickran Kouymajian, and Richard D. Kloian. Among them, we must cite *Le Genocide des Armeniens* (2006), a voluminous collection by Raymond Kévorkian and *Writers of Disaster* (2006) by Marc Nishanyan in particular. In 1999 Israel Charny edited the first-ever *Encyclopedia of* Genocide. With the leadership of associate editor Rouben Adalian of the Armenian National Committee in the United States, it became the first known encyclopedia to provide extensive coverage of the Armenian Genocide. We should add that these studies not only contained valuable information for Armenian society, but also for regional history and Ottoman society as a whole.

The essential Turkish conduct has been a total denial of the Armenian Genocide. In Turkish universities, there are no departments for genocide studies. Furthermore, there is not one department of Armenian studies, Armenian linguistics and literature, or Armenian history. In fact, the Armenian Genocide is a taboo subject, and this, in turn, prevents genocide studies as well.

In the mid-1970s in Turkey, a young generation of researchers who could make more objective studies were purged during the September 12th military despotism. The remainder of Turkish academics devoted their studies to "refuting" sources such as Morgenthau, the Blue Book, Andonian, and Lepsius that we cited above, not to investigate the facts of 1915. They also made "common cause" with a few Westerner academicians [*denialists –Ed.*] who worked primarily on the Ottoman history with the intention of repeating clichés as "There was no genocidal intention and purpose," "The Armenian revolutionaries revolted and called for armed struggle against the Ottomans," "Armenians betrayed our country," "During the process of forced deportations, perhaps some ill-treatment and uncontrolled events could be seen," and "Armenians exaggerate the numbers of their casualties," and so forth.

Shortly after the Turkish-Armenian Dialogue Collegium in June 2000, the French Senat accepted the Approval Decision of French Parliament about Armenian Genocide. After this approval, the Turkish Government decided that the genocide issue is a national security problem and founded ASIMKK-Struggle Committee Against Baseless Armenian Genocide Claims) as an organ of high National Security Council. Some "civil" organizations were built up, agitating protests against Hrant Dink and *Agos Review*, against writers like Orhan

Pamuk and Elif Şafak, who accepted Armenian Genocide. And a kind of "denial industry" of denial conferences was built up, organising denial conferences at the universities, seminars for teachers and imams, also for guides for tourists(!). Young scholars Ömer E. Turan and Güven Gürkan Öztan made a marvelous study of the mentality of the denial, beginning with founding of Republic until today: *Devlet Aklı ve 1915/Türkiye'de 'Ermeni Meselesi' Anlatısının İnşası* (*Raison d' état and 1915/Construction of Narrative of the "Armenian Question*, İstanbul: İletişim Publishing, 2018).

The Turkish Foreign Ministry sent summaries of some articles and papers delivered in international conferences to the universities in Turkey and asked for researches based on "denial." Under the presidency of ASIMKK by Mr. Devlet Bahçeli, leader of the ultra-nationalist party MHP, the Deputy Prime Minister, representatives of important ministries, General Staff, National Intelligence Agency (MIT) took part in this committee. In this context, official denial statements began to replace silence policy in textbooks; and some seminars arranged for training of teachers and civil servants.

In 1990, Turgut Ozal wanted to soften the government's attitude on the Armenian question, and invited Profs. Vahakn N. Dadrian and Levon Marashlian, two Armenian scientists to the XI. Turkish History Congress organized by the Turkish Historical Society. Levon Marashlian submitted a paper titled "Turkish-American Relations, the Armenian Question" to the congress. (This paper was published by Belge Publishers. See Levon Maraşlıyan, *Ermeni Sorunu ve Türk-Amerikan İlişkileri: 1919–1923*, trans. Şen Süer, 2000.)

In 1993, we see three important developments regarding Armenian-Turkish dialogue. While Taner Akçam has published his book entitled *Armenian Question and Turkish Identity* (*Ermeni Sorunu ve Türk Kimliği*), Belge Publishers published *History of the Armenian Genocide*, which published under the title *Armenian Taboo* in Turkish; so for the first time a book defining 1915 events as a "genocide" was presented to the Turkish reader. Indeed, it heralded the beginning of a dialog in the academic field; and an academic dialogue between Taner Akçam and Vahakn. N Dadrian. It was, in a sense, the first honest and sound bridge.

In that year, *Le Monde* published an article by Bernard Lewis, which maintained that the events of 1915 could not be defined as genocide. Lewis repeated official Turkish arguments when he said, "There is not any valid evidence that shows that the Ottoman Empire had a plan aimed at mass annihilation of the Armenian nation. Turks had legitimate causes for deportation; because

Armenians were fighting against the Turks as an ally of Russia which occupied Turkish territory."[13]

In Paris and in Istanbul, two parallel trials had taken place; while the former was based on denial, the latter was based on acceptance of the Armenian Genocide. Consequently, Lewis was fined a symbolic one frank, and ANZ was sentenced to two years in prison for violation of the paragraph 8 of Anti-Terror Law.

In 1995, *Genocide as a Problem of National and International Law: The World War I Armenian Case and Its Contemporary Legal Ramifications*, by Prof. Dr. Vahakn N. Dadrian, was published by Yale University and was immediately banned. However, the defendants were acquitted in 1997, and for the first time, the door was half-opened for publishing books on the Armenian Genocide.

In 1995, I went to Paris for a meeting with Yves Ternon regarding the Ternon Case because State Security Court had described Ternon as a "non-person." According to the court, "the author" of the book was the publisher. Ayşe Nur Zarakolu's sentence, cited above, was based on this evidence.

The Turkish Human Right Organization had been a member of the Paris-based International Human Rights Federation (FIDH). One of fundamental questions was whether or not İHD (HRO) was accepting the reality of genocide. When we answered the question we remind them our Ternon and Dadrian cases, thus our answer removed the last obstacle to membership. Later, for the sake of objectivity, FIDH sent Bernard Baudelot, former head of the bar in Paris as an observer for the Ternon case. He later published a report on the cases of ANZ.

In a sense, this case half-opened the doors for civil Turkish-Armenian dialog. At that moment, the Armenian State had not accepted the "genocide" matter as a precondition for normalization of Turkish-Armenian relations, and because of her attitude was criticized by the Diaspora Armenians. In 1995, in a conference in Paris, organized by UGAP, a reporter of *Haratch* newspaper asked me a question on Armenia's official attitude about not voicing the concept of "genocide." I said I was a human rights activist fighting for acceptance of the genocide in my own country but I had no right to judge Armenia's policy. I should add that Turkish-Armenian relations were very important for regional peace, and I understood the difficulties of Armenia.

---

13 I am pleased to add that, together with Yves Ternon, I appeared as an expert witness against Lewis. I could not resist the kitsch and I said: "As a Jew and a professor I am deeply ashamed of Prof. Lewis." We won the trial.—Ed.

On April 24, 1996, Commemoration Committee in Paris invited me to UNESCO building to give a speech at the commemorative ceremony. I think I was the first speaker from Turkey who had no worry about using the term "genocide" in an April 24 meeting.

We have seen some semiofficial efforts as well to address Turkish denial. In 2001 an attempt at a semi-official dialog between Turkish and Armenian parties within the framework of TARC—the Turkish Armenian Reconciliation Commission—began under increasing pressure of the United States. One of the aims of the Bush administration was to ease the pressures from the US Senate on a bill to recognize the Genocide. Two Armenian members of TARC were from Armenia, one from Russia, and another from the United States. The head of the committee, adviser David L. Phillips, was from the US State Department. Phillips, who was also a lecturer in the University of America at Washington, later gave the background of these meetings and inner debates in his book, *Unsilencing the Past: Track Two Diplomacy and Turkish-Armenian Reconciliation* (2005). The committee was met by many protests of members of the Armenian community in the United States, who felt that one does not agree to Turkish demands to investigate what really happened as if it is unknown and whether there really was a genocide. Turkish representatives of the committee changed continuously.

The committee decided to apply for the judgment of an expert organization on the nature of the 1915 events, the ICTJ—International Center of Transitional Justice—which has its headquarters in New York. The report submitted by the ICTJ hardly satisfied the Turkish side: The judgment was that the event of 1915 ***could be described as genocide*** in international understanding. The only consolation for Turkish side was that this judgment had no legal conclusion because the event had happened before 1948, the approval date of the United Nations Convention of Genocide. The Turks promptly abandoned TARC.

Turkish official history circles often complain that the international academicians treat them with indifference; even some official statements can be heard such as "Historians should come together!" However, despite all protests of Armenian community, an Armenian historian, Ara Sarafian, accepted to work with Halaçoğlu, head of Turkish Historian Society in a research project, but it was all to no avail. Swedish historian David Gaunt's common research project with Halaçoğlu had no practical application as well.

In May 2002, the Institute of Genocide and Holocaust Research/Studies of University of Copenhagen hosted one of the most interesting conferences which participants were two parties—"the Armenian Genocide and Its Denial." Participants of the meeting were genocide scholars such as Vahakn N. Dadrian, Richard G. Hovannisian, Wolfgang Gust, Helene Pirelian, Tessa Hofmann, Elazar Barkan, Eric Markusen, and also Nicolas Tavitian from European Armenian Federation. Gündüz Aktan, retired ambassador, and now deputy of Nationalist Movement Party (MHP), a member of TARC founded by pressures from the USA to the Turkish side; a few deputies of Turkish Grand National Assembly such as Bülent Akarcalı and Bayram Fırat Dayanıklı; and retired diplomat Pulat Tacar were representing the Turkish side. In Turkey, before leaving for the meeting, Bülent Akarcalı made a statement in a news conference, and said that the meeting was not impartial; participation of Turkish intellectuals such as Ragıp Zarakolu, Taner Akçam (who only sent his paper), and Ümit Necef, lecturer in University of Copenhagen, should be criticized because of their political past.

In the island of San Giorgio Maguire in Venice, the Institute of Venice and Europe organized a conference titled "Armenians and Turks: Relationship of One Thousand Years" in October 2004. The participants of the conference were: from the United States, Taner Akçam (University of Minnesota) and Rouben Adalian (Armenian Assembly of America); from Canada, Frank Chalk (Montreal Institute of Genocid and Liberal Research); from France, Raymond H. Kévorkian (Director of Paris Noubarian Library), Héléne Piralian-Simonyan (psychoanalyst), and Yves Ternon (doctor and historian); from Germany, Hermann Goltz (Halle-Wittenberg University Director of Lepsius Archives); from Israel, Israel Charny (Director of the Institute of the Holocaust and Genocide in Jerusalem, Hebrew University of Jerusalem);[14] from Turkey, Murat Belge (Bilgi University), Ferhat Kentel (Bilgi University), Halil Berktay (Sabanci University), Baskin Oran (Ankara University, Faculty of Political Sciences—SBF), and Ragip Zarakolu (writer and publisher, Belge International Publishing); from Armenia, Vladimir Margarian (jurist, judge of Constitutional Court) and Ruben Safrastyan (National Sciences Academy, Director of Institute of Turkology); from Italy, Antonia Arslan (University of Padua), Giampiero Bellingeri (University of Ca' Foscari in Venice), Mauro Bussani (University of Trieste), Aldo Ferrari (ISPI director of Research Program for Caucasus and Asia, former lecturer in the universities of Milano, Trieste, Gorizia and Venice), Gianclaudio

---

14 I am particularly pleased to recall the solution I offered all Turks and Israelis who wished to refer to the Armenian Genocide or Holocaust. I suggested the Turks use the Hebrew words for these events, and we Hebraists would use the Turkish words—and then none of us would be "hung" back in our countries.—Ed.

Macchiarella (University of Ca' Foscari, former Italian attaché of culture in embassies to Washington, Athens, Tehran and Ankara), and Pier Paolo Portinaro (University of Torino). Participants of the academic council of the conference were Prof. Antonio Rigo (University of Ca' Foscari, Director of the Institute of Venice and Europe of Cini Foundation) and Prof. Boghos Levon Zekiyan (University of Ca' Foscari).

A conference on "Ottoman Armenians," which was prevented in May, was arranged in September 2005 in Bilgi University, and then Istanbul University organized another conference based on official view, but this time some scientists who acknowledged the fact of genocide were invited to present their papers. The same happened in March 2006, at the conference on "New Approaches in the Turkish-Armenian Relations." The scholars who presented their views in addition to official denial approach were Profs. Levon Zekiyan, Israel Charny, Habib Afram, Yair Auron, and Ara Sarafian and Hilmar Kaiser.[15]

Let me make mention of the Fifth WATS—Workshop of Armenian and Turkish Scientists. The workshop's title was "Limits of Genocide: Purposes, Histories and the People." The meeting began with an open gathering titled "Where Are We Now?" The workshop presided by Gregor Suny (University of Michigan, Ann Arbor), Müge Göcek (University of Michigan, Ann Arbor), and Gerard Libaridian (University of Michigan, Ann Arbor). Other participants who made speeches or participated in debates were: Fuat Dündar, Paul Boghosian (NYU), Fikret Adanır (Ruhr-Universität Bochum), David Gaunt (Södertörn University College, Stockholm), Uğur U. Üngör (University of Amsterdam), Rober Toptaş (Bogazici University, Istanbul), Charles Ingrao (Purdue University), Stephen Feinstein (University of Minnesota), John Torpey (CUNY Graduate Center), Elazar Barkan (Columbia University), Nazan Maksudyan (Sabancı University, Istanbul), Ani Değirmencioğlu (Sabancı University, Istanbul), Khatchig Muradian (Haigazian University, Beirut), Razmik Panossian (Rights and Democracy, Canada), Donald Bloxham (University of Edinburgh), Marcello Flores (University of Siena), Eric Weitz (University of Minnesota), Katherine Fleming (New York University), Mark Mazower

---

15 Yes, a few of us foreign participants, among hundreds of attendees, declared there was an Armenian Genocide! Yair Auron, my close colleague in Israel, won a vivid newspaper display of his declaration! These were the heady days when Turkey was making an extra effort to be accepted in the European Union. Alas, these days have gone—resolutely. Moreover, we should note the conference took place in the months preceding the murder of Turkish-Armenian journalist Harant Dink. He too had been scheduled to be part of our small dissident group but he never turned up and we never knew why.—Ed.

(Columbia University), Speros Vryonis Jr. (emeritus, Columbia University), and Ragıp Zarakolu. Main subject-matters were: "What is Genocide?," "Dimensions of the Event," "The Process," "Scientists' Initiatives: The Case of Yugoslavia," "Aftermath: Telling the Story of the Past," "The Genocide: In International and Comparative Perspective, by Donald Bloxham," "On the Last Book on September 6–7, 1955, *Istanbul Pogrom* by Byzantium Historian Speros Vryonis Jr."

This denialist campaign reached its culmination with the murder of Hrant Dink on January 19, 2007. Paradoxically, it became a breaking point, after which denialism collapsed *de facto*. To accept the Armenian Genocide became a measure of being a real intellectual in Turkey. The mass funeral of Hrant Dink gave courage to democratic resistance in Turkey. The Foundation of Hrant Dink became most important institution for research about the Armenian reality with all its aspects. April 24 commemorations, which began first in Istanbul in 1919, came back to Istanbul and became also a ritual in Turkey. The President of Turkey also declared a condolence message for April 24, although, for sure, without mentioning the concept "genocide."

THE ARMENIAN GENOCIDE AS A CASE OF PREVENTING SELF-DETERMINATION

The official attitude on the Armenian Genocide and the systematic practice of ethnic cleansing in Anatolia has reached a new stage with the statement by Vecdi Gonul, the former Turkish minister of national defense, to the effect that had these tragic events not occurred, the present-day Republic of Turkey could not have come into being. Repulsive as these words may be, we have to admit that they are much more honest than pure "denial," and imply "admission" of what really happened.

However, that these tragedies should be presented as necessary, even indispensible, for the "building of a nation-state," accompanied by a "take it or leave it" kind of challenge, also comprises an implicit element of "threat": "We've done it before, so you'd better watch out or we'll do it again!"

In this context, I would like to draw attention to two books, both of which facilitate the study and comprehension of the Armenian Genocide, relating to the national question and the exercise of the right to self-determination: Vahakn N. Dadrian's magnum opus, *The History of the Armenian Genocide: Ethnic Conflict from the Balkans to Anatolia to the Caucasus* (published in Turkish under the title *Ermeni Soykirimi Tarihi/Balkanlardan Anadolu ve Kafkasya'ya Etnik Catisma* by Belge Publishers in 2008), and *The Turks and Us* by Shahan Natalie, famous for "Operation Nemesis" (the book was published in Turkish under the title *Biz Ermeniler ve Turkler* by Peri Yayinlari, again in 2008). These books provide an opportunity to understand not only 1915 alone, but the period before and after as well. Shahan Natalie's observation, "The Turks succeeded in building a nation" is interesting, provided one pose the question, "at what cost?"

In studying the Armenian tragedy of 1915, it would be useful, if one wishes to understand the question better, to look at the question from the perspective of "nation-building," "self-determination," and the fundamental articles of the Genocide Convention.

In the wake of the 1908 revolution, an attempt at a democratic revolution that nonetheless was going to stop halfway, the political leaders and the organizations of the Armenian people opted for "coexistence." They established political alliances with Ottoman parties and ran in elections on common lists. However, the fragility of projects for a common future in the Ottoman political arena and the impossibility of making these a reality summoned, once again, the old problems.

This was the period of nation-building, of building unitary states whatever the cost may be. Some Armenian intellectuals adopted a friendly attitude to the approach of the Turk Ocaklari (the Turkish Hearths), aiming at nation-building. The great musician Gomidas tried, for instance, to support a national identity through music, as he believed that separate identities could coexist. Up until that accursed year of 1914. Yet, in a multinational empire where geographic cohabitation was the rule, the formation of a unitary national state could only be predicated upon campaigns of ethnic cleansing. And for the defense of the right to self-determination and separation, one had to have a certain proportion within the population, a majority.

The country was ravaged by an economic crisis as a result of the Balkan wars and the government was bankrupt. For its part, the great Ottoman Army, which had recently been modernized, had suffered a humiliating defeat at the hands of the newly formed Balkan states, which had taken aback even the West. The fact that the Albanians, one of the most loyal subjects of the Sultan, had, for the first time, overcome their religious division to rise in revolt, had given these small states the possibility of joining forces and the courage to make a move.

The Committee of Union and Progress (CUP) entrusted the task of reorganizing the devastated Ottoman Army to the Germans, and by starting a ruthless policy of violence in the military tried to establish a discipline akin to

Prussian methods. The CUP entered World War I under the command of German militarism. It is a fact that Armenian leaders tried to talk the CUP leaders out of this orientation because this was bound to put the Armenian people in a difficult situation.

Significant forces of the Ottoman Army were decimated under harsh winter conditions on the Allahuekber Mountains as a result of a campaign under the command of none other than Enver Pasha himself. The only method to prevent the formation of an Armenian state was to cleanse this people from its historic territory. This meant the deportation of an entire people, including women, the elderly, and children, who were to be put on an exile journey headed towards the Syrian desert. The excuse provided for this forced exile was "Armenian revolutionaries"; in other words, it was the "revolutionaries" who were held responsible for what happened to their own people. It is of interest to note that the official explanation provided for the entire world in 1916 has to this very day formed the overall substance of how Turkey defends itself.

It is, of course, true that some Armenian organizations had their partisan groups, and these did stage actions against Turkey. But, contrary to what the official view has claimed to this day, **this can never legitimize the wholesale annihilation of civilians**. Today, even insurgent forces, let alone civilians, have rights and a status within the framework of the Geneva Conventions on war.

On the other hand, we know of the existence of Armenian soldiers and officers who served in the Ottoman Army up to the end of the war or died in Gallipoli or the Allahuekber Mountains. So much so that, on his return to Istanbul after the debacle, Enver Pasha published a statement praising the heroism of Armenian soldiers.

The accusation leveled at an entire people for "treason" on the basis of the actions of certain groups and the forcible deportation of this people in a manner that would necessarily destroy it cannot be understood without the logic of ethnic cleansing that lies behind them. Nation building is the process that creates the highest number of victims in this world. It is also the creation of a single identity in a melting pot, a fictional thing. The suffering, the exile, and the massacres experienced during the formation of the nation-states of the Balkans are testimony to this. In a certain sense, it was the Armenian people that paid dearly the cost of this whole process in the Balkans. It was the last level of ethnic cleansing that was genocide on the Ottoman part of Armenia.

The CUP method of solving the Armenian question was, within the confines of its own logic, successful. And it also paved the way for the foundation of the Turkish nation-state. To an ambassador who was still talking about the

Armenian question in 1916, Talat Pasha's answer was "no longer does there exist such a question."[16] One wonders whether this was a method based on intuition against the right to self-determination, or if the lessons of the Balkans and the massacres practiced by German imperialism in West Africa served as a model.

From the military point of view, the Armenian deportation can only be characterized as an "excellent" operation. When you look at the maps displaying the routes of forcible migration, you can sense the contribution of Prussian militarism in the preparation of these plans. Given their debacle in the Balkans, it seems hardly credible that the CUP adventurers would be able to execute such an operation all on their own.

One really wonders to what extent the experience of the atrocities perpetrated by the German colonial army in West Africa had its impact on all this. Is it pure coincidence that many German officers who were commanders in the Ottoman Army later took part in the early organization drive of fascism in Germany and participated in the 1923 Beer Hall Putsch of Hitler?

The German military could have stopped the deportation, had they so willed. On the contrary, in the military operations in Zeytun, Urfa, and Van, where the Armenians put up a partial resistance, German soldiers actively participated, let alone prevented what was happening.

But the depopulation of this territory was in line with the wishes of many colonial powers. The German right wanted Anatolia to be opened up for German settlement in the future. (Cf. Lothar Rathmann, *Die imperialistische Nahostpolitik des kaiserlichen Deutschlands* [Berlin: Dietz Verlag, 1962].)

For its part, when in 1916 the Russian tsar took hold of eastern Anatolia, he decided to settle Cossacks in the region to replace the surviving Armenians, which, of course, created great consternation among Armenian intellectuals. Also, the tsar was very anxious about Armenian voluntary brigades, because of the role of the ARF during the 1905 revolution. He ordered liquidation of this brigades and distributed them between regular Russian army.[17] And there was no priority for the tsar's army to save the Armenian people from the massacre.

Armen Garo (Karekin Pastermajian) was the hero of Ottoman Bank Occupation 1896, later MP of Erzurum/Garin at Ottoman Parliament. He was one of the negotiators of "Armenian Reform" with the CUP government. During

---

16 Cf. Henry Morgenthau, *Büyükelçi Morgenthau Anlatıyor* [*Ambassador Morgenthau's Story*] (Istanbul: Belge Publishers, 2005).

17 Cf. Simon Vratsian, *Tempest-Born DRO* (New York: n.p., book is offered by Amazon in the category of books in Armenian, 2000).

harsh discussions, Armen Garo told Prime minister Talat Pasha, "I understand, you will destroy us, and you are dreaming a federation with Arabians, because you can't assimilate them. And you are dreaming to assimilate the Kurds. You can't do it. They are native people of the region. Since Xenophon nobody succeeded to assimilate them."[18]

Had there been no Soviet Revolution, Armenia would not have come into existence. Furthermore, it would then have been very difficult for a state like Turkey to come into being. It is not the slightest irony of history that the same revolution of 1917, the new international balance of forces, and what it brought in its wake, made it possible for these two states, which do not recognize each other officially, to exist.

CONCLUSION

If you look into the UN Genocide Convention, you are bound to see that all the fundamental elements find their place in the Armenian case. The policies of the CUP were reminiscent of those of a proto-fascist party. In other words, this was a case of fascism *avant la lettre*. Precisely in the same way as the de facto occurrence of genocide in 1915, even before the concept "genocide" itself had come into circulation.

The end result is that the Anatolian region has lost its Armenian sons and daughters. The ethnic cleansing operation later reached out towards the eradication of historic buildings and even cemeteries. How could a people that did not exist, that even left no trace behind it, reclaim its rights? In the final analysis, the material basis for the exercise of the right to self-determination for the Armenian people was destroyed. It was not for nothing that Hitler, on the eve of the attack on Poland in 1939, asked at a meeting, "Who remembers the Armenian people nowadays?"[19]

EPILOGUE

When we decided to publish books about Armenian Genocide in 1993, the reason was not only to talk about the truth, but also to prevent a new genocide.

---

18 Cf. Armen Garo, *Bank Ottoman, Memoirs of Armen Garo, the Armenian Ambassador to Armenia* (Michigan: Armen Topouzian, 1990). Turkish edition: Armen Garo, *Osmanli Bonakasi* (Istanbul: Belge International Publishing, 2009).

19 Cf. Kevork Bardakjian, *Hitler and Armenian Genocide* (Cambridge, MA: Zoryan Institute, 1985).

There was a growing disaster, not only in Bosnia but also in the Kurdish part of Turkey, in these years. We, human rights activists, defined this period (1993–1995) as a "dirty war." 3.5 million Kurds had to leave their home regions in that period, and nearly 4,000 Kurdish villagers were forced to leave. Their settlements were destroyed and burned. We discussed this fact at the Habitat Conference in Istanbul in 1996 and made a detailed map, showing the places of destroyed Kurdish villages.[20]

Had there been no Soviet Revolution, Armenia would not have come into existence- Just as well, it would then have been very difficult for a state like The Turkish Republic under the new world situation after World War I. I defined this period as "annus horribilis" during the UN World Human Rights Conference in Vienna June 1993 and at the Mediterranean NGO's Conference in Cairo 1994. I came together with editor of *Oslobođenje* newspaper, going on under terrible siege conditions. And I was writing a column for *Özgür Gündem* newspaper in İstanbul. Like *Oslobođenje* staff, the *Özgür Gündem* team and I were from different roots. We were talking not only about democratization and the peaceful solution of the Kurdish question, but also about the Armenian Genocide. The building of *Özgür Gündem* was bombed on the same day as our Belge International Publishing and the office of the Kurdish newspaper *Welat* (the only Kurdish newspaper in Kurdish and Zaza language) in December 1994.

And this time, a new disaster period came back now not only to Turkey but also to Syria and Iraq. The children and grandchildren of the survivors of the 1915 genocide were under the threat of annihilation. And a new genocide could be possible for Yazidi people. Turkey began ethnic cleansing against the Kurds in Syria. The Kurdish homeland, Afrin, and the famous Kurdish mountains were invaded.

The Kurdish people are now in the same situation in the Armenian people were: they are under the threat of ethnic cleansing, "relocation," and genocide. They had it partly during Iraq/Iran war of 1980–1988 with the Anfal operation and Halapja chemical attack. Erdoğan's government wants to use Syrian refugees not only to blackmail the European Union, but also to change the Kurdish population ratio and, especially, that of the Kurdish-Alewiten. There is a "relocation" of Syrian refugees is going on, especially in the Kurdish-Alewiten regions. We can compare this "relocation" of Balkan and Caucasian refugees

---

20 Cf. Ragıp Zarakolu, *Bir Ülkeye Ağıt* [*Elegy for a Country/Diary of Year 1992*] (İstanbul: Belge International Publishing, 2002); Ragıp Zarakolu, *Bir Kadına Ağıt* [*Elegy for a Disappeared Woman/Diary of Year 1993*] (İstanbul: Belge International Publishing, 2003).

towards Armenian and Kurdish regions in the nineteenth and early twentieth centuries. Hate-speech has become a part of daily life as have anti-semitism, anti-Alewiten, anti-Kurdish or anti-Armenian, etc.

The Unionist party's ideology was based on the synthesis of Islam and Turkish nationalism. Their slogan was "Türkiye Türklerindir"—"Turkey is owned by Turks (only)." And this ideology has the power now, with the alliance between Erdoğan and Bahçeli, defined as Cumhur İttifakı (Congregation Alliance).

A political cleansing is going on: selected mayors, municipality and city council members and local staff of HDP are arrested. It is a kind of punishment for their political success at general and local elections. The presidential candidate of HDP, Selahattin Demirtaş, is in the prison. So is the righteous businessman Osman Kavala, who supported Armenian-Turkish dialogue and fought for a peaceful solution of Kurdish Question. Many human activists are in jail and in trial. Turkey has the world record for the number of journalists in prison.

The leaders of Unionist Party, Talat Pasha and others were put on trial in Istanbul and convicted. Unfortunately, the winner of the World War did not do their promise, during the genocide of 1915, to put them on trial because of their crimes "against the humanity."

Impunity gave always courage for crimes against the humanity, not only on a national level but also on an international level. My country Turkey can be successful to be a real democratic country only after it decides to face history, only after an apology and being prepared for reparation.

CHAPTER 8

A Contemporary Armenian: Richard G. Hovannisian— The Armenian Genocide and Extreme Denial

Figure 12.

EDITOR'S INTRODUCTION

R ichard G. Hovannisian is professor emeritus of Armenian and Near Eastern History and was the associate director of the G. E. von Grunebaum Center for Near Eastern Studies at the University of California, Los Angeles. He is currently also presidential fellow at Chapman University and is affiliated there with the Rodgers Center for Holocaust Education.

Professor Hovannisian is the author of numerous scholarly works, including the four-volume series *Armenia on the Road to Independence; The Republic of Armenia; Looking Backward, Moving Forward: Confronting the Armenian Genocide; The Armenian Genocide: Cultural and Ethical Legacies; The Armenian Genocide in Perspective.*

This chapter continues with excerpts from the volume edited by Prof. Hovannisian in which he published many of the papers that had been presented during the First International Conference on the Holocaust and Genocide in 1982: Richard G. Hovannisian, ed., *The Armenian Genocide in Perspective,* introduction by Terrence Des Pres, preface by Israel W. Charny (New Brunswick, NJ: Transaction Publishers, 1986).

Hovannisian, of course, celebrates the success of the conference in standing up to the pressures to close it down by the Turkish and Israeli governments. He writes about these papers that they "were delivered under the heavy shadow of intimidation."

> Yet in spite of the pressure to exclude discussion of the Armenian Genocide or else cancel the conference, people of good conscience prevailed, refusing to put political considerations above moral and humanitarian imperatives. It was because of such people that the Tel Aviv conference became reality. ... The anthology may be viewed as an attempt to address a few of the complex issues relating to the Armenian Genocide and its manifold consequences. It may provide answers to some questions regarding the Armenian past and, it is hoped, it will be of use to those dedicated to the prevention and punishment of the crime of genocide.[1]

In the Foreword of the book, Hovannisian noted at the time that although hundreds of *descriptive* articles and books were written about the Armenian Genocide,

---

1   Richard G. Hovannisian, *The Armenian Genocide in Perspective,* 2–3.

scholarly study of the subject is only just beginning. This may be explained in part by the fact that for years the exile survivor generation concentrated its energies on adapting to new environments, rescuing and caring for family members who had somehow stayed alive and organization of schools and churches to perpetuate, as well as possible, a national cultural heritage in diverse and often alien surroundings.[2]

As Yale University's Terrence Des Pres writes in his introduction to the book,

> The conference took place as planned, which speaks well for intellectual courage, but the point to keep in mind is that political interests were mobilized against an academic conference. It was a gathering of scholars, nothing less and nothing more, learned men and women convening to pursue understanding. ... The role of scholars counts more than we might have supposed. I do not refer to those among us busy revising the historical record, but rather to the kind of men and women who, against some very ugly pressures, went ahead with the Tel Aviv conference ...
>
> What is now wanted is victory over denial ... for a people to possess the dignity of their own tragic past becomes sufficient ground for renewal, for turning with new heart to carry on with life. To this decency the authors of the present volume contribute.[3]

The excerpt that will be included shortly is from Richard Hovannisian's own chapter, "The Armenian Genocide and Patterns of Denial." However, we should also take note of the fact that the volume as a whole is devoted to a significant selection of papers on the Armenian Genocide that were presented at the conference including "The Turkish Genocide of Armenians 1915–1917," by Leo Kuper; "Provocation or Nationalism: A Critical Inquiry into the Armenian Genocide of 1915," by Robert Melson; "Determinants of Genocide: Armenians and Jews as Case Studies," by R. Hrair Dekmejian; "What Genocide? What Holocaust? News from Turkey, 1915–1923: A Case Study," by Marjorie Housepian Dobkin; "Collective Responsibility and Official Excuse-Making: The Case of the Turkish Genocide of the Armenians," by Vigen Guroian; "The Armenian

---

2 Ibid., 1.
3 Terrence Des Pres, "Remembering Armenia," Introduction to Richard G. Hovannisian, *The Armenian Genocide in Perspective*, 9–17 (quotations from ibid., 13, 17).

Genocide and the Literary Imagination," by Leo Hamalian; "The Impact on West Armenian Letters," by Vahé Oshagen; "Psychosocial Sequelae of the Armenian Genocide," by Boyajain and Hagaz Grigorian; and, finally, "An Oral History Perspective on Responses to the Armenian Genocide," by Donald E. Miller and Lorna Touryan Miller. As Hovannisian notes, there were also papers by Vahakn Dadrian, Alen Salerian, and Avedis Sanjian at the conference but the authors did not submit these for publication. **The above selection represents the scholarship and contributions that the Turkish government and the Israeli government were conspiring—indeed, demanding with nasty power tactics—to suppress and censor!**

Hovannisian is very aware of the massive extent and considerable impact of denials of the Armenian Genocide. He noted that at some point the Armenian Genocide was on the verge of becoming a victim of such massive denial that it was developing into being a trivial historical item whose time and significance had passed:

> The Republic of Turkey has repeatedly impressed on other governments and international bodies that dwelling on a complex but no longer relevant past is unproductive, disruptive, and antagonistic. Yet the problem has persisted and the tone and tenor of the denials are more forceful than ever before. The Turkish position severely disrupts investigation of the Genocide, its causes, effects, and implications, and the scholarly and humanitarian ends to which such studies should be directed.[4]

Hovannisian goes on to produce a masterful review of the predominance of the denial narrative, including by bona fide prominent academics. In this connection, I remember being shocked while having lunch with him at the UCLA Faculty Club when he invited me to accompany him to go over to meet one of the truly nefarious academic deniers of the Armenian Genocide, Stanford Shaw, who has contended "that official Turkish records show no evidence of a genocide policy."[5] The conversation between them was entirely well-mannered, and to this day I am not sure how I feel about that.

The richly detailed but clearly written survey of denials of the Armenian Genocide goes on to track the history of denials with a strong emphasis on

---

4   Richard G. Hovannisian, *The Armenian Genocide in Perspective*, 130.
5   The Stanford Shaw quotation is from Jay Mathews, "Armenian Terrorism," *Washington Post*, May 17, 1982.

the propaganda of the Republic of Turkey over the years. Hovannisian also tells the intriguing and shameful tale of MGM's plan to create a film based on Franz Werfel's stunning account of *The Forty Days of Musa Dagh*[6] and how the United States capitulated to Turkish pressures and brought about cancellation of the project.

The second part of this chapter brings excerpts from a very significant pamphlet by Richard G. Hovannisian published by MacQuarie University, Sydney, Australia. This 1996 pamphlet is entitled, "Denial of the Armenian Genocide with Some Comparisons to Holocaust Denial." It was delivered as the inaugural Armenian Genocide commemorative lecture at Macquarie University on April 28, 1995.[7]

Hovannisian's writing throughout is remarkably clear and easy to understand. We get from him a variety of "verbal photographs" in which we can see up close the workings of distortion, motivated propaganda, manipulation, and outright lying, including by our fellow PhD scholars, let alone by power-seeking political fascists who are not at all averse to changing truth to fit their needs and desires. Hovannisian offers a powerful projection of how the Holocaust would look if the same success had marked the efforts of deniers of the Holocaust. Regarding comparison of the Armenian Genocide to the Holocaust, he wisely identifies many points for comparisons between the techniques of denials. To his credit he does his analysis without in any way succumbing to the competitiveness as to which people have been manipulated and suffered more. Throughout one experiences a fully grounded caring for all human life, even as this author, a committed and sensitive Armenian, of course is drawn first of all to the suffering of his people—something natural for all of us and the necessary basis for the next step in one's psychological development to care about all human lives.

The reader should note that there is much more in the original pamphlet that we do not include in these excerpts, including sections on the following topics:

- The Question of Intent: Rationalization and Relativisation
- Numbers

---

6   Franz Werfel, *The Forty Days of Musa Dagh* (New York: Viking, 1934, reprinted, Boston, MA: Verba Mundi Books, 2012).

7   Richard G. Hovannisian, *Denial of the Armenian Genocide with Some Comparisons to Holocaust Denial*, Inaugural Armenian Genocide Commemorative Lecture, Macquarie University, Sydney, Australia, April 28, 1995 (Sydney: Macquarie University Centre for Comparative Genocide Studies, 1996).

- The Trials of War Criminals
- Academic Freedom and Warriors for Truth
- Trivialization

In sum, the excerpts that follow are from two earlier classic publications by Richard Hovannisian. The first one is taken from the papers presented at the First International Conference on the Holocaust and Genocide in 1982 that were then published by him in 1986, and the second is from Hovannisian's Inaugural Armenian Genocide Commemorative Lecture at the outstanding Centre for Comparative Genocide Studies at Macquarie University, Sydney, in 1995 that the beloved late Professor Colin Tatz stewarded for some years.

We have asked Professor Hovannisian to offer us at this time a concluding perspective on the extent to which the 1982 conference contributed to the battle against denials of the Armenian Genocide and to the emergence of new scholarship.

PERSPECTIVE: RICHARD HOVANNISIAN LOOKS BACK IN 2020 AT THE 1982 CONFERENCE

The 1982 Tel Aviv International Conference on the Holocaust and Genocide was in many ways a watershed in helping to stimulate insightful comparative analyses of the causes and effects of intentional mass destruction. I had been drawn to this troublesome topic by sustained and increasingly sophisticated denial of the Armenian Genocide.

I did not set out to be a genocide scholar, but when one of my colleagues in the History Department of UCLA published a two-volume unabashed denialist work under the auspices of Cambridge University Press in the 1970s, I was compelled by the obligation to respond. Even though my main field of research and publication was the emergence of an Armenian republic at the end of World War I, the matter of genocide was not an entirely novel subject for me. I had already initiated an oral history course at UCLA to record the voices and marshal the testimonies of the rapidly dwindling survivors of the Armenian Genocide, most of them children in 1915 and now already in their sixties, seventies, and eighties. The focus was not on denial but rather on preserving as much as possible their daily lifestyle before the great calamity, their experiences during the deportations and massacres, and their odyssey of ultimate survival and rescue. Collectively, these tape-recorded interviews, now housed in the Shoah Foundation's Archives (at the University of Southern California), became an important source for allowing the victims to bear witness. In addition to this connection with the Armenian Genocide, I was asked by my late colleague and dedicated humanitarian, Leo Kuper, to join with him in submitting a proposal to the UCLA "Experimental College" to introduce an undergraduate course on comparative genocide. This pilot course was soon integrated into the multi-disciplinary Honors Program, and I continued to direct it until my retirement from classroom instruction at UCLA in 2015.

As for the Tel Aviv conference of 1982, when the announcement and call for papers went out, I cooperated in identifying and encouraging scholars with some knowledge of the field—whether in history, political science, sociology, psychology, literature, or religion—to submit abstracts for consideration by the conference organizers. In all, the handful of Armenian proposals was only a very small part of an all-encompassing conference program, but this became the trigger for controversy because of external and internal pressures to exclude the Armenian component. Thanks to the courage and determination of the conference organizers, the gathering took place, though crippled by coerced withdrawals of institutions and individual participants. I remember that on the opening night when I was asked to comment, I stated with some emotion that it was distressing and ironic that Armenian victimization seems in a strange way to have been twisted so as to transform the victims into victimizers, because inclusion of the Armenian Genocide in the conference program had jeopardized discussions relating to other affected groups and peoples. The warm reception accorded by the assembled scholars who had resisted the efforts to scuttle the conference and who expressed outrage at the intolerable situation was gratifying. In an unexpected turn of events, equally ironic was the fact that sessions in which papers on the Armenian Genocide were delivered drew very large audiences—undoubtedly much larger in fact than if the controversy and attempted suppression had not occurred in the first place.

Nearly all the Armenian-related papers given at the conference and subsequently published under the title of The Armenian Genocide in Perspective were descriptive in nature, as if to offer evidence and seek validation that there had in fact been an actual genocide. There was less analysis than the need to present hard facts, often drawing on foreign eyewitnesses and sources for proof. Since that time, with the expansion of comparative genocide studies and additional related aspects encompassing music, drama and film, visual arts, transgenerational responses, creative literature by the survivor second and third generation, and other specialized areas, many more scholars of diverse backgrounds, including conscientious Turkish intellectuals, have become engaged in exploring and presenting studied findings regarding the various dimensions and consequences of the Armenian Genocide. The conclusions of those delving deeper into the subject are largely based on a great corpus of documentation and evidence that was not yet available in the 1980s. This has allowed them to move beyond macro-histories, which represent the output of my generation, to add micro-histories, which seek to reveal what was occurring on the local level before, during, and after the genocide. They assess in what ways these local situations fit into a general pattern or were driven by individual actors or particular groups in a specific town, city, or province, as well as the interaction between the regional perpetrators and the central regime's planners and strategists.

Furthermore, it is heartening that if my generation had to suffer the injury of offensive terms that cast doubt and aspersion, such as "alleged," "claimed," "so-called," "what the Armenians term as" genocide, these and like qualifiers have now been dropped from nearly all reputable media outlets and publications.

There remains, of course, the essential ethical question of governments with perceived vested interests remaining silent in order not to offend the still-persistent and unrepentant denier government and the reluctance of several of the most powerful of these countries to go on record to declare publicly what in private they know to be the truth. It is to be hoped that, among them, the nation state with the largest number of genocide victims and their descendants will chose to take the ethical high road of a shared humanity.

THE ARMENIAN GENOCIDE AND PATTERNS OF DENIAL[8]

The admission of genocidal operations by the perpetrator government or its immediate successor is rare in modern times, unlike the boastful inscriptions of ancient tyrants. The post-World War II admission and acceptance of guilt by the West German government stand out in stark contrast with all other cases in the twentieth century. But even in Germany, which made itself answerable for the guilt of the Nazi regime and engaged in various compensatory acts, thousands of implicated individuals claimed innocence or ignorance in the face of the incriminating evidence. Still, the postwar German governments, whether of free will, through coercion, or a combination of the two, extended reparations to the survivors, the families of the victims, and the State of Israel. Discussion of the moral and political implications of the Holocaust has now found a place in

---

8   Excerpted with slight editing from Richard G. Hovannisian, *The Armenian Genocide in Perspective*.

the educational curricula, literature, mass-media productions, and the scholarly forums of Germany.

No similarities exist in the Turkish response to the Armenian Genocide. There has been neither candid admission nor willing investigation, neither reparation nor rehabilitation. On the contrary, state-sponsored attempts to suppress discussion of the Armenian Genocide have reached unprecedented proportions. Presumably, the underlying cause for the Turkish attitude is political, for there still exists an aggrieved party, however scattered and limited in resources, that demands some form of compensation. While many of the aggrieved would be satisfied with a simple Turkish admission of wrongdoing and the granting of dignity to the hundreds of thousands of victims by an end to efforts to erase the historical record, there are others who insist upon financial and even territorial restitution, thus adding to Turkish anxieties and attempts to obscure the past.

Comparative studies rightly draw parallels between the two tragedies, but this political dimension at once raises the point that fundamental differences exist between the Armenian experience in World War I and the Jewish experience in World War II, although in no way do they reduce the significance of either. Thus, one notes that the Armenians were still living in their historical homelands, had passed through cultural and political movements to the formulation of programs of social, economic, and administrative reforms in the Ottoman Empire, and were perceived as an obstacle to the realization of the designs espoused by some members of the ruling Turkish Union and Progress (Young Turk) party.

At the time of the deportations and massacres beginning in 1915, there was virtually universal condemnation of the act and of its perpetrators. The accounts of eyewitnesses and officials of many nationalities as well as the testimony of the survivors themselves were too detailed and corroborative to doubt the systematic nature of the operation. Being born into the targeted group was in and of itself sufficient to mark an individual for elimination. United States Ambassador Henry Morgenthau testified that the deportations to the Syrian and Mesopotamian deserts were unquestionably meant to annihilate the Armenian population:

The Central Government now announced its intention of gathering the two million or more Armenians living in the several sections of the empire and transporting them to this desolate and inhospitable region. Had they undertaken such a deportation in good faith it would have represented the height of cruelty and injustice. As a matter of fact, the Turks never had the slightest idea of reestablishing the Armenians in this new country. They knew that the great majority would never reach their destination and that those who did would either die of thirst and starvation, or be murdered by the wild Mohammedan desert tribes. The real purpose of the deportations was robbery and destruction; it really represented a new method of massacre. When the Turkish authorities gave the orders for these deportations, they were merely giving the death warrant to a whole race; they understood this well, and writes US Ambassador Henry Morgenthau, in their conversations with him they made no particular attempt to conceal the fact.[9]

The large corpus of evidence of genocide notwithstanding, the mechanism of denial and rationalization was put in motion as soon as the deportations began. Since then, that mechanism has moved through several major phases. During and immediately after World War I, with the evidence too fresh for total denial, the emphasis was placed on rationalization. Turkish publications and official declarations pointed to Armenian disloyalty, exploitation, and imminent general rebellion at a time when the fatherland was struggling for survival in a war on several fronts. The next phase, beginning with the international abandonment of the Armenian question and the founding of the Republic of Turkey in 1923, was characterized by downplaying of the unpleasant past and concentration on a new image, that of a new Turkey, in which minorities enjoyed cultural and religious freedom. Apparently convinced that the Armenian problem would evaporate in time, the Turkish government under Mustafa Kemal and his successors tried to deal with Armenian matters as quietly and expeditiously as possible through diplomatic channels with countries having active Armenian communities.

But in 1965, the worldwide Armenian commemorations of the fiftieth anniversary of the genocide and the increasingly demonstrative and militant stance taken by many second- and third-generation Armenians of the dispersion ushered in a new phase in Turkish strategy. While continuing to capitalize upon the geopolitical, military, and economic importance of their country in efforts to pressure foreign governments to disregard Armenian manifestations, Turkish leaders also authorized an active campaign of counterpropaganda. The resulting books and brochures were usually sent out from Ankara in the month of April, to detract from the annual Armenian commemorative programs marking the onset of the 1915 massacres, and were addressed primarily to policymakers and opinion makers abroad, to members of legislatures and state and local governments, and to libraries, scholars, and teachers.

Giving special attention to Jewish leaders and Jewish opinion, the strategy attempts to dissociate the Jewish experience from the Armenian one and to

---

9   Henry Morgenthau, *Ambassador Morgenthau's Story* (Garden City, NY: Doubleday, 1918), 309.

drive a broad wedge between the two peoples by expressing profound sympathy for the victims and survivors of the "true" Holocaust, while characterizing the Armenian "genocide" as a hoax and "the greatest lie of the century." Enlisting the services of Turkish academics and some non-Turkish writers, the architects of this strategy appeal to a Western sense of fair play in insisting that the "other side" of a grossly misrepresented situation be taken into consideration and that the Armenian movement be exposed historically as a treacherous but abortive national rebellion and currently as a scheme to subvert Turkey and alienate it from its allies. That the repeated denials and refutations have achieved a degree of success is evidenced by the fact that some Western reporters and commentators use qualifiers such as "alleged" and "asserted" in reference to the genocide.[10]

The transformation of a historic genocidal operation into a controversial issue causes anger and frustration among some, and leads others to ask if there might not be credibility in the Turkish assertions. This development may also serve as a warning of things to come. While several antisemitic groups have challenged the truth of the Holocaust, they have by and large been discredited, and the world remains strongly aware of the decimation of European Jewry. Yet, I would suggest that given conditions similar to those affecting the Armenians, the Holocaust, too, would be challenged, not only by prejudiced extremists and guilty governments but also by well-intentioned individuals who believe that in a relativist world there are always two sides to a story. To be more specific, let us ask how the Holocaust might be regarded under the following ten conditions, which approximate the Armenian situation.

What if—
- the Jewish survivors of the Holocaust, left largely to their own devices, had scattered the world over as refugees;
- the survivors, having no sovereign government to represent them, had to struggle for years merely to ensure the physical and economic survival of their families, with their limited community resources concentrated on the establishment of a new network of schools and temples

---

10 Prof. Hovannisian's original notes are presented as footnotes. A few footnotes have been added by the editor of the present book in the course of editing and excerpting the original text by Hovannisian. These characterizations were not infrequent for many years, but they are seen more rarely today. One is also reminded that for many years the *New York Times* and its affiliate, the *Boston Globe*, had an official policy of never referring to the Genocide other than as a massacre, but this policy was rescinded after publication of the *Encyclopedia of Genocide* in the first years of this century.—Ed.

to preserve the national-religious heritage as well as possible in diverse lands and circumstances;

- no independent Jewish nation-state had been created, and the Allied victors, despairing of assisting the survivors, abandoned the Jewish question;
- the Jewish communities were deprived of the leadership, inspiration, and impetus provided by a Jewish nation-state;
- in the absence of such a state, few resources were allocated for the founding of research institutes and other bodies for the gathering and analyses of materials relating to the Holocaust;
- Jewish survivors and expatriates were too few and lacked sufficient political and financial influence to affect their host governments or succeed in having the Holocaust dealt with in the media and in educational programs;
- the survivors, nearly all with vivid memories and indelible details of the genocide, gradually passed from the scene, and their children and grandchildren found it increasingly difficult to recount with preciseness the experiences of the survivors or to challenge deniers with first-hand eyewitness accounts;
- the German government, defying the harsh terms initially imposed by the Allies, succeeded in writing a new peace settlement that did not necessitate some form of compensation to the survivors or even a formal acknowledgment of the genocidal operation;
- the strategic geopolitical, military, and economic value assigned to Germany in international relations was sufficiently compelling to incline foreign governments to disregard Jewish claims against Germany and even to participate in the cover-up;
- a new generation of foreign students, scholars, and officials interested in German affairs espoused the goal of showing Germany in a new light as a progressive, democratic state and of revising its much maligned image and unfair stereotypes, such as an oversimplified picture of a victimizing Germany and a victimized Jewry.

It is likely that in these circumstances the Jewish people today would be facing the same general indifference and even annoyance that surround Armenians in their efforts to keep their case before world opinion, raising for them the question whether truth and justice can ever prevail in the absence of sheer political and military power.

By the 1970s the Turkish government came to the conclusion that it could no longer simply dismiss or ignore the Armenian problem and formulated a campaign to counteract Armenian propaganda. In this phase of the denial process, pamphlets and brochures sent out from Ankara to foreign countries were mostly reprints of the Turkish publications first issued between 1917 and 1919 and intended to cast blame for Armenian troubles on the Armenians themselves and, after the war, to minimize the Ottoman losses.[11]

Evolving from this type of literature by the mid-seventies were new tracts prepared by several Turkish historians and contemporary writers. These materials, which were intended to prove the baselessness of Armenian claims, included nothing new and were riddled with contradiction, misquotation, and distortion. In his essay entitled "Armenian Question," for example, Enver Zia Karal asserted that, despite their treacherous behavior, the Armenians were protected throughout Anatolia after the war. According to Karal, Major General James G. Harbord, head of an American military mission of inquiry to Asia Minor and Transcaucasia in 1919, admitted to this when he supposedly reported:

> Meanwhile, the Armenian, unarmed at the time of deportations, a brave soldier who served in thousands in the armies of Russia, France, and America is still unarmed *and safe* [*italics added*] in a land where every man but himself need to carry a rifle.[12]

What Harbord actually wrote gives the opposite picture:

> Meanwhile, the Armenian, unarmed at the time of the deportations *and massacres* [*italics added*], a brave soldier by thousands in the armies of Russia, France, and America during the war, is still unarmed in a land where every man but himself carries a rifle.[13]

---

11 See, for example, *Documents relatifs aux atrocités commises par les Arméniens sur la population Musulmane* (Constantinople: Société Anonyme de Papeterie et d'Imprimérie, 1919); *Documents sur les Atrocités Arméno-Russes* (Constantinople: Société Anonyme de Papeterie et d'Imprimérie, 1917); *The TurcoArmenian Question: The Turkish Point of View* (Constantinople: Société Anonyme de Papeterie et d'Imprimérie, 1919); Vladimir Tverdokhlebov, *War Journal of the Second Russian Fortress Artillery Regiment of Erzeroum and Notes of Superior Russian Officer on the Atrocities at Erzeroum* (n.p., 1919).

12 Enver Ziya Karal, *Armenian Question (1878–1923)* (Ankara: n.p., 1975), 22.

13 Major General James G. Harbord, *Conditions in the Near East: Report of the American Military Mission to Armenia*, United States Congress, 66th Congress, 2nd session, S. Doc. 266 (Washington, DC: Government Printing Office, 1920), 11.

Typical of the distortions in this genre of political pamphleteering is Karal's addition of the words "and safe" and his deletion of the words "and massacres." Harbord's real attitude about the genocide is public record:

> Massacres and deportations were organized in the spring of 1915 under definite system, the soldiers going from town to town. The official reports of the Turkish Government show 1,100,000 as having been deported. Young men were first summoned to the government building in each village and then marched out and killed. The women, the old men, and children were, after a few days, deported to what Talaat Pasha called "agricultural colonies," from the high, cool, breeze-swept plateau of Armenia to the malarial flats of the Euphrates and the burning sands of Syria and Arabia. ... Mutilation, violation, torture, and death have left their haunting memories in a hundred beautiful Armenian valleys, and the traveler in that region is seldom free from the evidence of this most colossal crime of all the ages.[14]

Sometimes efforts to defame the Armenians entered the realm of the absurd. In a pamphlet sent out from Ankara entitled "Truth about Armenians," Ahmet Vefa, aside from repeating the standard Turkish allegations, alerted the English-reading public to the existence of correspondence in the Hoover Institution archives at Stanford University making it known that "the Armenians were not and never could be desirable citizens, that they would always be unscrupulous merchants." Of greater interest is Vefa's contention that when Adolf Hitler asked rhetorically in 1939, "Who after all speaks today of the annihilation of the Armenians," he was making reference not to Turkish excesses against Armenians, but rather to the Armenian destruction of the pre-Armenian Urartians in the seventh century before Christ.[15]

Unable to make significant headway with this type of literature, Turkish officials encouraged sympathetic foreign scholars to present the "Turkish side" in the West and even afforded limited access to a few relevant archival files. Long before the astounding writings of Stanford J. Shaw in the 1970s, the trend toward revisionism had already influenced a number of scholars involved in Turkish studies. Because the existence of the Republic of Turkey was seen as a good thing, there was a tendency to justify the events that had led up to it

---

14 Ibid., 7.
15 Ahmet Vefa, *Truth about Armenians* (Ankara: n.p., 1975), 7–8, 11.

and its current boundaries. This disposition is reflected in the writings of Lewis V. Thomas, Richard Robinson, Norman Itzkowitz, and a significant number of younger scholars.

In the 1970s, revisionism reached levels that transcended all previous bounds in the writings of Professor Stanford J. Shaw. Under the guise of scholarly research he not only repeated but also enhanced the worn, unsubstantiated accusations against the Armenians. His treatment of the Armenian Question in *History of the Ottoman Empire and Modern Turkey* includes gross errors and surpasses even the excuses of the Young Turk perpetrators.[16] Setting a theme for subsequent Turkish propaganda, Shaw contests sources showing that there were between two and three million Armenians in the Ottoman Empire and maintains that there were actually no more than 1,300,000, thereby minimizing the number that could have been deported or killed. Characterizing the Armenians as the invariable aggressors, the victimizers rather than the victims, the privileged rather than the oppressed, and the fabricators of unfounded tales of massacre, he insists that the Young Turk government took all possible measures to ensure the safety of those people who had to be removed from the border districts and to provide them with food, water, and medical attention while en route to suitable new homes in prearranged relocation centers.

Specific instructions were issued for the army to protect the Armenians against nomadic attacks and to provide them with sufficient food and other supplies to meet their needs during the march and after they were settled. Warnings were sent to the Ottoman military commanders to make certain that neither the Kurds nor any other Muslims used the situation to gain vengeance for the long years of Armenian terrorism. The Armenians were to be protected and cared for until they returned to their homes after the war. A supplementary law established a special commission to record the properties of some deportees and sell them at auction at fair prices, with the revenues being held in trust until their return. Muslims wishing to occupy abandoned buildings could do so only as renters, with the revenues paid to the trust funds, and with the understanding that they would have to leave when the original owners returned. The deportees and their possessions were to be guarded by the army while in transit as well as in Iraq and Syria, and the government would provide for their return once the crisis was over.[17]

---

16 Stanford J. Shaw with Ezel Kural Shaw, *History of the Ottoman Empire and Modern Turkey*, vol. 2: *Reform, Revolution and Republic: The Rise of Modern Turkey, 1808–1975* (Cambridge, London, New York, Melbourne: Cambridge University Press, 1977), esp. 200–205, 240–241, 281, 287, 311–317, 322–324, 356–357.

17 Ibid., 315.

Determined to prevent the Armenian question from ever again becoming a topic of international diplomacy, the Ankara government has engaged in strong political lobbying to expunge even passing references to the Armenians. This policy is exemplified by the tactics used in relation to a United Nations Sub-Commission draft report on the prevention and punishment of genocide. In 1973 the special rapporteur of the Sub-Commission on Prevention of Discrimination and Protection of Minorities wrote in paragraph 30 of the introductory historical section:

> Passing to the modern era, one may note the existence of relatively full documentation dealing with the massacres of Armenians, which have been described as "the first case of genocide in the twentieth century."[18] The paragraph makes no mention of either the Ottoman Empire or of Turks, yet the Turkish mission to the United Nations and the Turkish government regarded the sentence as menacing and immediately applied pressure on governments and delegations represented on the full Human Rights Commission. Yielding to this pressure the commission adopted a recommendation that historic events preceding recent genocidal acts and the contemporary definition of genocide be omitted from the report. "It was pointed out that there was the dangerous pitfall of confusing the crime of genocide with the eventual consequences which might occur as a result of a given war and making such parallels without taking into account the historical and socio-economic background of the past events." Matters that had been subject "to controversial explanations and evaluations in different publications" should be avoided. Hence paragraph 30 should be deleted.[19]

When the issue was raised again in 1975, one delegate noted that the tragedy of 1915 was historical fact, "but in a civilized international community, consideration should also be given to the desire of a state not to be defamed on account of its past acts, which had been perpetrated by a previous generation and were probably regretted by the present generation." When the Sub-Commission's rapporteur submitted the revised version of his report in 1978, the historical section began with the Nazi-perpetrated Holocaust. In the words of Leo Kuper, the Armenian Genocide "had disappeared down the memory

---

18 The quotation from the rapporteur is from Leo Kuper, *Genocide: Its Political Use in the Twentieth Century* (1981 ed.), 219, 231.—Ed.

19 Ibid., 219–220.

hole." When a few members of the Sub-Commission questioned the delegation, it was now the rapporteur who explained:

> Concern had been expressed that the study of genocide might be diverted from its intended course and lose its essential purpose. Consequently, it had been decided to retain the massacre of the Jews under Nazism, because that case was known to all and no objections had been raised; but other cases had been omitted, because it was impossible to compile an exhaustive list, because it was important to maintain unity in the international community in regard to genocide, and because in many cases to delve into the past might reopen old wounds which were now healing.[20]

When the Turkish measures to erase even the memory of the Armenian victims in a draft report of the United Nations Sub-Commission became known, the story spread swiftly throughout the Armenian communities. Armenian groups around the world now mounted their own campaign, publicly invoking the human rights declarations of several member states of the UN Human Rights Commission. The subsequent lead of the United States in reversing its position during the Carter administration in 1979 was followed by several other countries, resulting in the request to the special rapporteur to take into account the various statements made in and to the commission about the Armenian tragedy.[21]

The most recent phase of denial, advanced in the 1980s by the Turkish military and civil governments, is characterized by efforts to reach the public at large. One aim of the current phase is to create a broad breach between Jews and Armenians by emphasizing the true horror of the Holocaust and playing up Turkey's ties with Israel, while cautioning against an Armenian scheme to

---

20 Ibid., 220.

21 The UN special rapporteur in 1978 was Nicodème Ruhashyankiko. Following the end of his tenure he was reported to have returned to his home in Rwanda and then disappeared never to be heard from again. Whether his fate was in any way connected to the subject of the Armenian Genocide in the UN report is altogether unclear. However, in 1985, the new rapporteur, MP Benjamin Whitaker, produced what many of us consider a brilliant report on genocide as a universal process and problem and a series of proposals for the UN to combat the spread of genocide in the world. In this report there was decisively clear and unambiguous identification of the Armenian Genocide. Updated Report on the Question of the Prevention and Punishment of the Crime of Genocide was received and noted by a resolution at the thirty-eighth session of the Sub-Commission in 1985 (E/CN.4/Sub.2/1985/6, 2 July 1985). A Special Double Issue of our magazine, Internet on the Holocaust and Genocide 3/4 (April 1986), was devoted in detail to the Whitaker Report.

detract from the Holocaust and dishonor the memory of its victims by winning recognition for a mythical genocide fabricated solely for political purposes. This approach has been used in public announcements, in private meetings and written exchanges with Jewish leaders, and in international diplomatic correspondence. All these means have also been employed in repeated efforts to dissuade the United States Holocaust Council from including the Armenian Genocide in any of its projected educational and commemorative activities.

In a booklet published in 1982 entitled, "Setting the Record Straight on Armenian Propaganda Against Turkey," the opening lines read: "In recent years claims have been made by some Armenians in Europe, America, and elsewhere that the Armenians suffered terrible misrule in the Ottoman Empire. Such claims are absurd."[22] Reflecting both the style and the methodology of the extreme revisionist historians, the brochure attempts to show that the Armenians, despite their many privileges, in the nineteenth century became Russian agents and initiated an indiscriminate reign of terror. "Muslims were brutalized as much as possible in order to stimulate reprisals and to bring about cycles of massacre and counter-massacre which could only be ended by European intervention. Realizing the terrorist intentions, Abdul Hamid II and his successors did all they could to prevent Muslim reprisals for the Armenian massacres, and they were largely successful."[23] In this manner the great Armenian pogroms in the 1890s are dismissed and Sultan Abdul Hamid, previously discredited by many Turkish writers, is portrayed as a patient and tolerant ruler.[24]

As for the events during World War I, there were, the brochure asserts, no generalized massacres, except by Armenians, and certainly no genocide. Perhaps as many as 100,000 Armenians may have died of various causes between 1915 and 1918, but that was not unusual compared with Turkish losses:

> There was no genocide committed against the Armenians in the Ottoman Empire before or during World War I. No genocide was planned or ordered by the Ottoman government and no genocide was carried out.

---

22 *Setting the Record Straight on Armenian Propaganda against Turkey*, Assembly of Turkish-American Associations (Washington, DC: Assembly of Turkish-American Associations, 1982), 1.

23 Ibid., 4.

24 During the reign of Sultan Abdul Hamid, large-scale genocidal massacres of Armenians erupted in 1894–1896 with an estimated death toll of 200,000. For many scholars, including this writer, this period can be considered the beginning of what we call the Armenian Genocide.—Ed.

Recent scholarly research has discovered that the stories of massacres were in fact largely invented Armenian nationalist leaders in Paris and London during World War I and spread throughout the world through the British intelligence.

Moreover, "the Armenian nationalists have continued to spread their message of hate, relying on repetition of the 'big lie' to secure acceptance of their claims in a Christian world predisposed to accept the claims of Christians whenever they are in conflict with Muslims."[25]

The Turkish publication to "set the record straight" concludes with a denunciation of Armenian oral history programs:

Carefully coached by their Armenian nationalist interviewers, these aged Armenians relate tales of horror which supposedly took place some 66 years ago in such detail as to astonish the imagination, considering that most of them already are aged eighty or more. Subjected to years of Armenian nationalist propaganda as well as the coaching of their interviewers, there is little doubt that their statements are of no use whatever for historical research. ...[26]

CONCLUSION

The history of the denial of the Armenian Genocide has passed through several phases, each somewhat different in emphasis but all characterized by efforts to avoid responsibility and the moral, material, and political consequences of admission. Only under the impact of the defeat of the Ottoman Empire and the flight of the Young Turk leaders were there partial admissions, but this trend was halted by the successful Kemalist defiance of the Allies and the subsequent international abandonment of the Armenian Question. In the absence of external force, neither the perpetrators nor successive Turkish governments have been willing to face the skeleton in their closet. Rather, they have resorted to various forms of avoidance, denial, repudiation, and vilification to keep the door shut. In the meantime, Turkish writers and scholars are still unable to deal honestly with their national past and continue to be drawn, wittingly or unwittingly, into the wheels of rationalization and falsification. Taking advantage of its strategic

---

25 *Setting the Record Straight on Armenian Propaganda against Turkey*, 4–8.
26 Ibid., 1.

geopolitical and military importance, the Republic of Turkey has repeatedly impressed on other governments and international bodies that dwelling on a complex but no longer relevant past is unproductive, disruptive, and antagonistic. Yet the problem has persisted, and the tone and tenor of the denials are now more forceful than ever before. The Turkish position severely obstructs investigation of the genocide, its causes, effects, and implications, and the scholarly and humanitarian ends to which such studies should be directed.

As the number of persons who lived through World War I and who have direct knowledge of the events diminishes, the rationalizers and debasers of history become all the more audacious, to the extent of transforming the victims into the victimizers. At the time of the deportations and massacres, no reputable publication would have described the genocide as "alleged." The clouding of the past, however, and the years of Turkish denials, diplomatic and political pressures, and programs of image improvement have had their impact on some publishers, correspondents, scholars, and public officials. In an increasingly skeptical world, the survivors and descendants of the victims have been thrust into a defensive position from which they are required to prove time and again that they have indeed been wronged, individually and collectively. It is not surprising that they should look with envy upon Jewish Holocaust survivors, who do not have to face an unrepentant and uncompromising German government and a high-powered political campaign of denial that a state-organized plan of annihilation was in fact enacted. The Armenians search desperately for morality in politics and ask if there may be any just and practical alternative to the dictum "might makes right."

DENIAL OF THE ARMENIAN GENOCIDE WITH SOME COMPARISONS TO HOLOCAUST DENIAL[27]

Those who deny, repudiate, or rationalize the Armenian Genocide during World War I and the Holocaust during World War II may not be acquainted with one another and may not even have read each other's publications. Yet there are striking similarities in their methodologies and objectives.

In the Armenian case, denial is far more advanced and has become entrenched in mainstream history. But the strategy has changed from one of absolute denial of intentional mass killing to one of rationalization,

---

27 Richard G. Hovannisian, *Denial of the Armenian Genocide with Some Comparisons to Holocaust Denial.*

relativization, and trivialization. These forms of denial are intended to raise doubts and to disguise the disinformation by appealing to a sense of fair play—giving a hearing to the other side of a "misunderstood" and misrepresented issue. Prejudice and stereotyping, they maintain, are residues of historical scapegoating or of wartime propaganda and are machinations by the alleged victims to enrich themselves personally and collectively.

The same strategy is applied to the Holocaust, although almost all the principals involved belong to antisemitic fringe elements and the political extreme right. Now, however, even the Holocaust has entered historical debate, especially in Germany.[28]

A side-effect of this debate is the creation of tension among some Holocaust scholars. The apologists and rationalizers trivialize the enormity of the event by pointing to the repeated violence and mass destructions in the twentieth century, citing, as a prime example, the annihilation of the Armenians in the Ottoman Empire. This attempted relativization of the Holocaust has caused some Jewish scholars to differentiate between the scope of the Holocaust and the Armenian tragedy, while withholding or qualifying the label of "genocide" in relation to the Armenians.

It has been said that denial is the final phase of genocide. Following the physical destruction of a people and their material culture, memory is all that is left and is targeted as the last victim to be annihilated. Complete annihilation of a people requires the banishment of recollection and the suffocation of remembrance. Falsification, deception, and half-truths reduce what was to what may have been or perhaps what was not at all. History becomes "something that never happened, written by someone who wasn't there." Senseless terror gives way to reason, violence adapts to explanation, and history is reshaped to suit a contemporary agenda. By altering or erasing the past, a present is produced and a future is projected without concern for historical integrity. The process of annihilation is thus advanced and completed by denial.[29]

In an introduction to his study on the Holocaust, Michael Marrus states contemptuously: "I have had no difficulty excluding from this book any

---

28 This refers to a period that has been called the dispute over the *Historikerstreit*, where some German intellectuals—prominent among them was Professor Ernst Nolte—claimed that there was nothing new and therefore little that was remarkable about the Holocaust. Such massacres were old and regular news in human history.—Ed.

29 Elie Wiesel, "Understanding Eyes," *Hadassah Magazine* (March 1987): 24. I wish to acknowledge the contributions to this paper of Michael Blacher, who made a comparative study of genocide denial in a graduate seminar that I directed at UCLA.

discussion of the so-called revisionists—malevolent cranks who contend that the Holocaust never happened."[30]

Those who study and write about the Armenian Genocide cannot be so unequivocal, because the denial has been institutionalized by a government, its supportive agencies, its influential political and academic collaborators, and by extension, its powerful military allies and trading partners. Kurt Jonassohn has aptly observed that a major difference in the treatment of the Armenian Genocide and the Holocaust is that "the Holocaust literature is directed at remembering, understanding, and preventing a recurrence by emphasizing the role of human rights, while much of the literature on the Armenian Genocide still addresses matters of historical fact—almost threequarters of a century after the events of 1915. Another difference is that German authors are participating in the examination of what happened, whereas Turkish authors are still trying to deny that a genocide occurred."[31]

This is largely the result of the unrelenting campaign against the actuality and factuality of the Armenian Genocide. Unfortunately, some members of the academic community have been co-opted into this offensive by denying the premeditated, organized nature of the Armenian destruction and by lending their names to advertisements and circular letters to that effect.

As the central characteristic of genocide is the calculated, intentional decimation of the targeted group, refuting the factor of intent is foremost in the denialists' brief. Denialists and rationalizers of both the Armenian Genocide and the Holocaust emphasize the following points:

1. Stories about alleged genocide are based on wartime propaganda.
2. Armenians in the Ottoman Empire and Jews in Europe were perceived as posing very real security threats, and their actions demonstrated that these concerns were not imaginary.
3. There was no intent to annihilate either group, only to relocate its members.
4. The deaths that occurred were primarily from the same causes that carried away even more Turks and Kurds, in the Armenian case, and Germans and Austrians, in the Jewish case.

---

30 Michael R. Marrus, *The Holocaust in History* (Hanover, NH: University Press of New England, 1987), xiv.

31 Frank Chalk and Kurt Jonassohn, *The History and Sociology of Genocide: Analyses and Case Studies* (New Haven and London: Yale University Press, 1990), 328.

5. The number of Armenian and Jewish dead is much less than claimed, and most of the alleged victims actually ended up in other countries.
6. The myth of genocide was created in both cases for economic and/or political motives.
7. Those who believe and promote the myth have been the willful or unwitting abettors of communism and Soviet expansion and the destabilization of the NATO alliance and the West.[32]

The proponents of truth are struggling against powerful political lobbies to rectify negative stereotypes and historical misconceptions as persons brave and bold enough to champion free speech and inquiry.

The strategies of denial are not always parallel. In the Jewish case, for example, it is critical for denialists to show that the Jews constituted a distinct cultural-racial group—that is, to acknowledge their separate existence in Germany and the rest of Europe. In the Armenian case, the denialists manipulate statistics, history, and culture in order to minimize the significance of the Armenian presence in the area once called Armenia and now known as Eastern Anatolia.

In this effort, it is necessary to obscure all evidence of that presence by changing toponyms, destroying historical monuments, and making Armenians disappear from the written record. Proudly proclaiming a cultural heritage that includes ancient civilizations from the Hittites to the Romans and even the Byzantines, Turkish spokesmen, buttressed by their foreign collaborators, eliminate most of the three millennia of Armenian history in the region. The destruction of a people has been followed by the destruction of its material culture and now even a campaign to eliminate its very memory.[33]

The repetition of rationalizations and the mixture of half-truths with lies have had a more telling effect than absolute and unequivocal denial. Even a person believing himself to be knowledgeable about the Armenian Genocide

---

32 See Deborah E. Lipstadt, *Denying the Holocaust: The Growing Assault on Truth and Memory* (New York: The Free Press; Toronto: Maxwell MacMillan, 1993); Richard G. Hovannisian, "The Armenian Genocide and Patterns of Denial," in his *The Armenian Genocide in Perspective*, 111–134. For bibliographic essays on this subject, see Erich Kulka, "Denial of the Holocaust," in *Genocide: A Critical Bibliographic Review*, vol. 2, ed. Israel W. Charny (New York: Facts on File, 1991; London: Mansell, 1991), 38–62, and Roger W. Smith, "Denial of the Armenian Genocide," ibid., 63–85.
33 See, for example, Clive Foss, "The Turkish View of Armenian History: A Vanishing Nation," in *The Armenian Genocide: History, Politics, Ethics*, ed. Richard G. Hovannisian (New York: St. Martin's Press; London: MacMillan, 1992), 250–279.

can be shaken by the seeming rationality of relativist arguments. *Washington Post* correspondent Richard Cohen, writing that he believed there was such overwhelming evidence of the Holocaust that it could not be denied, then added:

> That, at least, is what I had thought until recently. But then not too long ago, I found myself silting at the end of an enormous table in the embassy of Turkey. At the other end was the ambassador himself and what he was telling me was that the crime [Armenian Genocide] had always thought had happened had not ... [and] what the world persisted in calling a genocide was actually a civil war-one with atrocities on both sides and one in which the central government in Constantinople lost control over its own troops and could not protect the Armenians. There never was a policy to exterminate the Armenians.
>
> I had mentioned this genocide in a column-and mentioned it thinking that it as given—that no one could possibly dispute that it happened. ... But the ambassador said this had not happened. Sure, there were "incidents" and, yes, the Armenians had been banished. ... And so I sat there at the table unable to prove that one of the great crimes of history had actually been committed. ... None of this would matter—certainly not to the Armenians of 1915, the Jews of the 1940s, or the Cambodians of just yesterday—if it was not for the fact that to control the future, you have to first alter the past—take possession of it and rob it of its lessons.

Cohen concludes that truth is the last victim of genocide: "And so year by year, person by person, the genocide blurs, doubt corrodes it, and the easy word 'alleged' creeps in to mock the Armenian anguish."[34]

As yet, no German ambassador or other government official has recited like declarations regarding the Holocaust, but the forces of denial are nonetheless pressing hard to make their way to center stage.

WARTIME PROPAGANDA

Stories about intentional mass killing, say the denialists, have their origins in wartime propaganda, which is used to turn public opinion against the enemy-an enemy made so odious as to be worthy of merciless and relentless

---

34 Richard Cohen, "Killing Truth," *Washington Post*, May 31, 1983, Bl.

punishment. Among early proponents of this position were French denialists, Maurice Bardeche and Paul Rassinier, who were followed by Robert Faurisson, British popular historian David Irving and American professor Arthur Butz. All have pointed to the "myth" of extermination camps as being part of Allied propaganda to demonize the other side. Writing in different styles and with gradations of denial, this group, and others who share their view, emphasize that the supposed Holocaust and its six million Jewish victims is a hoax, a big lie, created and exploited by Jews and international Zionism to establish and consolidate the state of Israel and to reap great sums of money as indemnity.[35]

The victorious side intentionally distorted the actual conditions in the concentration camps in order to paint the defeated adversary as so evil as to necessitate just—that is, extreme—punishment. Such denialists have built upon the foundations laid by American revisionist historians, such as Harry Elmer Barnes, who explain the rise of Hitler and the Nazi regime as the logical outcome of the unfair treaties imposed upon the defeated powers at the end of World War I and who assert that stories of German excesses in World War II have been politically motivated. There is enough guilt to go around to all the parties in a conflict, and it is therefore underhand to single out just one government or country.[36]

Such an approach is no less explicit in the Armenian case. Turkish diplomat Kamuran Gürün shows the Turkish side to be the victim of its own lack of aggressiveness:

> We can easily state that propaganda is one of the weakest points of Turks. This was so in the Ottoman Empire, as well as in the Turkish republic. The propaganda activity of Turks has been restricted to refuting articles and

---

35 See, for example, Maurice Bardechè, *Nuremberg: Ou, La terre promise* (Paris: Les Sept Couleurs, 1948); and Maurice Bardechè, *Nuremberg II: Ou, Jes faux monnayeurs* (Paris: Les Sept Couleurs, 1950); Paul Rassinier, *The Real Eichmann Trial; Or the Incorrigible Victors* (Chapel Ascote, UK: Historical Review Press, 1979); Robert Faurisson, "The 'Problem of the Gas Chambers' or 'The Rumor of Auschwitz,'" *Le Monde*, January 16, 1979; Robert Faurisson, *Memoire en défense* (Paris: La Vieille Taupe, 1980); and idem, *Contre ceux qui m'accusent de falsifier l'histoire. La question des chambres a gaz* (Paris: La Vieille Taupe, 1980); Arthur R. Butz, *The Hoax of the Twentieth Century* (Torrance, CA: Institute for Historical Review, 1976); and David Irving, *Hitler's War* (New York: Viking, 1977).

36 See Deborah Lipstadt, "The Evolution of American Holocaust Revisionism," in *Remembering for the Future: The Impact of the Holocaust and Genocide on Jews and Christians*, ed. Elisabeth Maxwell and Roman Halter (Oxford: Pergamon Press, 1983), supplementary volume, 269–276.

erroneous assertions; thus it has been nothing more than a passive effort to defend the Turkish position. This attitude enabled the opposite side to act freely in portraying the Turks continuously as being guilty.[37]

American denialists, such as Stanford Shaw and Justin McCarthy, have labelled accounts of more than a million Armenian victims as the work of the "Entente propaganda mills." Justin McCarthy, apparently drawing freely from Kamuran Gürün's book, *The Armenian File*, maintains that the prevailing anti-Muslim attitudes in the West, the biased accounts of American missionaries, and the operation of the Allied Powers' "propaganda machines" were used to perpetuate and intensify negative views of the Turks. Denialists always have explanations. In his manual for students and teachers, entitled Turks and Armenians, McCarthy writes:

The English propaganda machine churned out atrocity stories against both Germany and its ally Turkey to aid in its war effort both at home and abroad. Several European states coveted Ottoman territory, and the massacres and atrocities for which the Ottoman government was said to be responsible were used as the justification for breaking up the Ottoman Empire and for taking all or nearly all lands away from Ottoman rule. The Western nations needed to believe and promote Ottoman and Turkish atrocity stories in order to excuse their own plans to annex Ottoman lands.[38]

DISCREDITING SURVIVOR TESTIMONY

Denialists are keen on discrediting survivor testimony. In the case of the Holocaust, they insist that such untrustworthy accounts as are given by so-called "survivors" are full of inconsistencies and exaggerations and were intended to swindle the German government out of billions of dollars and to win sympathy to create and bolster the State of Israel at the expense of other peoples. Similar claims are made in a Turkish denial booklet published in the 1980s.

---

37 Kamuran Gürün, *The Armenian File: The Myth of Innocence Exposed* (London, Nicosia, Istanbul: K Rustem & Bros. and Weidenfeld & Nicholson, 1985), 36.

38 Justin McCarthy and Carolyn McCarthy, *Turks and Armenians: A Manual on the Armenian Question* (Washington, DC: Assembly of Turkish American Associations, 1989), 85–86.

Carefully coached by their Armenian nationalist interviewers, these aged Armenians relate tales of horror which supposedly took place 66 years ago in such detail as to astonish the imagination, considering that most of them already are aged eighty or more. Subjected to years of Armenian nationalist propaganda as well as the coaching of their interviewers, there is little doubt that their statements are of no use whatever for historical research.[39]

Deborah Lipstadt, in *Denying the Holocaust,* writes of how the victims are charged with being provocateurs:

The denialists and rationalisers of genocide try to show that the alleged victims were not guiltless and that the security measures taken by the state were no different from what other beleaguered governments have done before and since. Bardeche, Rassinier, Faurisson, and other denialists of the Holocaust assert that the Jewish victims were in most instances partisans, saboteurs, spies, and enemy collaborators-a virtual fifth column. They point to the declaration of Chaim Weizmann in 1939 that Jews everywhere would support the Allied cause against Nazism and argue that it was only natural that the Jews should be perceived as a threat. Bardeche went so far as to assert that World War II was actually provoked by the Jews. Desperate acts of resistance, such as the Warsaw ghetto uprising, are offered as evidence of Jewish hostility, seriously jeopardising the war effort by forcing the diversion of regular armed forces to cope with insurrections. They show a certain affinity between Jews and Communists and therefore the Soviet Union-the largest enemy of the Reich.[40]

In the guise of a balanced, objective investigator, American Arthur Butz presents various forms of evidence to demonstrate that "Jews did, in fact, pose a security menace to the German rear in the war."[41] Most Jews in concentration

---

39 *Setting the Record Straight on Armenian Propaganda against Turkey,* 11.

40 Deborah E. Lipstadt, *Denying the Holocaust,* 49–64, 103–121.

41 In Arthur R. Butz, *The Hoax of the Twentieth Century,* 197. I have noted that there are some booksellers that no longer list this outrageously anti-Holocaust book. I knew a survivor of Auschwitz who was in the Sonderkommando, who had to put the bodies in the ovens, who appeared in a radio debate with Butz in Atlanta. She described how Butz—who incidentally was a tenured professor—ran out of the broadcast studio when the survivor told the story of "I was there."—Ed.

camps were there for specific punitive or security reasons, not because they were innocent members of a targeted group.

GOVERNMENTS NATURALLY ACT AGAINST SUSPECTED MINORITIES

A favourite argument of denialists of the Armenian Genocide is showing that all governments, including the United States of America, acted against suspected minorities, so the relocations undertaken by Germany or by Turkey should not be considered extraordinary, or as war crimes. An anonymous writer is quoted by Butz thus:

> The United States and Canada had begun to intern Japanese aliens and citizens of Japanese extraction in internment camps before this became a German policy toward many German and other European Jews. There was no tangible evidence of disloyalty, not to mention sabotage or espionage, among these people of Japanese extraction. The Germans at least had a somewhat more plausible basis to press for the internment of Jews.[42]

The anonymous writer concludes: "The internment of European Jews, like that of the Japanese in the United States and Canada, was carried out for security reasons."[43] Moreover, most of the Jews who were moved during the war were simply relocated to provide useful labour in agricultural and industrial enterprises, in lieu of service in the armed forces. They were, after all, simply being returned to their lands of origin in Eastern Europe.

These propositions are echoed in the Armenian case by the Turkish governmental publications and by authors such as Kamuran Gürün and their Western collaborators, especially the Americans Stanford Shaw, Justin McCarthy, and Heath Lowry. Gürün explains:

> The Armenians were forced to emigrate because they had joined the ranks of the enemy. The fact that they were civilians does not change the situation. Those who were killed m Hiroshima and Nagasaki during the Second World War were also civilians. Those who were killed during the First World War in France, Belgium, and Holland were also civilians. Those who died in London during the Battle of Britain were also

---

42 Ibid., 221.
43 Ibid., 204.

civilians. ... Turkey did not kill them [Armenians], but relocated them. As it was impossible to adopt a better solution under the circumstances, it cannot be accepted that those who died because they were unable to resist the hardships of the journey were killed by the Turks.[44]

Gürün has embellished the rationalisation of a key architect of the Armenian Genocide, Minister of the Interior and Grand Vizier Talaat Pasha, who, from his post war place of hiding in Germany in 1919, wrote: "These preventive measures were taken in every country during the war, but, while the regrettable results were passed over in silence in the other countries, the echo of our acts was heard the world over, because everybody's eyes were upon us."[45] Decades later, a Turkish official in Washington tried to draw a parallel for Americans: "Turkish response to the Armenian excesses was comparable, I believe, to what might have been the American response, had the German-Americans of Minnesota or Wisconsin revolted on behalf of Hitler during World War II."[46] And Turkish Ambassador to the US, Şükrü Elekdağ, wrote in 1982:

What took place was a complex tragedy which claimed Turkish as well as Armenian lives. Indeed, it was a civil war within a global war stemming from an armed uprising of the Armenian minority at a time when the Ottoman state was fighting for survival during World War I. Many more Turks than Armenians perished.[47]

The rather transparent excuses for the Turkish denialists were refined by their Western collaborators. Years before he was challenged in the French courts in the 1990s for his denial of the Armenian Genocide, Professor Bernard Lewis cautiously advanced the cause of revisionism by couching the Armenian calamity in terms of mutual warfare threatening the very existence of the Turkish state. In *The Emergence of Modern Turkey*, published in 1961, Lewis explains:

For the Turks, the Armenian [nationalist] movement was the deadliest of all threats. From the conquered lands of the Serbs, Bulgars, Albanians,

---

44 Kamuran Gürün, *The Armenian File*, 216.
45 [Talaat], "Posthumous Memoirs of Talaat Pasha," *Current History* 15, no. 2 (November 1921): 295.
46 Altemur Kılıç, *Turkey and the World* (Washington, DC: Public Affairs Press, 1959), 18.
47 *Congressional Record*, vol. 128, United States Congress, 97th Congress, 2nd session (Washington, DC: Government Printing Office, 1982), 1993–1994.

and Greeks, they could, however reluctantly, withdraw, abandoning dis-
tant provinces and bringing the Imperial frontier nearer home. But the
Armenians, stretching across Turkey-in-Asia from the Caucasian frontier
to the Mediterranean coast, lay in the very heart of the Turkish home-
land-and to renounce these lands would have meant not the truncation,
but the dissolution of the Turkish state. Turkish and Armenian villages,
inextricably mixed, had for centuries lived in a neighbourly association.
Now a desperate struggle between them began—a struggle of two nations
for the possession of a single homeland, that ended with the terrible holocaust of 1916 [sic], when a million and half Armenians perished.[48]

Stanford J. Shaw, in a volume co-authored with his wife and published by
Cambridge University Press (*History of the Ottoman Empire and Modern Turkey*),
engages in more egregious distortions and deceptions. He makes it seem, for
example, that, in ordering the Armenian deportations, the Turkish authorities
were simply following a precedent already established by the Russians.

In the initial stages of the Caucasus campaign the Russians had demonstrated the best means of organising a campaign by evacuating the Armenians from their side of the border to clear the area for battle, with the
Armenians going quite willingly in the expectation that a Russian victory
would soon enable them not merely to return to their homes but also to
occupy those of the Turks across the border. Enver [Minister of War] followed this example to prepare the Ottoman side and to resist the expected
Russian invasion. Armenian leaders in any case now declared their open
support of the enemy, and there seemed no other alternative.[49]

Ascribing sinister motives to the Armenians, Shaw would have his readers
believe that there was "no alternative" to deportation:

It would be impossible to determine which of the Armenians would
remain loyal and which would follow the appeals of their leaders. As soon as
spring came, then, in mid-May 1915 orders were issued to evacuate the entire
Armenian population from the provinces of Van, Bitlis, and Erzurum, to get

---

48 Bernard Lewis, *The Emergence of Modern Turkey* (London, New York, Toronto: Oxford
University Press, 1961), 350.
49 Stanford J. Shaw with Ezel Kural Shaw, *History of the Ottoman Empire and Modern Turkey*,
vol. 2, 315.

them away from all areas where they might undermine the Ottoman campaigns, against Russia or against the British in Egypt.[50]

> Concealing the fact that the Armenian population was deported and massacred throughout the width and breadth of Anatolia, Shaw claims that the Armenians were "evacuated" only from the war zone along the Russian frontier and from the Cilician countryside but not from the cities in that region near the Mediterranean Sea.[51] This assertion is preposterous, and its publication by Cambridge University Press is scandalous.

Although, like Arthur Butz among Holocaust revisionists, Justin McCarthy, a student of Stanford Shaw, tries to show that he is more balanced, his underlying motives are as obvious as those of Gürün, Shaw, and other denialists. In fact, McCarthy may again be beholden to Gürün in his reiterating the ridiculous claims that Armenian rebellions flared all over Anatolia, requiring the diversion of entire army divisions to suppress the conspiratorial risings. McCarthy prides himself on being a demographer, yet he apparently does not see the untenable contradiction between his minimalisation of the number of Armenians in the Ottoman Empire and his reiteration of Gürün's figure that, from the province of Sivas (Sebastia) alone, there were 30,000 Armenian guerrillas, half of whom had already made their way to the Russian lines to fight against the Turkish armies and the other half of whom were prepared to strike those armies from the rear. McCarthy adds unabashedly: "No one accurately counted the numbers, but unquestionably there were more than 100,000 Armenian guerrillas or other fighters from Anatolia or the Russian territories fighting in Anatolia."[52] For McCarthy and all other denialists and rationalisers, the desperate efforts at self-defence in a few isolated places—Van, Shabin-Karahisar, Urfa, and Musa Dagh—are sufficient proof of Armenian disloyalty and conspiracy. "Deportation," a word McCarthy begrudgingly uses instead of his preferred term—"relocation," became the Turkish government's response to the menace posed by the Armenians:

> The principle of the deportation was based on one of the few known ways to defeat a guerrilla insurgency and has been used from ancient up to modern

---

50 Ibid.
51 Ibid.
52 Justin McCarthy, *Turks and Armenians: Nationalism and Conflict in the Ottoman Empire* (Madison, WI: Turko-Tatar Press, 2015), 48; compare with Kamuran Gürün, *The Armenian File*, 200.

times. Because guerrillas depend on local villages for supplies, support, and recruits, the guerrillas must be separated from the populace. ... The Ottomans had for centuries deported groups who threatened civil order, including rebellious Turks. ... Deportation of civilian populations because of real or imagined guerrilla threats has been practised by many modem governments.[53]

CONCLUSION

It has been said that denial aims to reshape history, to rehabilitate the perpetrators, and to demonise the victims. It demonstrates the fragility of memory, truth, reason, and history. Israel Charny labels denialists as the arrogant killers of truth who try, by the murder of recorded memories of human history, to write the final chapter of the original genocide. The denial of genocide celebrates its destructiveness, minimizes the significance of human life, and subordinates people to unquestioning obedience to government and authority.[54]

Yisrael Gutman adds that the refusal to acknowledge the very facts of genocide is a brutal attack on morality and fosters distrust in the historical record.[55] The process of denial becomes increasingly sophisticated through rationalisation, relativisation, and trivialisation. The denialists are more interested in justifying the present and shaping the future than they are in honestly portraying the past. By concealing the truth, they become defenders of and accomplices to the great crime.

In February 1996, more than a hundred scholars and literary figures published a petition denouncing denial of the Armenian Genocide. The petition states in part:

> Where scholars deny genocide, their message is: murderers did not really murder; victims were not really killed; mass murder requires no confrontation, but should be ignored. Scholars who deny genocide lend their considerable authority to the acceptance of this ultimate human crime.

---

53 Ibid., 52.
54 Israel W. Charny, "The Psychology of Denial of Known Genocides," in Israel W. Charny, *Genocide: A Critical Bibliographic Review*, vol. 2, 22–23.
55 Yisrael Gutman, "The Denial of the Holocaust and Its Consequences," in *Remembering for the Future*, ed. Elisabeth Maxwell and Roman Halter (Oxford: Pergamon Press, 1983), vol. 2, 2116, 2121–2124.

The denial of genocide is the final stage of genocide: it murders the dignity of the survivors and destroys the remembrance of the crime. Denial of genocide strives to reshape history in order to rehabilitate the perpetrators and demonise the victims. The Turkish government's denial of the Armenian Genocide encourages—by its very nature—current campaigns which deny the Jewish Holocaust and the Cambodian genocide; it encourages those genocidal episodes which are, even now, being perpetrated in Africa, the Balkans, and elsewhere. The Turkish government's tactics pave the way for the denial of future state-sponsored Holocausts and genocides.[56]

Among the signatories to the petition are noted Holocaust scholars Yehuda Bauer, Israel Charny, Helen Fein, Raul Hilberg, Steven Katz, Robert Jay Lifton, Deborah Lipstadt, and Robert Melson, and among the prominent literary figures are Allen Ginsberg, Norman Mailer, Arthur Miller, Henry Morgenthau III, Harold Pinter, Susan Sontag, John Updike, and Kurt Vonnegut. This salutary expression of solidarity inspires guarded optimism in the ongoing struggle against the manipulators of truth. Denial of the Armenian Genocide has penetrated far deeper within academic and political circles than has rejection of the truth of the Holocaust, but the arguments used are nonetheless the same.

The underlying motives of all these aspects of denial are deep-seated and range from historic prejudices to current political agendas. In the face of this ugly reality, it is incumbent upon people of good conscience to unite in combating this bigotry and in upholding the precept that an inseparable part of academic freedom is academic integrity.

---

56 *The Chronicle of Higher Education* (February 2, 1996), A30.

CHAPTER 9

A Contemporary Jew: Michael Berenbaum—The Armenian Genocide, the US Holocaust Memorial Museum, and Israel

Figure 13. Michael Berenbaum.

Contrary to some claims, during my time of service at the United States Holocaust Memorial Museum I experienced no political pressure whatsoever from the United States government regarding the Permanent Exhibition. Political pressure came from two governmental sources, officials portraying themselves as close to the German government, including a member of the Bundestag, and Israeli public officials and scholars close to that government concerned about the portrayal of the Armenian Genocide or even the use of the word "genocide" in depictions of the Armenian experience.

A word of biography may be in order. I served as deputy director of the President's Commission on the Holocaust in 1979 through January 1980 and later returned to the project—it was not yet a Museum—in 1987 serving first as a content consultant and in 1988–1993 as project director responsible for the development of the Museum's Permanent Exhibition working for the Museum Development Committee of the United States Holocaust Memorial Council. As the Museum reached completion, I became the director of the Museum's Research Institute in 1993 and occupied this position until 1997, which shortly after my departure became the Center for Advanced Holocaust Studies. I was appointed to the United States Holocaust Memorial Council, the governing body board of the Museum, by President Bill Clinton in 1998 and completed my term in 2003. During my term on the Council, I chaired the Education Committee and was on the Executive Committee for the last three years of my term. Thus, I write with not inconsiderable first-hand information regarding the work of the Museum and from personal direct knowledge.

It seems hard now to fathom, but in the early 1980s West Germany was concerned that a Museum on the Holocaust in the heart of Washington would impact negatively on the perception of Germany in the United States its most important ally. Recall that the early 1980s was less than a generation after the Holocaust and that Germany had only recently undergone a veritable earth-quake in response to the broadcast of four-part mini-series, the docudrama *The Holocaust* on German national television. A cynical joke was told at the time that the broadcast of the television series on the Holocaust had more impact than the original events. One concrete immediate result of the broad-cast was that the Bundestag, West Germany Parliament, extended the stat-ute of limitation on German war crimes, then set to expire. At that point the German government was moving toward the fortieth anniversary of the end of the war, a time when it hoped that West Germany could put World War II and the Holocaust behind it. Bitburg was one example of this effort at nor-malization. The desire of West Germany to join the commemoration of the fortieth anniversary of the Normandy invasion was another. So too, was the ongoing effort to distinguish between the good German people and the bad Nazis.

East Germany had purveyed a different historical narrative. As communists they told themselves that they were among the first victims of Nazism and hence had no responsibility for the crimes of Nazism. Their response mirrored Austria, which also then described itself as the first of the Nazi victims having been invaded in March 1938. Austrian history resumed on May 8, 1945, or so they convinced themselves. Adolf Hitler was part of German history, not Austrian history. Many Austrians benefitted from the so-called "Waldheimer's disease," a gap in their memory between March 1938 and May 1945, selective amnesia made manifest in Kurt Waldheim's campaign for President.

I played no role in the establishment of the informal committee appointed by Elie Wiesel on the issue of Germany, as this occurred during the interval when I was neither on staff nor on the Council. I did, however, have several conversations with mid-level West German Embassy officials as well as with the staff of several foundations that were dedicated to advancing German-American and German-Jewish relations and expressed astonishment that West Germany would be concerned about a Museum in the planning stages as I was convinced that the relationship between West Germany and the United States, West Germany and the American people, and West Germany and the American Jewish community would be shaped overwhelmingly by the actions of the West German government and the German people toward their own Jews, toward Israel and their records on human rights, civil rights, and democracy. Germany—both East and West. It could only undo the damage of its past record by the way it acted going forward. I was struck then and remain struck even now by the insecurity of the Germans forty years after the Holocaust regarding that dark period in German history. They were not confident in what they had achieved and how far they had moved forward.

The German initiative was private yet it carried with it the promise of a significant gift for the establishment of the Museum, whose fundraising campaign was but in its infancy. Edward Linenthal described these efforts in his work *Preserving Memory: The Struggle to Create America's Holocaust Museum*,

> [West] German-government officials attempted to moderate the portrayal of Germany in the Museum. In 1986 Wiesel established a US German Committee on Learning and Remembrance, with Peter Peterson, a member of the West German Bundestag. Aside from Wiesel, there was little

enthusiasm for this among Council members and his resignation (in December 1986) ended the connection.[1]

Those advocating Elie Wiesel's candidacy for the Nobel Prize drew considerable support from the Bundestag. This effort was not unknown to Wiesel though he deliberately kept his distance from the active campaign to remain above it, but his responsiveness toward Peterson's initiative was understandable.

The Content Committee, the Council body charged with reviewing the content of the Permanent Exhibition, did consider one concrete image to depict the "New Germany," namely the well-known photograph of Willy Brandt kneeling at the Warsaw Ghetto Memorial in a display of homage to its victims. I had advanced consideration of including this photograph not because of its portrayal of Germany but simply as a most useful image to grapple with Holocaust denial. The reasoning was simple: if the Chancellor of West Germany acknowledges the Holocaust, then that is a manifest refutation of Holocaust denial that was then achieving some visibility—not acceptability—in public discourse. Some survivors on the Committee objected and Dr. Hadassah Rosensaft, whose first husband and child were murdered at Auschwitz and was subsequently a postwar hero of rehabilitation at Bergen Belsen, objected vociferously and quite personally. She said: "If you were a child of Holocaust survivors, you would see that photograph differently." She feared that somehow it was exonerating the Germans while I saw it as an act of penance from a Chancellor whose hands were clean. Brandt was an anti-Nazi who had spent the war years in Norway and Sweden and the pre-war years working clandestinely against the Nazi regime. The vehemence of her objection carried the day as it was not worth the fight.

Now to the Armenian question, here too, a word of background is in order. The initial push for the United States government to do something significant relating to the Holocaust came from Senator Jack Danforth (R.MO) who moved for Days of Remembrance to be observed coinciding the April 28–29, the day American troops liberated Dachau. Danforth, a man of great moral stature, was an ordained Episcopal priest interested in such observances being held in Churches and Synagogues throughout the country. Mosques were not yet a consideration as in the 1970s the United States was still thinking religiously of Protestants, Catholics, and Jews. The linkage to the liberation of Dachau was to give an American veneer to the commemoration of an essentially European event.

---

1   Edward T. Linenthal, *Preserving Memory: The Struggle to Create America's Holocaust Museum* (New York: Viking, 1995), 251.

The initiative for an American National Memorial to the Holocaust came from the staff of President Jimmy Carter, Mark Siegel, Ellen Goldstein, and Stuart Eizenstat, three proudly Jewish domestic policy officials who felt that the time had come for the United States to do something significant about the Holocaust and who felt that it might do good and assist the President in his outreach to the American Jewish community. The announcement of the President's Commission and the national effort to memorialize the Holocaust came at the White House, the occasion was the celebration of thirtieth anniversary of the establishment of the State of Israel. Prime Minister Menachem Begin was the guest of honor and 1,000 rabbis were in attendance.

With the appointment of the President's Commission on the Holocaust, the initiative to realize the Days of Remembrance fell to the Commission. Elie Wiesel had been named chairman. Wiesel's brilliant sense of drama and his aspiration for the Holocaust to achieve an exalted stature took over and he envisioned a Joint Session of Congress dedicated to Holocaust commemoration with the President and the Chairman of his Commission addressing the Senate and the House. When such an event proved unfeasible, we created something quite akin to it.

The site chosen was the Capitol Rotunda, sacred space in Washington where Presidents and high-ranking revered officials lie in State upon their death. President Carter was invited to participate,[2] as well as the Vice President Water Mondale, the Speaker of the House and the Minority Leader, the Majority and Minority Leaders of the Senate. The Diplomatic Corps was invited. The Presentation of the Flag was to be preceded by the flags of the Army Units that liberated the concentration camps. If one could not get a Joint Session of Congress, then this was surely second best in terms of prestige and prominence reinforcing and advancing the unique nature of the Holocaust.

Second only to Israel with its nationwide commemoration, the United States was to observe Days of Remembrance. The Chairman and Rabbi Irving Greenberg, the Commission's director, were committed to reinforcing the importance of Yom HaShoah, observed on the 27th of Nissan, within days of the conclusion of the Passover observance. In 1979 that date coincided with April 24, which is the day observed by the Armenian community to commemorate

---

2   Address by President Jimmy Carter, National Civic Holocaust Remembrance Ceremony, Capitol Rotunda, April 24, 1979, reprinted in *Report to the President, President's Commission on the Holocaust, September 27, 1979* (Washington, DC: Government Printing Office, 1979), 26–27.

the genocide. That coincidence presented an interesting challenge. Would the Armenians be left standing on the outside, their genocide neglected, when the Jews and the American people were commemorating the Holocaust?

One member of the President's Commission on the Holocaust was particularly interested in the Armenian issue, Kitty Dukakis, wife of the then Governor of Massachusetts Michael Dukakis, a state which had a sizable Armenian community working with Set Momjian, an Armenian-American lobbyist, close to the Carter administration lobbied for the inclusion of Armenians in the commemorative event. Irving Greenberg suggested a creative and gracious way to handle the situation. In keeping with American civil tradition prayers were to be recited by clergy of diverse faiths, a Roman Catholic Priest, a Protestant Minister and a Rabbi who would preside over the recitation of the Kaddish and the *El Maleh Rachamim*, the Jewish memorial prayer for the dead. An Armenian Minister from Massachusetts was invited to participate. The Armenians would be included, and their unique historical experience honored.

Little did we suspect when the invitation was extended that their inclusion would present an international problem for the President of the United States. The Turks began a campaign to ensure that the term "genocide" was not used by President Carter to refer to the Armenian experience. Carter's speech writers handled the situation deftly, obliquely. The President said:

> It is fitting that we recall today the persecution, the suffering and the destruction which has befallen so many other people in this century, in many nations, peoples whose representatives have joined us in this observance. For the central lesson of the Holocaust must be that, in the words of the poet, "Each man's death diminishes me."[3]

Carter went on to underscore a principle of his own foreign and domestic policy: "Human rights and human dignity are indivisible. America was, and always will, speak out in defense of human rights not only in our own country, but around the world."[4] The word "genocide" was not used, yet the reference was direct enough to be heard by the Armenian community—although it remained seriously offended by the failure to use the word "genocide" explicitly—and oblique enough to be ignored by the Turkish government.

---

3   Ibid.
4   Ibid.

In its aftermath, the Armenian community did push for the inclusion of an Armenian representative in the composition of the United States Holocaust Memorial Council, the Commission's successor body charged with implementing its recommendations. That appointment was not controversial. More significant was the inclusion of a Ukrainian-American representative and a Polish-American representative as while Ukrainians and Poles were both victims of Nazism, they also participated in the murder of Jews.

Ukrainians, mostly former Soviet POWs who were turned, staffed the Aktion Reinhard death camps of Treblinka, Sobibor, and Belzec and also assisted the Germans in the destruction of the Warsaw Ghetto among other actions. In the end there was no Ukrainian-American representation on the Council, but the Polish-American community was represented in the final composition of the Council. Council survivors, many of whom were born in Poland and went through the Holocaust there, were uncomfortable but came to understand that ethnic politics in the United States mandated representation of Polish-Americans. Jew who survived the Holocaust in German-occupied and annexed Poland were often emotionally angrier at the Poles than they were at then Germans because they felt they had been betrayed by friends and neighbors, former school mates and business partners, people they grew up with and knew and from whom they had the right to expect support.

RECOGNIZING NON-JEWISH VICTIMS ALONGSIDE JEWS IN THE HOLOCAUST

More troubling to the chairman was the Carter definition of the Holocaust as the systematic state-sponsored "murder of eleven million people, six million Jews and five million non-Jews." which was part of the Executive Order. Wiesel was deeply troubled by this definition as he regarded the Holocaust as exclusively Jewish. In the end, he too finessed the issue saying that "while all Jews were victims not all victims were Jews." His underlying fear was that the Holocaust was being dejudaized. Speaking of the Holocaust, one might initially refer to eleven million people, six million of whom were Jews; soon the six million Jews would be unmentioned, lumped into the eleven million figure; all too soon thereafter, forgotten. This issue led to a delay in Wiesel assuming the chairmanship of the United States Holocaust Memorial Council and divided the Council for many years to come.

As the confrontation was developing, I told Elie Wiesel that "no one will tell you how to include the non-Jews, but you will have to include them in the museum if it is to be built in Washington." He did not take kindly to that communication and shortly thereafter, I was dismissed as deputy director. Perhaps, I was too young to know that one does not tell one's boss information that he does not want to hear without paying a price. And Wiesel had reached the stature where he was unaccustomed to receiving unwanted information, especially from subordinates.

A while later, while serving as Director of the Jewish Community Council of Greater Washington, I wrote an essay on the "Uniqueness and Universality of the Holocaust"[5] to advance my position, which argued that the inclusion of non-Jews in the proposed Museum was essential if one wanted to understand the uniqueness of the Holocaust and what was distinctive, unprecedented about the annihilation of Jews.

In essence, I argued that one could not speak of gassing, the mode by which Jews were murdered in the death camps without including the T-4 program in which under Hitler's direct orders, the Nazis set out to kill those Germans who were, to use non-politically correct terms, mentally retarded, physically infirm, congenitally ill, or emotionally disturbed. It was in this program that the gas chambers were developed and its personnel, after having killed thousands and tens of thousands in the T-4 program migrated to the death camps where they murdered hundreds of thousands and millions. Yet, unlike the Holocaust, public protests by some Germans such Bishop Count Von Gallen formally halted the T-4 program, driving it underground. Such voices were not heard when it came to the murder of the Jews.

Social democrats, trade unionists and political dissidents were targeted for what they did, Jews were subject to the "Final Solution" simply for the fact that they were Jews, or that they had Jewish grandparents.

Jehovah's Witnesses were martyrs, if they signed a document renouncing their faith and promising not to proselytize, they could be released from the concentration camps. Jews were victims, offered no such options. They were not murdered for their faith but for their blood; even those who had converted a generation before were not spared.

Nazi policy toward the Poles was to make them a subservient, leaderless nation, water carriers for the master race. It was not annihilation. The Polish nation would survive, the Jewish nation would not.

---

5   Michael Berenbaum, "The Uniqueness and Universality of the Holocaust," *American Journal of Theology and Philosophy* (Fall 1981), reprinted in Richard W. Rosseau, S.J., *Christianity and Judaism, The Deepening Dialogue* (Scranton: Ridge Row Press, 1981).

Soviet POWs were also subject to brutal conditions that led to their death. The first to be gassed at Auschwitz were Soviet POWs, yet by mid-1942 when the Germans realized that the World War would not end swiftly, they came to value the usefulness of young and able-bodied men for labor and some Soviet POWs even directly served the Nazis as the staff of death camps and in clearing ghettos in occupied Poland. Some slave laborers were even Jewish, but spared only for a time. Even if useful, their utility was secondary to their Jewishness. These young and able-bodied Jews were then also murdered.

German policy toward German, Austrian, and Czech homosexuals—again, I use non-politically correct terms because the term "gay" presumes acceptance—was not geared toward annihilation but toward reeducation—what we might call today conversion therapy—or toward punishment. There was no program of annihilation even though some 5,000 of those incarcerated in concentration camps were killed or died as a result of the conditions they faced.

The Roma and the Sinti—I mistakenly called them Gypsies then—shared much of the fate of the Jews. They too were murdered in the gas chambers of Auschwitz, yet there was no "Final Solution," no attempt to annihilate them everywhere. In some countries they were not subjected to death and even German policy distinguished between full Gypsies and part Gypsies. But Jews were central to Hitler's worldview; everyone else was peripheral.

I wrote then that the Armenian Genocide also served to underscore what was singular about the Holocaust. The German pursued the "Final Solution to the Jewish Problem," the annihilation of Jews everywhere. They Turks did not try to murder every Armenian everywhere.

Thus, I felt that the far from detracting from the uniqueness of the Jewish experience, *the inclusion* of non-Jews was essential to understanding what made the Holocaust unique and it was in the interest of survivors to include them not as a concession to the political necessity of operating in pluralistic American society but as an opportunity to serve their most basic interest in advancing the uniqueness argument.[6]

Toward the end of the 1980s I had the opportunity to edit a book based on a United States Holocaust Memorial Council conference on "The Other Victims: Non-Jewish Victims of Nazism" and entitled it *A Mosaic of Victims*[7] because I did not believe that it was in anyone's interest to divide the world

6   Ibid.
7   Michael Berenbaum, ed., *A Mosaic of Victims*.

into Jews and others. Later, in planning the United States Holocaust Memorial Museum, we named the area that dealt with these non-Jewish victims "Enemies of the State" and "Prisoners of the Camps" deciding to use words more applicable to that time and place and still not dividing the world into Jews and others.

One must always be cautious that a comparison of the modes of victimization and the reasons for persecution, incarceration and murder, does not degenerate into a comparison of suffering or what is often called the "Olympics of Suffering." Suffering is personal and to say that "I suffer more than you" is to exclude the other and demean the experience of the other. While we may chuckle uncomfortably at a Larry David episode on the real survivor; in life, to compare suffering is hurtful and rejecting of the experience of another.

WHY RECOGNIZE THE ARMENIAN GENOCIDE IN THE HOLOCAUST MUSEUM?

As we set out to consider the Permanent Exhibition of Museum there were clear reasons to favor the inclusion of the Armenian Genocide within the Museum. Historical justice warranted their inclusion; so too the comparison—not the equation—of the Holocaust, which would enable us to highlight the "Final Solution" aspect of the Holocaust. Finally and perhaps most importantly there were several clear organic links from within the Armenian Genocide to the Holocaust narrative: Hitler's statement to the German high command in 1939; the invention of the term "genocide" by Raphael Lemkin—with the Armenian experience clearly in his mind—when in 1933 he submitted a draft proposal to the League of Nations for an international convention on barbaric crimes and vandalism; the use of photographs as a form of protest by Armin Wegner; and the modeling of behavior in such instances as when the resistance fighters in Warsaw and Bialystok saw their deeds as a contemporary *Musa Dagh* (Franz Werfel, its author, was among the "muses who fled Hitler," the Jewish emigres who found refuge in the United States).

Furthermore, there is the case of Henry Morgenthau, Jr., the Secretary of the Treasury who met with President Franklin Delano Roosevelt on January 16, 1944 and presented him with the *Personal Report to the President* documenting American governmental misdeeds with regard to the rescue of European Jews, a meeting that directly led to the creation of the War Refugee Board on January 22, 1944. Morgenthau was the distinguished son of a distinguished father who saw his father's actions during World War I when as US Ambassador to Turkey he documented, protested, and personally attempted (such as with Talaat), however unsuccessfully, to protest the victims' fate.

Clearly, the Turkish government was uncomfortable with the possibility that the Armenians would be included in the Museum and brought pressure to bear on the issue.

The first attempt of pressure came from the scholarly milieu. Bernard Lewis, the well-respected Princeton scholar, a most influential scholar of Islam, and a deeply committed Jew met with Jeshayahu "Shaike" Weinberg, the Museum director and a long- time acquaintance, to warn him off including the Armenians. He tried to underscore that the Holocaust was different than the Armenians in that there was no "Final Solution," and there was violence on both sides. He did not deny the massacres and the victimization of the Armenians, but strongly advised against their inclusion stressing that the Museum would be inviting political opposition both from the Turks and the Israeli government. He was unpersuaded by the argument that inclusion was not equation and comparison was also not equation since we fully intended to *compare and contrast*. This was some dozen years before he came out fully in support of the invasion of Iraq and his sterling reputation was further tarnished. Among those who had learned of his editing a book in the 1960s where he had originally described the Armenian Genocide and then in the next edition denied there was any genocide, his intellectual position had slipped markedly—the Armenians and many scholars never forgave Lewis for this. Still, he was a towering figure at this time and his opposition was significant and forced the staff to reconsider but ultimately not to reject their initial plans.

The second movement of the opposition was to challenge the reliability of the source of Hitler's statement. The oft-reported story of Hitler's address to the German High Command in Obersalzberg on the eve of the Polish invasion bears repetition. Hitler told his officers:

> I have issued the command—and I'll have anybody who utters but one word of criticism executed by a firing squad—that our war aim does not consist in reaching certain lines, but in the physical destruction of the enemy. Accordingly, I have placed my deathhead formations in readiness— for present only in the East—with orders to send to death mercilessly and without compassion, men, women, and children of Polish derivation and language. Only thus shall we gain the living space [Lebensraum], which we need. *Who, after all, speaks today of the annihilation of the Armenians?* [*italics added*]

This version of Hitler's speech is traceable to Louis Lochner, the famous American correspondent in Berlin, who received a copy of the notes of the meeting from Hermann Maas, who received it from Hans Oster a key assistant of Admiral Wilhelm Canaris, director of the Abwehr, the counterintelligence department of the German high command. The information was sent to London on August 29, three days before the German invasion of Poland. (In 1944, Maas was a leader in the conspiracy against Hitler.) There are two other citations by journalists writing in the days before World War II began of the same quote by Hitler, both omit any reference to the Armenians. The historical staff did not want to rely solely on their knowledge with regard to this quote, so we asked Professor Gerhard Weinberg, then the William Rand Kenan, Jr. Professor of History at the University of North Carolina at Chapel Hill, to weigh in of its accuracy.

He wrote that this speech was "clearly designed to reassure his [Hitler's] listeners and assuage any doubts they might have." The audience, Weinberg said, "consisted of men who had themselves as adults lived through the events to which Hitler referred."[8] This was not the first time that Hitler had invoked the Armenian experience. He had previously used it as an example of how common massive resettlement had been in history.

The implications of Hitler's reference to the Armenians are clear: had the world remembered the Armenian experience, German officers might have been more reticent to carry out such a campaign of terror and destruction. Remembrance might have protected future generations, a message that the Museum was anxious to convey to its visitors.

We developed the contours of a visit to the Museum. Visitors would enter the elevator on the ground floor and rise to the fourth floor. In the elevator they would hear an American soldier describe his first reaction to entering the concentration camp. The exhibition would begin with the American liberators as a transition between the National Mall and the Holocaust. The exhibit on liberation would end with a question, the very question asked by American soldiers and their commanders: "How could this happen?" The rest of the Museum would be designed to answer that question.

The exhibition would then begin with the "World Before," a glimpse into Jewish life before the Holocaust, and opposite that exhibition the visitor would have a choice of seeing a fifteen-minute film on the rise of Nazism in 1919–1933 and a brief history of genocide as antecedents to the Holocaust, which would include the Armenian story.

---

8   Personal correspondence, August 1990.

STATE OF ISRAEL'S SEVERE PRESSURES FOR UNIQUENESS
OF THE HOLOCAUST

Around this time, I received a visit from a mid-level official at the Israel Embassy in Washington. He stressed the importance of not including the Armenians within the United States Holocaust Memorial Museum. His stated concerns were threefold. Turkey was (then) Israel's only Muslim ally in the Middle East, a vital partner and source of support. Secondly, Turkish fury at the inclusion of the Armenian Genocide might endanger the safety of the Turkish Jewish community, which was living freely in that country. And thirdly, the inclusion of the Armenian experience would detract from the uniqueness of the Holocaust and an appreciation of the singularity of the Jewish experience. His arguments were painful to hear because clearly, he had been sent on a mission, not quite to his liking. Our conversation was both in Hebrew and in English, as my Hebrew is fluent and I prefer to speak to Israelis in Hebrew because it gives me the opportunity to speak Hebrew and keep up with its professional usage. Furthermore, I have found that Israelis tend to be more candid and even more direct in Hebrew. They are more diplomatic and reserved in English, at least then.

My first response was formal, stated for the record. I asked him to remind the Turkish officials that the United States Holocaust Memorial Museum was an US government project and not a Jewish project, even though the Holocaust was important to the American Jewish community. The name of the museum was the *United States* Holocaust Memorial Museum, and therefore, while I was deeply supportive of Israel and close to many Israelis, I was working as an American official.

My second response was to object to the politicization of historical memory. I remarked that we were fortunate that the German government did not deny the Holocaust; otherwise, in the name of good relations between the United States and Germany or Israel and Germany, we—or the Israeli government—could be asked to omit all mention of the Holocaust lest the Germans were offended.

Thirdly, I challenged the strength and the reliability of the Turkish-Israel alliance if the inclusion or even mention by an American institution of the Armenians as part of the historical background of the Holocaust was to pose a danger to both the Turkey-Israel alliance and the Turkish-Jewish community. I also explained to him our approach to the uniqueness and universality of the Holocaust and why it served the interest of Jews to include all enemies of the state and prisoners of the camps as well as the Armenian Genocide—and how we intended to include it. Neither he nor I were satisfied by the meeting, nor could we have expected to be. He had delivered a message and could report back that such a message had been conveyed and, as anticipated, I had not convinced him of how right we were, historically, morally, Jewishly.

In the summer or fall of 1990 William Lowenberg, Vice Chairman of the Council, visited Israel and met with the Foreign Minister of Israel who impressed upon him the importance of not including the Armenians. An ardent supporter of Israel and a towering figure in the San Francisco Jewish Federation, he returned determined to minimize or eliminate all mention of the Armenians. As staff, I was not informed of the meeting but learned of it through murmurings of the board leadership. We were proceeding with the introductory film on the Rise of Nazism and Genocidal Precedents. The question of the inclusion of the Armenians came before the Executive Committee of the Museum Development Committee where the matter of the inclusion of genocidal precedents was referred to the Content Committee. However Albert Abramson, the influential chairman of the Museum Development Committee, asked "that the minutes reflect that is the 'sense' of the Committee that a comparison should not be made in the film or any other place in the Museum to any other mass murder because the Holocaust is unique."

The Content Committee considered the matter on February 13, 1991 where I presented the issues to the Committee in what I recall as its most stormy meeting. Edward Linenthal, the preeminent historian of memorialization who wrote an influential history of the Museum's creation, described the meeting.

> A prominent survivor and council representative lost control and screamed at Berenbaum "ordering" him not to mention the Armenians in his presence again. In this case, a survivor used his privileged voice as a weapon, and only Franklin Littell and Raul Hilberg spoke in Berenbaum's behalf. At the cost of significant political support within the institution— several people mentioned that Berenbaum had lost any chance to eventually become museum director because of the issue—he succeeded in salvaging the Hitler quote for inclusion in the permanent exhibition, for even that had been in jeopardy.[9]

I recall the feeling of betrayal that others including the Israeli scholars on the Content Committee did not speak out for they alone could have changed

---

9   Edward T. Linenthal, *Preserving Memory*, 234.

the outcome, especially since their position was to defend the uniqueness of the Holocaust. Yehuda Bauer, Israel's preeminent scholar and teacher on the Holocaust, did send a private letter, after the issue had been decided. He wrote a letter to Benjamin Meed, the Chair of the Content Committee:

> For the last two years I have been on the receiving end of direct pressure by the Turkish representatives in Jerusalem, by the Turkish embassy in London, by my own Foreign Office representatives and by the Jewish community in Istanbul (on one occasion by a member of the Jewish community in Washington as well). ... The Jewish community in Istanbul under pressure from their government provide a very sad example of the kind of behavior we all know from Jewish communities who have to bend their backs and their heads before authority. ... Denial of other people's genocides would expose us to a tremendous wave of criticism and would be morally absolutely contemptible.[10]

But his communication was private not public and did not sway other members of the Committee who did not learn of it. In the end, the opening film is only about the Rise of Nazism and includes no genocidal antecedents to the Holocaust. The Hitler quote is featured prominently, as are references to Franz Werfel and Musa Dagh. And over time, the Museum to its great credit has included exhibitions on subsequent genocides and feature significant programming on them even as genocides were ongoing and even in anticipation of potential genocides. Even some of the most ardent proponents of the uniqueness of the Holocaust have come to understand that if we situate the Holocaust as a world apart from our world, then it has nothing to say to our world.

And everyone involved in Holocaust scholarship, education, exhibitions and films is far more assured today that the Holocaust has achieved a stature of significance that will endure even as the survivors are no longer and we transition between lived history and historical memory.

As to my not becoming Museum director, a position to which I once aspired, I suspect that there were other reasons that the job was not mine to have. Like many insider candidates, my skills were taken for granted and my flaws including administrative shortcomings were magnified; an outsider seemed more attractive until they didn't. After two very public failures with the

---

10   Ibid., 234–235.

director, an insider, Sara J. Bloomfield was hired as director and has served for almost a quarter century as director. And my dear friend and respected colleague Shaike Weinberg did not groom me as his successor as would have been required and expected. Ironically, given the trajectory of my subsequent career, I am not ungrateful that I was not given that opportunity and remain most grateful for the many creative and scholarly opportunities that the Museum did give me and those that not running a large and complex institution have brought my way.

Still I remain deeply disturbed by Israeli attempts then to politicize history and deeply unimpressed by Israel's political leadership continued efforts to politicize history.

ISRAEL IS IN A LOSE/LOSE SITUATION

When in January 2012, during the tense moment in Israel's relationship with Turkey, the Israel's Knesset Committee on Education debated whether to recognize the Armenian Genocide. I wrote an op-ed for the Israeli newspaper *Haaretz*:[11]

> On the one hand there are those who believe in historical justice. But that
> is not the real issue, as the MKs who organized the session are joined by
> others who are furious at contemporary Turkey for many recent incidents
> that have contributed to a significant deterioration in [Israeli-Turkish]
> relations.

---

11 Michael Berenbaum, "When Silence is Wisdom," *Haaretz*, January 6, 2012. I have continued to write about the politicization of memory by Israel leaders including the Prime Minister and his inappropriate linkage of the Mufti and Hitler's decision to gas the Jews, the then Education Minister Naftali Bennet speaking at Auschwitz in 2018 of the ghettos of Vienna and Paris, where there were none, and Israeli political leaders and even Yad Vashem portraying the non-bombing of Auschwitz as an accusation against the Allies *without* considering the decision by Yishuv leadership on June 11, 1944 not to request that Auschwitz be bombed and the seeming reversal of that decision twenty-six days later when Chaim Weizmann and Moshe Shertok (later Moshe Sharett, Israel's second Prime Minister) requested that Auschwitz be bombed in a meeting with Anthony Eden, the British Foreign Minister. In January 2020, Yad Vashem criticized its own film shown at an international conference commemorating the 75th anniversary of the liberation of Auschwitz for not including any mention of the Ribbentrop-Molotov Pact of August 1939, the agreement between Nazi Germany and the Soviet Union that included a secret codicil dividing Poland and the subsequent Soviet invasion from the East. Apparently, it was done so as not to offend the Russian President Putin who was attending the conference.

On the other side are pragmatists who feel that Israel's relationship with the Turks is tense enough right now without adding fuel to the fire, especially as the Syrian situation is so explosive. Turkey has come out strongly against the Assad regime, even as Israeli observers wonder whether their interests are better served by the devil it knows than by the unknown alternative. They are joined by MKs who are zealous to preserve the uniqueness of the Nazi Holocaust, and who feel that use of the term "genocide" with regard to the Armenian tragedy somehow diminishes the Shoah's stature—even if it's by no means clear how this is so.

By having its Education Committee hold a hearing on the subject, the Knesset is setting a dangerous course, morally, politically, and historically. Here's why:

I have no doubt that the crime committed during the years 1915–1918, which led to the deaths of as many 1.5 million Armenians, was genocide. Indeed, the very word, a hybrid combining the Greek *geno*, meaning race or tribe, and the Latin derivative *cide*, from *caedesi*, meaning killing, was first coined to depict the massacre of Armenians by the Turks.

Early this decade [2001], I worked on a film depicting Turkey's mostly positive role during the Holocaust which brought me into direct contact with many Turkish officials. Naturally, the issue of the Armenian Genocide came up. I advised those officials and Turkish intellectuals with whom I have worked closely to admit to the genocide and not to expend such national prestige fighting a historical truth. It implicates neither the current regime nor any of its predecessors dating back to the founding of the Turkish Republic by Mustafa Kemal Atatürk following the collapse of the Ottoman Empire after World War I. Say it once, say it quietly and get it behind you.

No one would think any less of the current Turkish government were it to acknowledge such a chapter in the country's history. In fact, such an act would be met with admiration. Germany is a proof in point by its admitting to the past and taking vital steps to establish a democratic state and to act and educate.

But the Knesset should stay out of it. For the Knesset to pass a resolution today would only serve to politicize history. Sensitive to its relationship to Turkey and to the vast stake the Turkish government has had in denying the genocide, the State of Israel has long believed that it's not in its national interest to use the word genocide with regard to the massacres. There is no mention of this genocide at Yad Vashem, Israel's official Holocaust memorial institution. Foreign Ministry officials tried ever so hard to force the cancellation of an academic conference on the subject in Israel some three decades ago. The state has also formally and informally pressured international Jewish organizations, as well as the influential American Jewish community not to touch the issue.

In the early 1990s, for example, when the US Holocaust Memorial Museum was in the process of being created, Israel tried to make sure it would include no mention of the Armenian Genocide and came close to succeeding. The museum eliminated from the permanent exhibition's opening film any mention of previous cases of genocide, and limited mention of the Armenian case to Hitler's 1939 quote on the subject, as well as to a reference to Franz Werfel's novel, *The Forty Days of Musa Dagh*.

At the time, I was the museum's project director, and Israeli Embassy staff and Foreign Ministry officials warned me that we should steer clear of the issue. During a visit to Israel, the then-vice chairman of the Holocaust Memorial Council met with the foreign minister himself, who told him this was a subject of highest concern to the Israeli government. As a result, he ordered the staff not to discuss it and when it was brought up before the museum's content committee, the atmosphere was explosive. I was ordered not to mention the Armenians again.

And there are many other, more recent examples of Israeli governmental pressures.

So why should Israel not deal with this? After all, not to pass such a resolution is craven. It legitimizes the denial of history for political purposes, for a political agenda. Yet to pass this resolution at this time, when nothing has changed other than the fact that Israel and Turkey are feuding would have Israel serve as an example par excellence that historical facts can be changed for a political purpose—something other nations might notice as they consider the memory of the Holocaust.

Israel is now in a lose/lose situation. The longer the politicians debate the issue, the more it diminishes the country's moral stature and the more dangerous it becomes for the memory of the Holocaust. Not to acknowledge the Armenian Genocide puts it on the side of historical deniers, yet to acknowledge it now, out of anger, as punishment for the Turks, is an undesirable politicization of history. Sometimes, as the Talmud tells us, silence is wisdom.

However, I might add today, that is not true of silence with regard to the facts of the genocide.

CHAPTER 10

Israel's Continuing Denial of the Armenian Genocide

RAPHAEL AHREN, "WHY ISRAEL STILL REFUSES TO RECOGNIZE A CENTURY-OLD GENOCIDE," *TIMES OF ISRAEL*, APRIL 24, 2015[1]

Addressing the United Nations in New York on International Holocaust Remembrance Day earlier this year, President Reuven Rivlin dedicated a large chunk of his speech to the fate of the Armenian people, who were killed by the hundreds of thousands between 1915 and 1923.

Rivlin spoke of "one hundred years of hesitation and denial" and stressed that at the time, no one in the Land of Israel denied the massacre that had taken place.

"The residents of Jerusalem, my parents and the members of my family, saw the Armenian refugees arriving by the thousands—starving, piteous survivors of calamity. In Jerusalem they found shelter and their descendants continue to live there to this day," he said.

During his speech, he uttered the word "genocide" nine times—but never in the context of what had occurred to the Armenians. Or did he?

Speaking in his mother tongue, Rivlin referred to the *retzah bnei ha'am ha'armeni*, which means "the murder of the members of the Armenian nation," but hints at the Hebrew term for genocide, *retzah am*.

For some, his choice of words was a smart rhetorical device with which he elegantly avoided a diplomatic pitfall, since Israel has never officially recognized the Armenian Genocide. The Armenian community in Israel, however, was disappointed.

Rivlin used to be known as one of the country's strongest advocates for the unequivocal recognition of the genocide, said Georgette Avakian, a member

---

1   Raphael Ahren, "Why Israel Still Refuses to Recognize a Century-Old Genocide," *Times of Israel*, April 24, 2015. We appreciate the permission by Raphael Ahren and the *Times of Israel* to republish this article from their original publication.

of the Armenian Case Committee in Israel. "Today, he is the president of the state and things aren't exactly as they once were," she told The Times of Israel. "He didn't use the word 'genocide.' Yes, he said *retzah bnei ha'am ha'armeni*, but that's not enough."

This Friday, the world observes the 100th anniversary of the mass murder of nearly a million and a half Armenians at the hand of Ottoman Turks. Well, not the entire world. While countless regional and local government have recognized the Armenian Genocide, from Scotland, New South Wales, and forty-four US states to the province of Buenos Aires and the municipality of Aleppo in Syria, the overwhelming majority of countries in the world—including the United States, Germany, and, of course, Israel—refuses to do so.

In most cases, countries don't want to formally refer to the events between 1915 and 1923, during which Ottoman forces massacred Armenian citizens in a systematically planned act of ethnic cleansing, as genocide, out of concern for their ties to Turkey, which is a member of NATO and an important Muslim ally of many Western countries. Ankara resolutely denies that genocide took place on its soil and aggressively objects to anyone who adopts such a terminology.

Earlier this month, Pope Francis referred to the mass murder of the Armenians as "the first genocide of the 20th century." Turkey was furious: The pontiff had joined "the conspiracy" of an "evil front" against the country's ruling AK party, Prime Minister Ahmet Davutoğlu declared. (Even though the Vatican had officially recognized the Armenian Genocide already in 2000, when Pope John Paul II said it was a "prologue to the horrors that would follow.")

Israel doesn't formally recognize the Armenian Genocide for various geopolitical reasons that go beyond a hoped-for détente with Turkey. These strategic considerations weigh so strongly that they continue to trump heavy pressure from Jewish and Armenian groups and even a significant number of Israeli politicians. Israel's ongoing denial of the Armenian Genocide survived several debates in the Knesset and even efforts by a former education minister to add the topic to school curricula.

"Israel's position hasn't changed," Foreign Ministry spokesman Emmanuel Nahshon said in an interview last week. "Israel and the Jewish people are showing solidarity and empathy with the Armenian people and government in light of the profound tragedy they endured during World War I."

Nahshon carefully skirted the G-word. So did the Knesset's press release about Israel's delegation to Yerevan for official memorial events over the weekend, which referred merely to the "Armenian tragedy."

Three Israeli dignitaries are scheduled to represent the state in Armenia: MKs Anat Berko (Likud) and Nahman Shai (Zionist Union) and Israel's non-resident ambassador to Armenia, Shmuel Meirom.

"Israel must reconsider its position on whether the time has come to recognize the fact that an Armenian Genocide occurred. As Jews, we must recognize it," said Shai, whose center-left party will most likely be in the opposition. In an interview, he went as far as calling the tragic events "the Armenian Holocaust," even daring to say that they were "just like what the Nazis did to the Jews."[2]

But Berko, who represents Israel's ruling party, steered clear of such terms.

"We consider this a horrible tragedy and we identify with the Armenian people," she told *The Times of Israel* last week. Jerusalem recognizes the suffering that befell the Armenian people and relates to it by sending a "respectable delegation" to Yerevan, she added, suggesting that it is pretty much all Israel can do for the Armenians at this stage.

"This is the state's position. We're representing the state; my personal view on this doesn't matter," she said regarding Jerusalem's refusal to call a genocide a genocide. Referring to the events 100 years ago as a "horrible tragedy" is strong enough, and there is no need to commit to calling it a genocide, she argued, suggesting that historians are still unclear on what exactly happened back then.

Does recognizing the Armenian Genocide marginalize the Holocaust?

In 2001, when relations with Turkey were much rosier than today, then foreign minister Shimon Peres outright denied "Armenian allegations," denouncing them as efforts to create a parallel between them and the Holocaust. "Nothing similar to the Holocaust occurred. What the Armenians went through is a tragedy, but not genocide," he said at the time.

The Holocaust's uniqueness, some argue, prevents Israel from referring to the Armenian situation as genocide. Following this warped logic, recognizing another people's genocide somehow diminishes one's own tragic history. On the other hand, a growing number of Israelis argue that since Jews suffered genocide they are obligated to be the first to recognize it if it is being done to others.

Many important Jewish groups, including the Anti-Defamation League and the Union for Reform Judaism, have long recognized the Armenian Genocide.

---

2   "Members of Israel's Knesset to Attend Centennial Commemorations in Yerevan," *Asbarez. com*, April 14, 2015, http://asbarez.com/134041/members-of-israels-knesset-to-attend-centennial-commemorations-in-yerevan/.

"As members of a nation that knew the Shoah and that fights Holocaust denial, we are obligated to show special sensitivity toward the catastrophe of another people," reads an online petition calling on the Israeli government to recognize the Armenian Genocide. Among the signatories are prominent Israelis from all spheres, such as writer Amos Oz, historian Yehuda Bauer, retired Israel Defense Forces general Amos Yadlin, former Likud minister Dan Meridor and about a dozen former MKs and ministers. (So far, some 760 people have signed the petition.)

And yet, chances that Jerusalem will heed their call anytime soon remain low, according to Israel Charny, the longtime director of the Institute on the Holocaust and Genocide in Jerusalem and one of the first and most vocal Israeli advocates for the recognition of the Armenian Genocide.

"Right now, the best we can hope for is that government representatives will make *menschlich* [decent] statements of recognition of the genocide and the sympathy and the identification of the Jewish people with the Armenian people with the tragedy and evil that they suffered," he said.

But Charny, who was invited by the Armenian government to attend the state's official genocide commemoration Friday in Yerevan, does expect a renewed attempt by MKs to vote on an official Israeli recognition. He attended previous such discussions in the Knesset, during which he felt that a majority of lawmakers are actually in favor of recognition legislation, but that they were always stifled by the powers that be in the Foreign Ministry and the Prime Minister's Office.

Whether such a law will be passed by the 20th Knesset is doubtable, but Charny hopes, at the very least, that "the people who stifle it carry the shame and responsibility in history for stifling something that is absolutely bona fide, for which there is plain evidence, and which is a forerunner of the Holocaust."

Israel should take an example from Armenia, which started devoting significant resources to studying genocides other than their own, Charny said. The Armenian equivalent of Israel's Yad Vashem Holocaust Museum has recently built a new library dedicated to mass murder of other peoples, and legislators established a day of commemoration for victims of all genocides. In comparison with Armenia, he suggested, Israel appears self-centered and indifferent to other people's tragedies, as if Jews had the monopoly on suffering.

"There is nothing in Armenia that is minimizing their own memory of their genocide. On the contrary. But they're expanding their worldview," he continued. "For me, it is our Jewish tradition at its wisest—it is the Israel that I and many others like me dream of—that would be able to expand itself to be concerned also with the genocides of other people, and not just be busy with the realpolitik, crushing kind of self-interest policy."

What is it, exactly, that keeps Jerusalem from recognizing the Armenian Genocide? Israel is a small country in a hostile neighborhood that can't afford to antagonize the few friends it has in the region. Even more powerful states refuse to employ the "genocide" term for fear of alienating Turkey, and though ties between Jerusalem and Ankara are at an all-time low, Israel knows that recognizing the Armenian Genocide would further distance any prospect of reconciliation.

But perhaps more important than the ties with Turkey is Israel's budding friendship with Azerbaijan. A Shiite Muslim but moderate country bordering Iran, it is the archenemy of Armenia and therefore opposes any acknowledgment of Armenian victimhood. Indeed, Azeris are currently involved in a campaign to portray the Armenians themselves as perpetrators of systematic mass murder. Citing the so-called Khojali massacre of 1992, in which Azeris were killed during the Nagorno-Karabakh War, government officials and scholars sympathetic to Baku accuse the Armenians of genocide.

"Armenia is a poor country, and they ain't worth as much in their shtetl over there, compared to the flourishing Azerbaijan."

During his Holocaust Day speech at the UN, Rivlin actually listed Khojali among a number of other ostensible "genocides," much to the Armenians' dismay.

In February, Foreign Minister Avigdor Liberman attended an event in Azerbaijan commemorating the events at Khojali, again angering Armenia. "It is inappropriate that any politician could allow himself to be pulled into cheap Azerbaijani manipulations," Armenian Foreign Ministry spokesman Tigran Balayan said at the time.

(Several articles making such claims have appeared in the Israeli press in recent months, pointing to a concerted effort to turn the Armenians from victims into perpetrators.)

Israel refuses to recognize the Armenian Genocide "only because of material interests," said Avakian, of the Jerusalem-based Armenian Case Committee. "It's because of relations with Azerbaijan and Turkey, arms deals and other economic issues. Israel is forgetting that the Jewish people also went through a horrible Holocaust."

Baku and Jerusalem indeed have strong trade ties, in addition to a mutual distrust of Iran. Some 40 percent of oil used in Israel comes from Azerbaijan, and Jerusalem "also sells its Azeri partner armored troop carriers, multiple rocket launchers, Tavor rifles and ammunition," Bar-Ilan University scholars Anna Geifman and Dima Course wrote in a 2013 paper.[3] "However, since neither country has enough friends beyond its borders, it should be clear that each partner may contribute to much-required foreign lobbying for the sake of the other."

There is a strong lobby within the Israeli government that puts realpolitik ahead of principle, which explains why strong ties with Azerbaijan prevent the recognition of the Armenian Genocide, said Charny, the Jerusalem-based genocide scholar. "Armenia is a poor country, a struggling, smaller country. And they ain't worth as much in their shtetl over there in Armenia, compared to the flourishing Azerbaijan," he said sarcastically.

And yet, efforts to place historical truth and moral considerations over political expediency have come from both the left and the right in Israel.

In 2000, then-education minister Yossi Sarid (Meretz) announced plans to place the Armenian Genocide on Israel's history curricula. "Genocide is a crime against humanity and there is nothing more horrible and odious than genocide. One of the objectives of our education — our main objective — is to instill sensitivity to the harm to the innocent based on nationality alone," he said on the 85th anniversary of the massacre. "We Jews, as principal victims of murderous hatred, are doubly obligated to be sensitive, to identify with other victims."

A decade later, in June 2011, it was MK Arye Eldad, of the far-right National Union party, who introduced a bill to declare every April 24 Armenian Genocide Remembrance Day. A few weeks earlier, the Knesset had held its first discussion on the recognition of the genocide. It appeared that there would be a majority for recognition, but the issue was never put to the vote.

Another right-wing politician—today he is Israel's president—was one of the Knesset's most outspoken advocates for the recognition of the Armenian Genocide. As MK and Knesset speaker, Rivlin vocally argued that the moral imperative not to deny another people's suffering must trump whatever Israel's diplomatic and geopolitical needs dictated.

---

3   Anna Geifman and Dima Course, "Israel and Azerbaijan: Geopolitical Reasons for Stronger Ties," BESA Center Perspectives Paper No. 208, July 15, 2013, http://besacenter.org/wp-content/uploads/2013/07/perspectives208.pdf.

It is unthinkable for the Knesset to ignore this tragedy, Rivlin commented two years ago in the plenum. "We demand that people don't deny the Holocaust, and we can't ignore the tragedy of another nation." He even sought to establish an annual parliamentary session to mark the Armenian Genocide. "It is my duty as a Jew and an Israeli to recognize the tragedies of other peoples," Rivlin said. "Diplomatic considerations, important as they may be, do not allow us to deny the disaster [experienced by] another people."

Today, as Israel's head of state, whose words carry so much more weight on the international stage, Rivlin faces a true dilemma pitting moral clarity against political expediency. While Armenians accuse him of an about-face, other advocates of recognition say he remains committed to the cause. The way he tiptoed around the word "genocide" during his UN speech is not the only manifestation of his ostensible hesitancy to utter the G-word in relation to Armenia. In December, he also decided not to renew his signature on an annual petition calling on Israel to recognize the massacre as a genocide. Israeli pro-recognition activists were disappointed, but some acknowledged that it might not behoove a president to sign petitions of this sort.

For Charny, the genocide scholar, Rivlin's pro-recognition credentials remain fully intact. True, the president avoided uttering the word "genocide," but he placed the Armenian massacre front and center during his speech for Holocaust Remembrance Day, suggesting that Jeremiah would have wept for the Armenians as he wept for the people of Israel.

Rivlin's reference to the *retzah bnei ha'am ha'armeni* counts as a full recognition of the Armenian Genocide, Charny opined, "and I consider that a major symbolic step forward."

Israel's political system places certain limitations on the powers of the president, but "it is not a trivial matter when the president of a country takes a stand like that," he added. "It's a breakthrough and it is tragic that it is not celebrated correctly, either in Israel or in Armenia." Indeed, there are clear indications that Rivlin hasn't changed his mind on the matter. During a briefing for English-speaking journalists last week, he congratulated the pope for recognizing the Armenian Genocide. "There is a saying that the Nazis used the Armenian Genocide as something that gave them permission to bring the Holocaust into reality, according to their belief that they have to discriminate against the Jewish people," he said. "We cannot allow any kind of racism, any kind of anti-Semitism, any opportunity of acting in wars that can be defined as genocide. This is very obvious.

Raphael Ahren is the Diplomatic Correspondent of the Times of Israel

ISRAEL W. CHARNY WITH YAIR AURON, "IF NOT NOW, WHEN WILL ISRAEL RECOGNIZE THE ARMENIAN GENOCIDE?," *CALIFORNIA COURIER*, JANUARY 9, 2020[4]

The following was submitted as an op-ed in English to the Jerusalem Post *by Israel W. Charny, and similarly in Hebrew to* Haaretz *with the additional signature of Yair Auron, but in both cases was not published. Both of us are well-known scholars in Israel and long-term advocates for Israel to recognize the Armenian Genocide. While there is no real basis for judging why op-eds are not accepted by newspapers, we cannot help wondering whether our strong critique of Jewish/Israeli policy and especially the comparison of our people to the peoples of the world who remained silent during our Holocaust was "too much" for the Israeli editors.*

The electrifying news of the US Senate voting unanimously—yes, unanimously—to recognize the Armenian Genocide, now completes the sequence of the resolution of the House of Representatives in October recognizing the Armenian Genocide.

The US Congress had the guts to overcome the so-often repeated orders of the administration not to embarrass, upset, or defy Turkey.

This leaves us in Israel with a deep underscoring of our long-standing shame in not completing recognition of the Armenian Genocide even when our Knesset Committee on Education approved it a few years ago, and even when there was a clear-cut majority of voices in the Knesset for recognition. Each time, our administration would step in and utilize its administrative and political powers to squelch the completion of a successful vote on the resolution.

Spiritually, we the Jewish people, have failed miserably in this and other instances of recognizing forthrightly not only past genocides of other peoples but ongoing genocides of peoples in our world. Like the goyim who remained silent during our Holocaust, we have been the goyim of our age failing to recognize and speak up for other peoples undergoing the hells of genocide—such as the Yazidi at the hands of Da'ash, the Rohingya in Myanmar, the Christians in Syria and in other countries, or the Uighurs in China.

---

4   Israel W. Charny and Yair Auron, "If Not Now, When Will Israel Recognize the Armenian Genocide?," *California Courier*, January 9, 2020.

IWC: I have just returned from Athens where an International Conference on the Crime of Genocide took place December 5–7, and I then spoke in Thessaloniki on December 10 after my wife and I had spent the day meeting members of the remnant Jewish community and visiting two synagogues and the Jewish Museum, in all of which we learned a great deal of the spectacular tragedy of Thessaloniki Jews in the Holocaust, 96% of whom perished at Auschwitz.

The Greeks are now marking the 100th anniversary of both the Pontian and Anatolian genocides. While the genocide of the Greeks began in various pogroms and then in parallel with the heightening of the Armenian Genocide in 1913 and onward, the Turks intensified their murders of the Greeks at the time that the Armenian Genocide was grinding to a halt. The Armenians therefore marked their 100th anniversary of the Armenian Genocide in 2015 and the Greeks mark their 100th anniversary now in 2019.

What was outstanding for me was that along with the depth of feeling for their own memories and their own tragedy, the conference and the public meeting in Thessaloniki were simultaneously genuinely committed and dedicated to the lessening and prevention of genocide to all other peoples.

Halevai aleinu (wish that were true for us)!

Both events in Greece were dedicated to the United Nations worldwide "International Day of Commemoration and Dignity of the Victims of the Crime of Genocide and of the Prevention of this Crime- December 9." Was there any recognition of this day in our Israel? By the government, educational system, press and media?

It is time for us to be true to the finer parts of Jewish tradition of respecting and protecting human life—whoever and wherever.

Professor Israel W. Charny is the director of the Institute on the Holocaust and Genocide, Jerusalem. He is the author recently of The Genocide Contagion: How We Commit and Confront Holocaust and Genocide (*Winner of the "Spirituality and Practice Book Award"*). *Professor Yair Auron is associate director, Institute of the Holocaust and Genocide, Jerusalem. He is the author recently of* The Holocaust, Rebirth, and the Nakba: Memory and Contemporary Israeli–Arab Relations.

SUPPLEMENT: INSTITUTE ON THE HOLOCAUST AND GENOCIDE, JERUSALEM—HIGHLIGHTS OF THE STORY OF THE FIRST KNOWN INSTITUTE ON GENOCIDE IN THE WORLD

Marc I. Sherman, MLS

When reviewing the accomplishments of the Institute on the Holocaust and Genocide, Jerusalem over the last forty years, one has to wonder, "How big are their offices?" and "How large is their staff? Well, when the reality sets in, it is hard to believe that the accomplishments, trailblazing and impact of the Institute on the Holocaust and Genocide, Jerusalem throughout the world stems from a small room located in the house of Prof. Israel W. Charny. In fact, the room is so small, that people have to take turns passing through the area. The idiom, "Good things come in small packages" definitely applies!

The Institute on the Holocaust and Genocide, Jerusalem, was founded in 1979 through the efforts of Profs. Charny, Shamai Davidson, MD, and Elie Wiesel. As recorded in the description of the Institute in its brochure, the Institute "is probably the most identified body in the world that is devoted to the study of the genocides of *all* peoples, aiming at understanding the generic genocidal process, as well as to the further goal of developing new concepts for intervention and prevention of genocide to *all* peoples in the future." The Institute maintained throughout the years an International Advisory Board that reflected leading scholars and academics in the field.

To interject a personal note of my connection to the Institute, it began soon after my arrival in Israel from New York in 1985. I was fortunate enough to have been able to make *aliyah* (immigrate), already employed at Tel Aviv University. I was a freshly minted library science/information professional with an MLS degree from Syracuse University. While studying in my program, I was approached by a professor from the Maxwell School to assist him with a grant he received from UNESCO to build a bibliography on the international and comparative law of human rights. He needed a librarian/bibliographic specialist from the Information Studies School to assist him, while serving as the subject specialist for the project. He envisioned that my role in the project would last a few months and then the bibliography would be completed. However, the adage, "When man plans, God laughs" applies to this story. My co-editor died from a heart attack walking on campus and the project lasted three years. The last letter he wrote which would turn out to be the most influential letter ever written on my behalf was to the Rector of Tel Aviv University introducing me. The letter, in fact, was sent out after he died.

One month later, I received a call from the New York office of Tel Aviv University asking me to come meet with the Rector who was in New York on university business. The letter he received from my co-editor led to his offering me a position to coordinate and publish the Tel Aviv University Research Catalogues to document all research activities and publications of the university faculty. One year later I arrived in Israel.

While collecting information on the research activities, I saw that a Prof. Israel W. Charny from the Social Work School was building a bibliographic project on genocide. The combination of a bibliographic project and the field of genocide led me to make an appointment with him. We met and although I am sure Israel thought he would never see me again, I offered my expertise to him and the Institute and the roller coaster ride began and is still ongoing today, thirty-five years after we first met!

Since its founding, the Institute has initiated many research projects that further solidified its contributions to the emerging field of comparative genocide studies. These projects can be grouped into two major categories, individual projects that culminated in publications; and longer-term information-based reference projects.

Israel W. Charny was very fond of and appreciated the importance of building reference information sources, especially for the emerging field of comparative genocide studies. Thus, the Institute initiated a series of projects through the years to further provide scholars and students in the field with material to further their research endeavors. Five major information-based projects undertaken by the Institute were a news magazine, *Internet on the Holocaust and Genocide*; a series of books, *Genocide: A Critical Bibliographic Review*; the first computerized bibliographic project in the field for the United States Institute of Peace, the *Holocaust and Genocide Bibliographic Database*; the first encyclopedia in the field, the *Encyclopedia of Genocide*; and finally, an electronic magazine, *Genocide Prevention Now* (*GPN*). I will give short descriptions of each of these projects which will show the impact that the Institute on the Holocaust and Genocide, Jerusalem had on the field of comparative genocide studies over the last forty years.

Before I present the descriptions, I would like to give the reader a sense of the sequence of the projects take on by the fledgling first institute on genocide in the world. There was no long-term master plan. There was a deep desire and energy to open up a world of study, and at each crossroads an instinctive decision was made to proceed further.

Charny's work begins with his magnum opus, *How Can We Commit the Unthinkable? Genocide: The Human Cancer* on which he worked for 10 years, the last five of which were already in Israel to which he moved in 1973 in collaboration with the director of Israel's main think tank in the social sciences at the time, Dr. Chanan Rapaport of the Szold National Institute on the Behavioral Science in Jerusalem.

Among other things, Charny enjoys telling how in writing this book he spent a year role-playing every day (for those who know the Stanislavsky tradition of theatre) for a half hour each of the roles of victims, bystanders and accomplices, and perpetrators of genocide.

The book was hailed far and wide by the Prime Ministers of Germany and France, the United Nations, the US Dept. of State, the *New York Times,* and endless professionals. Its outstanding feature for most reviewers and readers was its culminating proposal of the Genocide Early Warning System (GEWS). Note the pronunciation with a soft "g": it is Charny's personal way of reminding himself of the specific tragedy of his own Jewish people even as he addresses genocide as a distinctly universal problem of humankind.

After all these years, a new edition of *How Can We Commit the Unthinkable* has just been reissued by Routledge Publishers in 2019.

It was the completion of this book which was published in 1982 that freed Charny to go on to initiate the idea of a First International Conference on Holocaust and Genocide in 1982. And then it was the success and profound meaningfulness of the conference that invited the next project of the Institute on the Holocaust and Genocide. *Internet on the Holocaust and Genocide* was a computer-generated magazine in which we published 56 issues over a ten-year period. Like the conference, it was multi-disciplinary. In fact, Charny made a point of not starting the project until several different ethnic/national groups had agreed to work together as sponsors. The issues were mailed out to hundreds of people around the world with no obligatory subscription fee, but yes with a request for contributions to which many people responded.

It was time for a new project. Now came the initiation of the series, *Genocide: A Critical Bibliographic Review* whose first volume in 1988 was promptly crowned with a memorable award as "Outstanding Academic Book of the Year" by the American Library Association. These books charted a new form of scholarly information—an analytical summary essay by a known scholar of a given area of genocide studies followed by a meaningfully annotated bibliography of the major publications in the field. After the first four volumes by our Institute, the series was turned over to Prof. Samuel Totten, a Distinguished Fellow of the Institute who published several additional volumes. (The bibliographic sections of these volumes were all included in the computerized bibliographic database of genocide studies built by the Institute in 1994.)[5]

Enter the 1990s and the Institute plays a major role in founding the International Association of Genocide Scholars (IAGS), and launches the monumental first encyclopedia in the field of genocide studies. What a rollercoaster! See the description of how we had to return the manuscript to the publisher because of poor editing. But even more important see the story of how we were prepared to abort the completed project of the publisher. The publisher had received a legal opinion from their attorney that they needed to censor what we had to say about denials and especially about deniers of genocide or face the danger of serious suits. The publisher expected us to comply, for after all, this was a legal opinion. "No way!," said Charny, and he won. (A year later he lost at least one skirmish when another publisher, Palgrave, UK, agreed to another attorney's advice to kill a chapter he had written on academicians who deny the Holocaust or another genocide.) These supporters of denial made tough moves in those days!

The period 2003–2007 finds Israel W. Charny very busy with being vice president and the president of IAGS, and 2007–2010 chair of the editorial board of a new journal, *Genocide Studies and Prevention*, which he founded for IAGS together with Roger Smith.

2009–2012 ushers in a new major period for the Institute, which has now been honored by a very strong grant from the Carnegie Corporation of New York to develop a new journalistic format for news of the now increasingly recognized field of genocide studies along with providing an outlet for new and important studies of genocide. See my description of *Genocide Prevention Now* (*GPN*), which published four issues a year in 2010–2012. An amazing number of *GPN* articles were then picked up by Google. *GPN* also published under my direction the first formal directory of colleges and universities where students could earn degrees in the field.

The following major projects will be summarized now:

---

5   Marc I. Sherman and Israel W. Charny, eds., *Holocaust and Genocide Bibliographic Database. Version 2.2* (Jerusalem: Institute on the Holocaust and Genocide, 1994. Prepared for the United States Institute of Peace, Washington, DC)

1. 1985–1995: *Internet on the Holocaust and Genocide*
2. 1988, 1991, 1994, 1997: Series, *Genocide, A Critical Bibliographic Review*
   - 1988: *Genocide: A Critical Bibliographic Review*
   - 1991: *Genocide: A Critical Bibliographic Review, Vol. 2*
   - 1994: *The Widening Circle of Genocide. Genocide: A Critical Bibliographic Review, Vol. 3*
   - 1997: *Medical and Psychological Effects of Concentration Camps on Holocaust Survivors. Genocide: A Critical Bibliographic Review, Vol 4.*
3. 1994: *Holocaust and Genocide Bibliographic Database*, Version 2.2
4. 1999 (US), 2000 (UK): *Encyclopedia of Genocide*
5. 2010–2012: *Genocide Prevention Now* (GPN).

1985–1995: *INTERNET ON THE HOLOCAUST AND GENOCIDE*[6]

Long before the word "Internet" became a household term, the Institute published the *Internet on the Holocaust and Genocide*, which was "an international information resource exchange toward understanding, intervention, and prevention of genocide." The Institute published fifty-six issues of *Internet* in 1985–1995 (six issues per year) concluding with a special triple issue (54/55/56) in April 1995. Pauline Cooper, who worked at the Institute for twenty years until her retirement, served as managing editor for the entire period and worked tirelessly to bring each issue to print.

Eight Special Issues appeared over the ten years: *The Whitaker Report* (January 1984); *Genocides and Politicides since 1945: Evidence and Anticipation* by Ted Gurr and Barbara Harff (December 1987); *Genocide as Boundary-Crossing Behavior* on violence in Northern by John L. P. Thompson (June 1989); *The 75th Anniversary of the Armenian Genocide* (April 1990); *Power Kills; Absolute Power Kills Absolutely* by R. J. Rummel (June 1992); *Denial of the Holocaust and Contemporary Genocide* (September 1993); *Educating about*

---

6   *Internet on the Holocaust and Genocide* (1985–1995). Fifty-six issues of this computer-generated magazine were mailed to hundreds of genocide scholars and institutes around the world. Edited by Israel W. Charny and Pauline Cooper, managing editor, with regular participation by Lily Kopecky and contributions from many scholars including Ted Gurr, Barbara Harff, R. J. Rummel, and George Kent. In 1995 *Internet on the Holocaust and Genocide* was transferred to Macquarie University in Sydney, Australia under the direction of Prof. Colin Tatz.

Genocide (November 1994); and the last issue celebrating the tenth anniversary of Internet, April 1995.[7] The special *Tenth Anniversary Issue of Internet on the Holocaust and Genocide* includes articles by Rouben Adalian, Aryeh Barnea, Michael Berenbaum, Stanley Cohen, Vahakn N. Dadrian, Helen Fein, David Krieger, Eric Markusen, Robert Melson, Rudy Rummel, Roger W. Smith, Yves Ternon. It also includes a section that gives many details of the trial in which Prof. Bernard Lewis was sued in Paris for denial of the Armenian Genocide, the role of *Le Monde*, and the letter sent by Prof. Lewis to the courts in Paris, and the letter sent by our Institute to Lewis.

Seven special sections were also published by *Internet*: *The Children's Holocaust* by George Kent (September 1990); *The Death Toll of Marxism in the Soviet Union* by R. J. Rummel (February 1991); *Genocide of the Kurds* (April 1991); *Publication Resources on the Armenian Genocide* (April 1992); *Genocide in Yugoslavia* (September 1992); *The Tragedy of Genocide and War in the Former Yugoslavia* (April 1994); and finally, *In Memory of Prof. Leo Kuper* (August 1994).

Lastly, *Internet* published two major series of columns by the doyen of genocide studies, Prof. Leo Kuper, and by Lilli Kopecky, head of a Holocaust survivors association in Israel, who published as "The Voice of Auschwitz 8482." With the publication of the final issue, *Internet on the Holocaust and Genocide* was transferred to the Centre for Comparative Genocide Studies at Macquarie University in Sydney, Australia under the editorship of Prof. Colin Tatz.

1988, 1991, 1994, 1997: *GENOCIDE: A CRITICAL BIBLIOGRAPHIC REVIEW*[8,9,10,11]

Genocide: A Critical Bibliographic Review was the first comprehensive published review of literature in the field of comparative genocide studies. This multi-volume series of books presented an international collaboration of experts in the field of genocide studies. Invited scholars were asked to provide a chapter

---

7   *Internet on the Holocaust and Genocide* (April 1995).
8   Israel W. Charny, ed., *Genocide: A Critical Bibliographic Review* (New York: Facts of File, 1988).
9   Israel W. Charny, ed., *Genocide: A Critical Bibliographic Review*, vol. 2.
10 Israel W. Charny, ed., *The Widening Circle of Genocide*, vol. 3 of *Genocide: A Critical Bibliographic Review* (New Brunswick, NJ: Transaction Publishers, 1994).
11 Robert Krell and Marc I. Sherman, eds., *Medical and Psychological Effects of Concentration Camps on Holocaust Survivors*, vol. 4 of *Genocide: A Critical Bibliographic Review* (New Brunswick, NJ: Transaction Publishers, 1997).

summarizing the expertise in the field and a critically annotated list of the most important bibliographic sources for their field. Therefore, each chapter in the series provided an authoritative summary and discussion of the current knowledge available with regard to that specific aspect of genocide studies and the series also provided an annotated bibliography for the emerging field—neither of these were previously available. The American Library Association honored the first volume in this series with the distinguished award of "Outstanding Academic Book of the Year."

The initial volume contained chapters on "The Study of Genocide"; "Intervention and Prevention of Genocide"; "The History and Sociology of Genocidal Killing"; "The Holocaust"; "The Armenian Genocide"; "Genocide in the USSR"; "Genocide in Cambodia"; "Other Selected Cases of Genocidal Massacres"; "Philosophy," including "Multiple Genocide" and "Nuclear Destruction"; "Understanding the Psychology of Genocidal Destructiveness"; and three final chapters on literature, art, and film of the holocaust, genocide, and nuclear and other futuristic destruction. Subsequent volumes in the series continued the initial effort to further build a comprehensive annotated summary and bibliography for scholars and students of the field. Vol. 4 in this series was edited by Robert Krell and Marc I. Sherman and was devoted to the single topic of *Medical and Psychological Effects of Concentration Camps on Holocaust Survivors*. This volume contains over 2,400 citations and originated with an earlier bibliography prepared by the esteemed Norwegian, a Holocaust survivor himself, Prof. Leo Eitinger, and Miriam Rieck in 1979–1980. With Vol. 5, the publication of *Genocide: A Critical Bibliographic Review* shifted to the University of Arkansas under the editorship of Prof. Samuel Totten, who is a distinguished fellow of our Institute in Jerusalem.

1994: *HOLOCAUST AND GENOCIDE BIBLIOGRAPHIC DATABASE*[12]

The *Holocaust and Genocide PC Bibliographic Database* was our Institute's successful attempt to build a computer database covering all aspects of the field. To label this work a "labor of love" undercuts the true effort put into developing this unique project. The project was funded by grants from the United States Institute of Peace in Washington, DC. The platform selected to enter the citations was Pro-Cite, which at that time was the best available software to build, maintain, and search bibliographic records.

---

12 Marc I. Sherman and Israel W. Charny, *Holocaust and Genocide Bibliographic Database. Version 2.2.*

The *Holocaust and Genocide PC Bibliographic Database* invited distinguished scholars to contribute leading sources in their specific field along with annotations and abstracts. The fields covered in this interdisciplinary database included religion, psychology, sociology, law, medicine, history, economics, political science, anthropology, education, and philosophy. The database contained some 9750 unique bibliographic citations of books, chapters of books, book reviews, journal articles, and dissertations, more than half with abstracts, and a unique controlled index word scheme developed specifically for this database.

At one point in the project, we experienced severe technical problems that caused all our files to be erased and the back-up system to fail. We were presented with two options; 1. give up; or 2. recreate the project. Since I served as the lead person on this project, and was single at that time, I chose the second option and immediately called Prof. Charny to inform him that yes, I was crazy and insisted that I would be undertaking the task to reenter all 9,750 citations (and abstracts!) from scratch! Prof. Charny accepted my offer and promised me any psychological treatment that would be needed as a result.

Upon completion of the database, we applied to the National Endowment for the Humanities for a grant to continue the project and expand it to cover many additional areas and contributing editors. Unfortunately, we were rejected. However, on seeing the reviews of our application, we saw that a degree of antisemitism was present in one of the blind reviewers who could not understand how we could apply for a grant when, according to him, Israel was possibly guilty of genocide against its own Arab population!

1999 (US), 2000 (UK): *ENCYCLOPEDIA OF GENOCIDE*[13]

Every field of study needs an encyclopedia to cement its place among the various academic disciplines. The field of comparative genocide studies is no different. The Institute, under the editorship of Prof. Charny published the first such encyclopedia in 1999 (US) and 2000 (UK). The *Encyclopedia of Genocide* (a two-volume set) was published by ABC-CLIO in Santa Barbara, California

---

13   Israel Charny, ed., *Encyclopedia of Genocide*. Associate Editors: Rouben Paul Adalian, Steven Jacobs, Eric Markusen, and Samuel Totten. Bibliographic Editor: Marc I Sherman. Forewords by Bishop Desmond M. Tutu and Simon Wiesenthal: "Why Is It Important to Learn about the Holocaust and the Genocides of All Peoples?" 2nd ed., 2000. Partial French edition, *Le livre noir de l'humanité: Encyclopédie mondiale des genocides*, forewords by Bishop Desmond M. Tutu and Simon Wiesenthal, trans. Janice Valls-Russell (Toulouse: Éditions Privat, 2001). 3rd ed., 2002. Internet e-book ed., 2003.

in several editions and to this day is also available as an e-book. In 2005, a French version was published.

The encyclopedia presents the entire field of comparative genocide studies and has received outstanding reviews from noted scholars in the field and associated fields. Although the encyclopedia is constructed in an A-Z format, it can also be viewed according to several major subject categories such as the following: "Definitions of Genocide and the Study of Genocide"; "Genocidal Events, Interventions, and Prevention"; "Denial of Genocide, the Holocaust, and the Armenian Genocide."

Two interesting side stories about the encyclopedia show how close it came to never being published. Upon submitting the manuscript to ABC-CLIO, they sent it to two copy editors who proceeded to do a "hatchet job" on the work. What was returned to us for review was unrecognizable and certainly did not meet our standards of scholarship. Prof. Charny challenged ABC-CLIO either to return the manuscript to its original version or we would withdraw the book and not have it published. He insisted the encyclopedia had been carefully edited both by him and by five distinguished associate editors and needed no further work, and insisted that the publisher return the manuscript To their credit, ABC-CLIO quickly respected our insistence, and we were able to have the original version published.

More important is the story that reflects the grave dangers of denials of genocides and deniers and the grave dangers of submitting to the terror of their financial and political aggressions. The story of potential legal ramifications was emotionally and financially distressing. ABC-CLIO was concerned about being sued with regard to sections of the encyclopedia that identified major characters active in Holocaust denial and wanted the Institute to revise or withdraw entirely certain materials about them. This was the period when the famous litigation by arch-denier-and-antisemite David Irving against Holocaust scholar Deborah Lipstadt was taking place. At a crucial meeting with the public at their Oxford UK offices—with the participation of famed publisher, Prof. Irving Louis Horowitz of Transaction Books who was invited as a consultant by ABC-CLIO—Prof. Charny adamantly refused to withdraw the material on the deniers. The publisher yielded. Admittedly, a bit of a compromise ensued about some of the language, but we took advantage of submitting the slight revision to include an added sentence that delighted us: "David Irving denies being a denier."

The encyclopedia sold very well far and wide including any number of unexpected libraries such as: the Culinary Institute of America (Hyde Park, New York), the Peace Research Library (The Hague, Netherlands), American

University of Armenia, American University of Nigeria, Thammasat University Library (Thailand), National Library Board (Singapore), Rensselaer Polytechnic Institute (Troy, New York), Ike Skelton Combined Arms Research Library (Fort Leavenworth, Kansas), Bogazici University (Istanbul, Turkey), American University of Sharjah (United Arab Emirates), the International School of Ulaanbaatar (Mongolia), and Yang Ming Shan Christian School (Taiwan).[14]

2010-2012: *GENOCIDE PREVENTION NOW (GPN)*[15]

In 2006, the Institute received a major grant from the Carnegie Corporation in New York. The goal was to develop an Internet magazine devoted to the awareness and prevention of genocide.

The birth of *GPN* occurred over dinner at a fine Italian restaurant near the offices of the Carnegie Corporation in New York, when Prof. Charny presented the proposal to distinguished Vartan Gregorian, president of the Carnegie, who also served on our International Council and was a strong advocate for remembering and memorializing the Armenian Genocide. A formal proposal was submitted to Carnegie and was soon accepted. Since this was really the first time our Institute "joined" the worldwide web (up to that time, we had never even had a website!), this was an adventure into unknown territory for our staff (and among other things necessitated the engagement of a webmaster, Karen Wolberger, MPH) who has continued a growing number of years to be the managing editor of our publications and our web specialist.

GPN consisted of two major parts. The first was an online magazine that pioneered a new journalistic format which combined news, academic-level papers, and resource information about genocide studies. Four issues were published each year between 2010 and 2012. Almost immediately, *GPN* was recognized by Google as a world leader in providing information about genocide and received many thousands of visits to the site. Special Issue 5 (Winter 2011)

---

14 For a larger list of universities and public libraries who have purchased the Encyclopedia, please access the World Catalog at: https://www.worldcat.org/title/encyclopedia-of-genocide/oclc/475989556&referer=brief_results.

15 *Genocide Prevention Now (GPN)*. Twelve issues of this internet magazine were published in 2010–2012, including regular tracking of the emergency taking place in Syria and of the growing Iran nuclear threat. See especially *Genocide Prevention Now 5* (2011): *Special Issue on Co-Victims of the Armenian Genocide: Assyrians, Yezidis, Greeks.* The magazine was edited by Israel W. Charny, with Karen Wolberger (managing editor and webmaster), and with regular participation of columnists Leo Kuper and Lili Kopecky.

was devoted to "Co-Victims in the Armenian Genocide: Assyrians, Yezidis, and Greeks." Issue 7 contained a Special Section "Iran Nuclear Watch," devoted to what *GPN* defined as the most pressing existential problem for Israel and the world. Special Sections on the Israeli Knesset Recognition of the Armenian Genocide were published in Issues 8 and 10.

The second section of the magazine was devoted to news of genocide studies and was called "Holocaust and Genocide Review," which I edited. The section included up-to-date bibliographies, a worldwide list of academic programs in Holocaust and Genocide Studies, a profile of selected memorials and museums, a bulletin board of major activities occurring between *GPN* issues, and lastly, a profile of academic courses at universities and colleges throughout the world. Lecturers were invited to submit a history of how their course developed along with their syllabi for that course. As editor, I was particularly interested in presenting courses from universities and colleges "off the beaten track," where Holocaust and Genocide Studies would never have been expected to be available to students. Thus, I received first-class essays from professors at the University of Alaska (Anchorage), the University of South Dakota, and the University of Idaho. Although the number of students at these universities whose families were affected by the Holocaust and genocide appeared to be marginal, these courses were nevertheless among the most popular at these universities.

A VARIETY OF ADDITIONAL PROJECTS AND PUBLICATIONS BY INSTITUTE PROFESSIONALS

We will now look at a selection of the individual projects that Israel W. Charny and the Institute on the Holocaust and Genocide in Jerusalem took on, and finally we will present a selection of outstanding works by two other senior figures in the Institute, Emeritus Prof. Yair Auron of the Open University of Israel, associate director, and Emeritus Prof. Samuel Totten of the University of Arkansas.

SELECT LIST OF PROJECTS BY ISRAEL W. CHARNY AND THE INSTITUTE ON THE HOLOCAUST AND GENOCIDE, JERUSALEM

- 1982: Israel W. Charny in collaboration with Chanan Rapaport. *How Can We Commit the Unthinkable: Genocide: The Human Cancer.* Boulder, CO: Westview Press.

- 1984: Israel W. Charny, ed., *Toward the Understanding and Prevention of Genocide: Proceedings of the International Conference on the Holocaust and Genocide.* Boulder, CO: Westview Press. Republished, New York: Routledge, 2019.

- 1989: Dan Bar-On, *Legacy of Silence: Encounters with Children of the Third Reich.* Cambridge, MA: Harvard University Press. This book presents a courageous study through direct interviews of children of perpetrators of the Holocaust in Germany. It was launched with initial funding and the active scholarly collaboration of the Institute.

- 1991: Publication of a series of studies of the psychology of evil by Israel Charny together with Daphna Fromer, in various journals including *Holocaust and Genocide Studies, American Journal of Orthopsychiatry,* and the *Journal of Traumatic Stress.* Included in these articles was a thought provoking study of Jewish/Israeli students in helping professions (medicine, psychology, and social work) and their obedience to authority in planning and possible implementing involuntary mass "euthanasia" for selected populations; and another study of the readiness to obey government orders concerning the expulsion of Arabs out of Israel.

- 1992: Shamai Davidson, MD. *Holding on to Humanity: The Message of Holocaust Survivors—The Shamai Davidson Papers.* Edited by Israel W. Charny. New York: New York University Press.

- 1995: *Genocide in the Twentieth Century: Critical Essays and Eyewitness Accounts.* Edited by Samuel Totten, William S. Parsons, and Israel W. Charny. New York: Garland. Revised and expanded paperback version: *Century of Genocide: Eyewitness Accounts and Critical Views.* New York: Garland, 1997. Second revised and expanded paperback version: *Century of Genocide: Critical Essays and Eyewitness Accounts.* New York: Routledge, 2004. Subsequent editions of the book follow published by Totten and Parsons (Parsons was chief of staff at the United States Holocaust Memorial Museum and regrettably has passed away) and continue by Totten.

- 2005–2007: Israel W. Charny was elected President of the International Association of Genocide Scholars, an organization he helped found in 1994. Marc I. Sherman, the Institute's Director of Information Resources was elected Secretary of IAGS for 2007–2009. In

2008, he participated in a delegation to Kurdistan to further under-stand the genocide committed by Saddam Hussein against the Kurds.

- 2006: Israel W. Charny. *Fascism and Democracy in the Human Mind: A Bridge between Mind and Society.* Lincoln, NB: University of Nebras-ka Press. Paperback edition, 2008. Awarded "Outstanding Academic Book of the Year" by the American Library Association.
- 2007: Israel W. Charny. *Fighting Suicide Bombing: A Worldwide Cam-paign for Life.* Westport, CT: Praeger International Studies. The final chapter, "A Proposal for a 'Worldwide Campaign for Life'" by the leaders of many religions and other world leaders and heroes has drawn praise on many occasions and this is now under active consid-eration by a major organization in Greece.
- 2011: Israel W. Charny receives the Armenia Presidential Medal in recognition for his lifetime work in recognition of the Armenian Gen-ocide and combatting its denial. In 2013, Yair Auron, the Institute's Associate Director, was honored with the award.

Figure 14. Armenian President, Serzh Sargsyan, awards the President's Prize to Prof. Israel W. Charny.

- 2012: The Israel W. Charny Library Reading Room was established at the Armenian Genocide Memorial and Museum in Yerevan, Armenia to house the Institute's library.

- 2013: The University of Hartford (Connecticut) sends a film crew to Jerusalem to document the life work of Israel W. Charny and the Institute for an exhibition at the University's Greenberg Center.[16]
- 2015: Israel W. Charny is invited to testify in Israel's Knesset concerning formal recognition of the Armenian Genocide.
- 2015: Associate Director Yair Auron initiates an academic program in genocide studies at the American University of Armenia.
- 2015: Israel W. Charny and Yair Auron are invited by the Armenian government to participate in the Centennial of the Armenian Genocide held in Yerevan, Armenia. Charny delivered a plenary address at the international conference and together with Auron, appeared on television and in documentaries about the event in Armenia and in Israel.
- 2016: The Institute completes a study of articles by Holocaust and genocide scholars that appeared in the *Journal of Genocide Research* (*JGR*). The article "Holocaust Minimization, Anti-Israel Themes, and Antisemitism: Bias at the *Journal of Genocide Research*" was published in the *Journal for the Study of Antisemitism*.[17]
- 2016: Israel W. Charny, *The Genocide Contagion: How We Commit and Confront Holocaust and* Genocide (Lanham, MD: Rowman & Littlefield). Awarded the "Spirituality and Practice Book Award."
- 2017: Israel W. Charny, *A Democratic Mind: Psychology and Psychiatry with Fewer Meds and More Soul* (Lanham, MD: Lexington Books).
- 2017: Israel W. Charny, *Psychotherapy for a Democratic Mind: Treating Intimacy, Tragedy, Violence, and Evil* (Lanham, MD: Lexington Books).

SELECT LIST OF BOOKS BY SAMUEL TOTTEN

Samuel Totten has been a distinguished fellow of the Institute on the Holocaust and Genocide, Jerusalem for many years.

16 The resulting film, *Dr. Israel W. Charny: Interviews on the Holocaust and Genocide,* can be accessed at: https://www.youtube.com/watch?v=3cN6I1SESKQ.
17 The journal is no longer online, but the article can be found on the website of the Institute, http://ihgjlm.com/articles/Holocaust-Minimization-Anti-Israel-&-Antisemitism-at-JGR.pdf.

Totten, Samuel. *The Prevention and Intervention of Genocide: An Annotated Bibliography*. New York: Taylor & Francis, 2007.

———. *An Oral and Documentary History of the Darfur Genocide*. Santa Barbara, CA: Praeger Security International, 2010.

———. *Genocide by Attrition: The Nuba Mountains of Sudan*. 2nd ed. Piscataway, NJ: Transaction Publishers, 2015.

———, ed. *Last Lectures on the Prevention and Intervention of Genocide*. London: Routledge: 2017.

———, ed. *Dirty Hands and Vicious Deeds: The US Government's Complicity in Crimes against Humanity and Genocide*. Toronto: University of Toronto Press, 2018.

———. *Teaching about Genocide: Insights and Advice from Secondary Teachers and Professors*. 2 vols. Lanham, MD: Rowman & Littlefield, 2018.

———. *Teaching and Learning about Genocide and Crimes against Humanity: Fundamental Issues and Pedagogical Approaches*. Charlotte, NC: Information Age Publishers, 2018.

———, ed. *Centuries of Genocide: Critical Essays and Eyewitness Testimony*. 5th ed. Toronto: University of Toronto Press, 2021.

Totten, Samuel, and Paul Bartrop. *Dictionary of Genocide*, 2 vols. Santa Barbara, CA: ABC Clio-Press, 2007.

Totten, Samuel, and Steven Jacobs, eds. *Pioneers of Genocide Studies*. New Brunswick, NJ: Transaction Publishers, 2007.

Totten, Samuel, and Henry Theriault. *The United Nations Genocide: An Introduction*. Toronto: University of Toronto Press, 2020.

Recently Prof. Totten has put his hand to new fictional writing about genocide:

Totten, Samuel. *All Eyes on the Sky*. Kampala, Uganda: African Studies Books, 2020. This is a novel about life and death in the Nuba Mountains of Sudan.

———. *Extinguishing Existence: Short Stories about Crimes Against Humanity and Genocide in Africa*. Kampala, Uganda: African Studies Books, 2021.

SELECT LIST OF BOOKS BY YAIR AURON

Prof. Yair Auron is emeritus professor at the University of Arkansas and associate director of the Institute on the Holocaust and Genocide, Jerusalem

Auron, Yair. *The Banality of Indifference: Zionism and the Armenian Genocide*. New Brunswick, NJ: Transaction Publishers, 2000.

———. *The Banality of Denial: Israel and the Armenian Genocide*. New York: Transaction Publishers, 2003.

———. *The Pain of Knowledge—Holocaust and Genocide issues in Education*. New Brunswick, NJ: Transaction Publishers, 2005.

———. *Israeli Identities—Jews and Arabs Facing the Mirror and the Other*. New York: Berghahn Books, 2012.

——. *The Holocaust, the Rebirth and the Nakba* [Hebrew]. Tel Aviv: Resling, 2013. Also translated into Arabic and English.

——. *"Whoever Saves a Life … The Banality of Compassion: The Story of the Circassian Muslim Village in the Caucasus who Saved Jewish Children during the Holocaust and its Significance* [Hebrew]. Tel Aviv: Resling, 2016.

——. *The 100 Years of Musa Dagh*. Lorraine, Quebec: Corridor Books, 2017. Hebrew and French editions were also published.

Auron, Yair, and Hrayar Karaguezian. *A Perfect Injustice: Genocide and Theft of Armenian Wealth*. New Brunswick, NJ: Transaction Publishers, 2009.

List of books in the Open University Series on Genocide Studies edited by Yair Auron (these are the first textbooks on genocide published in Hebrew).

Volume 1. Auron, Yair. *Thought on the Inconceivable: Theoretical Aspects of Genocide Studies.*

Volume 2. Auron, Yair, and Issac Lubelski, eds. *Racism and Genocide.*

Volume 3. Gutful, Arnon. *Genocide in the "Land of Free"—The Indians of North America 1776–1890.*

Volume 4. Ginsburg, Eitan. *Conflict and Encounter: The Destruction of the Indian Peoples of Spanish America.*

Volume 5. Auron, Yair. *The Armenian Genocide: Forgetting and Denying.*

Volume 6. Hurwitz, Ariel. *Hurban—The Destruction of the Jews by the Nazi Germany.*

Volume 7. Margalit, Gilad. *Nazi Germany and the Gypsies.*

Volume 8. Neuberger, Benyamin. *Rwanda 1994—Genocide in the "Land of Thousand Hills."*

Volume 9. Aran, Lydia. *Tibet 1950–2000: Destroying a Civilization.*

Volume 10. Epstein, Alek. *Political and Ethnic Cleansings in USSR, 1912–1953.*

Volume 11. Charny, Israel W. *"And You Must Destroy the Evil Inside of You": We Are the Human Beings who Commit Holocaust and Genocide.*

Volume 12. Auron, Yair. *So That I wouldn't Be among the Silent.*

THE LIGHTER SIDE OF THE INSTITUTE

Throughout the years, in order to maintain our sanity while dealing with genocide, we often composed humorous and satirical pieces that helped us continue our journey into the dark side of humanity. The following are three examples—two of which have gone on to be published. Here is a glimpse into how our survival mechanisms stayed intact while we dealt with promoting an awareness of genocide, campaigned to combat its denial, and ultimately to advancing ideas for its prevention.

1. "How to Avoid (Legally) Conviction for Crimes of Genocide: A One-Act Reading," *Social Science Record* 24, no. 2 (1987). The piece was later republished also in the *California Courier*. The setting for this

thought-provoking satire by Prof. Charny is the "Legal Offices of Satan, Whore, & Conformist, Specialists in International Criminal Law." Their clients, who come together to the law firm to ask for help in escaping prosecution for genocide, are none other than Talaat (Minister of the Interior, Turkey), Adolf Hitler (Germany), Joseph Stalin (USSR), Idi Amin (Uganda) and Pol Pot (Cambodia). The one-act reading shows the absurdity of attempts to defend and justify the acts of these masters of genocide utilizing the legal community.

2. The second piece, also by Prof. Charny, was published in our *Internet on the Holocaust and Genocide*, Special Issue 25/26 (April 1990). This essay centered around definitions of genocide as debated by a future "Intergalactic Council for Protection of Ethnic and Planetary Human Rights and the Prevention of Genocide," which adopted a policy that only mass killing that totally and completely wiped out the object people would be entitled to the name "genocide." This left the Holocaust and the Armenian Genocide with definitions of *attempted genocide* as well as *humanicide*. The Armenian delegate to the Council is then heard being pleased that finally the Holocaust and Armenian Genocide were on equal footing and one was not placed in a superior position of tragedy or importance than the other.

3. In an imaginary book review, I contributed to the satire at the Institute by writing a "review" of Prof. Charny's book, *I Knew I Could Exterminate (!!)*, subtitled *Odius Scrooge: Memoirs of a Genocidologist* (New York: Righteous Press). This "book" examines the work of Prof. Charny including his role as executive director of the World Organization of Victims, Perpetrators, Bystanders, and Deniers (in short, Anyone). Unfortunately, this essay was not published but—if you want a laugh—can be obtained from the Institute.

IN CONCLUSION

In 2020, the field of Holocaust and Genocide Studies has carved a niche in the world's academic community. Courses of study are growing with new universities and colleges offering degree programs. A trend is developing for more museums in the world dedicated to a specific genocide to now offer space to recognize the genocide of other peoples.

The problems confronted by the International Conference in 1982 by inviting Armenian Genocide scholars are less likely to occur today and are likely to become less and less—although there definitely remain institutions, governments, and museum administrators in many countries (such as China, Japan, Israel, Poland, Russia, and more) who maintain policies that exclude and censor certain information that is contrary to their political/ideological system, and much work does remain to achieve a more genuine freedom to seek and present truth. All in all, comparative genocide studies are no longer taboo with more and more ethnic groups in the world recognizing that to acknowledge the genocide of other peoples does not belittle the suffering encountered by their people. On the contrary, recognizing the suffering of other people who experienced genocide only strengthens your own group's resolve to educate future generations about their own tragedy.

To this, we owe the Institute on the Holocaust and Genocide, Jerusalem, under the direction of Prof. Israel W. Charny, a thanks for their accomplishments, trailblazing vision and forward thinking approach to promote an awareness of genocide to *all* peoples and to its prevention throughout the world.

Afterword

STANDING UP FOR TRUTH AND JUSTICE
AGAINST EXCESSIVE POWER

I've come to a firm conclusion that all of our lives we need to stand up and fight for decency and justice everywhere—in our family lives, in our religious affiliations, in our educational systems—very much including our colleges and universities, in our communities, towns, cities, states, countries, and international system.

For the drive to accumulate power over other people is ubiquitous.

Everywhere there are Cain-like people and constellations that seek to one extent or another to render their fellow people into enslaved or destroyed Abels—to borrow metaphorically from the amazing report of the first murder in human history that took place in the first family of humans in human history, as reported to us with ruthless truth in what is to become for much of civilization the foremost Holy Book from which we are to learn how to conduct our lives in a God-fearing way.

I know today that my wonderful inspiring education in excellent Jewish and secular American schools and universities in no way prepared me for the truth that if I really want to be a decent and strong human being, I must be true to my inner voice of truth and justice and exercise good wisdom in how I go about things, stand up against abuse, exploitation, domination, destructiveness.

In my own life, I've taken some of the opportunities:

- as a four-year-old to slap my awesome big father on his rear end when I felt he was abusive to mother;
- also at four to hit the doctor who was trying to put an ether mask on me without any prior explanations or preparation for the tonsillectomy he was going to perform;
- as a seventh-grader to tell a Hebrew school teacher I would hit him if he lifted his hand to me as he had threatened to do;

- as a teenage youth at night on an empty street near Riverside Avenue in NYC to escape an antisemitic gang that was encircling me;
- as a long-term married man to finally reach a decision to terminate a deeply insulting and abusive relationship (and to open the door to many years of a wholesome and loving relationship);
- as a graduate student and junior intern in a government psychiatric hospital to tell an FBI agent during the insanely rotten McCarthy period years ago that I would not answer his questions about what my colleague students were saying, who they met, and what they were reading, because he and not they were the real threat to American democracy;
- and, as this book tells, as an untenured professor, to refuse the orders of my university and my Israeli government to cease the subject of the Armenian Genocide and to remove Armenian speakers from the program of a professional conference.

I am proud of my selfhood in all these cases—and ashamed of the many other times I failed or delayed to stand up strongly. But I am also angry at my parents and educators who did not prepare me for the omnipresent forces in my life that would seek to overwhelm me and my inner sense of fairness and justice.

This book is not only a "whodunit" of a specific intriguing attempt by a known reactionary government (Turkey), supported by other governments and individuals, to continue denying hard historical facts of their commission of a major brutal genocide. It is also the story of a largely democratic country that itself holds as holy the memory of its own tragic suffering of genocide (Israel) agreeing to support the demands of the reactionary government to wipe out the factuality of the genocide of other victims (the Armenian Genocide).

Because it pays off.

Because there are valuable political and economic benefits to catering to the denier liars. Because that's the way life is to be lived—practically, realistically, going after what you believe you need regardless of what's true and just.

I think and hope this book will intrigue a great many readers because it's a good story about current events that matter to many of us. And I also hope a lot that this book may contribute and inspire more people to devote their energies to standing up against the injustice and brutalities of excessive power.

Acknowledgements

ACKNOWLEDGEMENTS AND HEARTFELT THANKS

Thanks are due, with great pleasure, to a number of people, beginning particularly with the administration of the conference itself and continuing with those who encouraged and supported the development of this book and to several special contributors to our contents.

- To Kenes, the excellent congress-organizing firm in Tel Aviv, and its founder and director at the time, Gideon Rivlin, for his generous professional, moral, and financial support during the complex process of standing up against firm and frightening demands of the Israeli government.

    I was very aware throughout that in addition to the solid traditions of business integrity that prevailed at Kenes, that owner Gideon Rivlin was also with us making a principled statement of honoring the memory of another people's genocide as a further fulfillment of his commitment to honoring the memory of the Holocaust of our own people.

- To Edna Keinan, MA of the Kenes organization, our congress secretary, who was professionally and personally outstandingly capable and personally a very delightful person with whom to work even under very great pressure. It was all super-complicated with fast-moving changes and issues exploding all the times. Edna, you were wonderfully and faultlessly capable. Thank you.

- To the late Yocheved Howard, MFT and her husband Ephraim Howard, PhD of Kibbutz Hazorea who agreed to serve as administrative co-directors. The Howards took charge in particular of receiving proposals for papers and other presentations. Yocheved and Ephraim were colleague family therapists together with whom I had organized the

very successful Third International Family Therapy Conference in Tel
Aviv in 1979, also with the excellent Kenes conference organizing company, where among other things we pioneered the technique of two day
pre-conference workshops which proved so successful that the money
they generated financed the continued operation of our Israel Family
Therapy Association for several years. Although they were not genocide
scholars, they very much shared with us the goal of our 1982 conference to see genocide as a universal human problem of the first order,
and to place the archetypal Holocaust of our Jewish people in this context with other peoples and as an invaluable source for understanding in
greater depth the way in which genocides are constructed and unfold.

Now moving on to the writing of the book in the current years, I want to
express warm appreciation to several people who encouraged this project. It
all began with an article that is now Chapter 1 of the book, which I sent to a
small handful of people for critical review. Within days I had a reply from Greg
Sarkissian, president of the outstanding Zoryan Foundation based in Toronto,
which is devoted to the Armenian Genocide and to the memorial of the genocides of all peoples and to universal human rights; two days later I had a reply
from Michael Berenbaum of Berenbaum-Jacobs Associates, a firm devoted to
building new museums on the Holocaust—and genocide; and I heard from
Harut Sassounian, publisher of the important Armenian-American newspaper, the *California Courier*, and formerly president of the United Armenian
Appeal. All three deeply encouraged the further development of the project,
and Sarkissian and Berenbaum in particular urged me to develop a full-length
book. Greg Sarkissian also pledged that the Zoryan Institute would sponsor
and promote the book, and Michael also contributed generous financial support to enable production.

Another type of thank you is due several participants who have contributed chapters to the work. As our subtitle conveys, we turned to three con-
temporaries to represent identity-wise a contemporary Turk, Armenian, and
Jew. All three are truly distinguished scholars and/or leaders known around
the world:

- **Ragip Zarakolu** is a Turkish national who has taken refuge from
  Erdoğan's prison of fascism in Sweden these years. Ragip captures one's
  deepest respect and touching sympathies for his unbelievable record
  as a long-term publisher in Turkey who dared to publish records of

the Armenian Genocide and other human rights issues in the face of draconian laws and measures against their public pronouncement. He himself served so many jail sentences; lived to see his wife imprisoned multiple times and die of cancer in jail, and lived to see his son imprisoned. He has never wavered in his commitment to freedom.

- **Professor Richard Hovannisian** is a brilliant and prolific American scholar at UCLA who has pioneered in the study of the Armenian people including earlier periods of independent Armenian government. He has been a powerful voice for many years for knowing and recognizing the facts of the genocide. Yet for all that he is a "total Armenian," Richard recognized and supported early on the emergence of the encompassing field of genocide studies of all peoples. Personally, I remember with much warmth how he hosted a luncheon at the UCLA Faculty Club honoring both Leo Kuper and myself for our beginning initiatives in genocide studies.

- **Prof. Michael Berenbaum** is a brilliant philosopher—he is also a rabbi—who heads Berenbaum & Jacobs, a firm devoted to building new Holocaust museums everywhere in the world. As the reader will learn, Michael is the professional who was in charge of selecting all the contents of the brilliantly successful United States Holocaust Memorial Museum in Washington, DC, and in that context put in a brave battle against the ponderous seniors of the museum's Board of Directors to include materials on the Armenian Genocide, but lost. Now as an entrepreneur, he and his creative designer-specialist colleague, Eddie Jacobs, work in many ways to infuse in Holocaust museums themes of concern for the genocides of all peoples. Most recently, they opened a new museum in Dallas, Texas, which includes a full-blown Genocide Gallery, focusing on many different genocides. Berenbaum and Jacobs are also pioneering new types of communications using narrative drawings (good old comic books, in normal street language), which are very impressive.

- A fourth chapter was contributed by **Marc I. Sherman**, MLS, longtime bibliographic specialist of our Institute on the Holocaust and Genocide in Jerusalem. He has been our Institute research guru for close to forty years. When the platform of the *Holocaust and Genocide Database* crashed on us after we had received a $100,000 grant for our work of several years, Marc volunteered for the unimaginable task of redoing the entire project from our printouts. Clearly, he then earned permanently my undying appreciation and respect.

He is also a funny guy and uses his humor in many a commonplace everyday situation, so that he lightens our heavy load of being so deeply concerned with genocide. He loves to track the admittedly amazing unfolding of our physically so-small Institute, and we are grateful to him for doing it in the Supplement.

- **Professor Yair Auron**, who wrote the inspiring Foreword to the book, and whose work appears or is cited a good number of times in the book, is for me a "true Israeli." He hails from a working-class immigrant family from the generation that built the miracle of the new country, has a measure of direct and indirect kibbutz-life experience (his elder brother, a famous liberal leader in the Knesset, Haim Auron, is a kibbutz member to this day), is among the finer products of Israeli education and became an outstanding academic leader in his own right, loves Israel deeply yet is honestly critical of its flagrant ethical shortcomings and failures. We are a bit of a "Mutt and Jeff" collaboration—a native Israeli and the "spoiled" and "overprotected" American-Jewish immigrant that I be—as we work together these many years directing the Institute on the Holocaust and Genocide, Jerusalem, including activities such as a monthly Genocide Seminar in which professionals from a variety of fields participate and seek out the especially controversial and most problematic topics in the field of genocide study. Essentially, even when we disagree on a specific matter, Yair and I agree that we want to see a decent and just as well as powerful and winning State of Israel.

Finally, to a special person with a special role: Karen Wolberger, MPH, managing editor and web specialist. My debt/gratitude to you goes far beyond the numerous pages you have crafted, the computer conundrums and crazy-making problems you have solved, and even the steadiness and reliability of your collaboration with me (now ten years). Your persistence and spirit continue to add to the goals we are working to achieve. I appreciate more than I can say your help and dedication to the Institute and your friendship. The present book is also a celebration of our Institute, and you play a definitive and central role in it.

About the Author

Prof. Israel W. Charny is executive director of the Institute on the Holocaust and Genocide in Jerusalem, which he founded in 1979 with the late Shamai Davidson and Elie Wiesel. He was the editor in chief of the *Encyclopedia of Genocide* (2 vols., 1999), and was formerly professor of Psychology and Family Therapy at the Hebrew University of Jerusalem.

Among his major contributions to the field of genocide studies are developing and hosting the First International Conference on the Holocaust and Genocide in Tel Aviv in 1982; publishing *How Can We Commit the Unthinkable?: Genocide: The Human Cancer* in 1982 (republished by Routledge in 2019); founding and editing the series *Genocide: A Critical Bibliographic Review*, 4 vols. (Facts on File, 1988,[1] 1991, 1994, 1997); founding and editing the *Internet on the Holocaust and Genocide* from 1985 to 1995, the first interdisciplinary network for researchers from many different fields; and developing and editing the *Encyclopedia of Genocide* (Santa Barbara, CA: ABC CLIO Publishers, 1999; French ed., 2001; internet 2003–).[2]

Among his many other publications on genocide are the *Book of the International Conference on the Holocaust and Genocide* [ed. with Shamai Davidson] (1983); *Toward the Understanding and Prevention of Genocide* (Westview Press, 1984); and *Genocide in the Twentieth Century: Critical Essays and Eyewitness Accounts* [with Samuel Totten and William S. Parsons] (Garland Publishing, 1995; rev. with new title, *Century of Genocide* [1997, 2004]); *Fighting Suicide Bombing: A Worldwide Campaign for Life* (Praeger, 2007); and, most recently, *The Genocide Contagion: How We Commit and Confront Holocaust and Genocide* (Rowman & Littlefield Publishers, 2016).[3]

---

1   This book was awarded "Outstanding Academic Book of the Year" by the American Library Association.
2   This book was awarded "Outstanding Academic Book of the Year" by the American Library Association.
3   This book won the "Spirituality and Practice Book Award."

Three works that are primarily on mental health, but very much relate to issues of doing harm to other humans beings are *Fascism and Democracy in the Human Mind* (2006);[4] *A Democratic Mind: Psychology and Psychiatry with Fewer Meds and More Soul* (Lexington Books, 2017); and *Psychotherapy for a Democratic Mind: Treating Intimacy, Tragedy, Violence and Evil* (Lexington Books, 2018). Charny's basic definition of mental health and mental illness revolve around the concept of being good to oneself and promoting one's own life constructively, *and* being decent and constructive to the lives of others. Mental disturbance is either doing harm to oneself, or to others, or both.

---

4   This book was awarded "Outstanding Academic Book of the Year" by the American Library Association.

Index

Ten Commandments for Sovereign Nations and Genocide Scholars

Samuel Totten

- Thou shalt deem all individuals and peoples of the world as precious as any other, and treat them accordingly.
- Thou shalt not disparage, diminish, or harm in any way an individual or people due to their unique distinctions, be it due to color, ethnicity, religion, nationality, politics, or any other classification and/or reason.
- Thou shalt strive to understand, appreciate, and act in ways that do not automatically (*sans* evidence) conflate a government's misdeeds and actions as being synonymous with its citizens.
- Thou shalt view, respect, honor, and treat individuals and members of a group as fellow human beings, and not as "others" and/or "outside a nation's universe of obligation," and thou shalt not deny known acts of crimes against humanity, genocide, and/or war crimes.
- Thou shalt refuse to engage in bystander behavior (be it a lack of caring or feigned ignorance, let alone due *realpolitik* and/or a lack of political will) when fellow human beings are being ill-treated, mistreated, and/or harmed and unable to adequately protect themselves.
- Thou shalt not engage in removing a people from their land and homes for ulterior purposes.
- Thou shalt not engage in crimes against humanity, against any individuals, and/or groups of people for any reason whatsoever.
- Thou shalt not engage in genocide against any groups of people or individuals within such groups for any reason whatsoever.
- Thou shalt not engage in war crimes or any cavalier acts that "mistakenly" engage in such crimes.
- Thou shalt honor the environment (land, water, air, and wildlife) as a gift of God, treat it and act accordingly.

Samuel Totten is Professor Emeritus, University of Arkansas, and Distinguished Fellow of the Institute on the Holocaust and Genocide in Jerusalem.

CPSIA information can be obtained
at www.ICGtesting.com
Printed in the USA
JSHW021711060421
13337JS00003B/109